Loving Me

A 180-Day Journey to Self-Love

Publisher: Melody Rohr, LLC
www.melodyrohr.com

First edition

ISBN 978-0-578-47719-0

Book cover by: BITOS
Interior Design by: Maria Slama and Manuel Garfio

Note:
Every effort has been made to ensure that the content provided in this book is accurate and helpful for our readers at publishing time. The author of this book is not engaged in rendering psychological, financial, legal, or other professional services, and does not dispense medical advice or prescribe the use of any technique as a form of treatment for physical, psychological, or medical problems. The advice and strategies contained herein may not be suitable for every situation. This book is not intended as a substitute for medical advice or healthcare professionals. If expert assistance or counseling is needed, the services of a competent professional should be sought. Always consult your physician before beginning any exercise program. In the event you use any of the information in this book for yourself, the author and the publisher disclaim all liability, direct or consequential, in connection with the use of any information or suggestion in this book. You are responsible for your own choices, actions, and results. The author and publisher advise readers to take full responsibility for their safety and to know their limits.

While the author has made every effort to provide accurate Internet addresses at the time of publication, neither the publisher nor the author assumes any responsibility for the errors or for changes that occur after publication. Further, the fact that an individual, product, organization, or

This workbook belongs to:

Date started: ________________

Date ended: ________________

To the two precious souls who melt my heart each time they say "momma." You are my sweethearts, my shining stars, and my greatest miracles. I am so grateful you chose to walk hand in hand with me during this lifetime. ***Thank you.***

To my darling husband. Thank you for being so wonderful. We could not be more different, yet it makes it all that more fun and exciting. I am so appreciative of your love and support. ***Thank you.***

To my family and friends. You all make my world that much brighter. I am so thankful for being blessed with such a kind, loving, and supportive tribe. ***Thank you.***

To all the kind people who participated in the study. I am so grateful for your input, your generosity, and the time you dedicated in order to make this the best program it could be. ***Thank you.***

I must also acknowledge all the brilliant souls who helped me put this book together. I am so grateful for your time, expertise, creativity, and genius. I could not have done it without you. ***Thank you.***

And, finally, I am forever grateful to you, my readers. Thank you for inviting me into your lives and for visiting with me for a little while. May this be the first step toward your best life. ***Thank you.***

You have all inspired me to create this book.
Thank you.

Table of Contents

Before we begin...

Thank you for picking up this book! I am honored and delighted that you have decided to use this program. I am thrilled about the journey you are embarking on because I know it can transform your life for the better.

Each person will pick up this book for a different reason, but all of you share a common hope and desire for change – you all want something more. Whether you have big goals and expectations, or are just curious about self-love, I can promise you that the more you love yourself, the more magical your life will become.

To be clear, this book is not about fixing you, because you are not broken. Depending on your unique situation, you may feel differently, but no matter your circumstances or your negative beliefs about yourself, you just need to be reminded that you are whole and that you have infinite potential eager to emerge. Most of all, you need self-love to heal you and reawaken you to your most authentic and greatest self.

Self-love is at the center of all that is essential for your inner happiness; it is a vital key to living a fulfilled life. However, most of us were never taught how to love ourselves, and this lack of guidance can make the path to self-love seem difficult or confusing.

Within these pages, you will find activities and journaling prompts and questions designed to restore, refresh, and renew your connection and relationship with yourself. This process will help you fall in love with all of you – your body, your mind, and your spirit.

The road toward self-love is certainly not the easiest, but it is assuredly a necessary and highly rewarding one. For by loving yourself, not only will you change, but your whole life will also be transformed.

To help you successfully accomplish this program, I have put together a brief explanation of what the program is about, what you can expect, and certain recommendations that can assist you during the next 180 days.

I know that you have greatness within you, and I wish to help you unlock it through the power of love. May the next 180 days be empowering, magical, and transformative!

Love,
Melody

PART 1

Helpful Information

Introduction

How did this book come to be?

So many people are profoundly unhappy and dissatisfied. They look at their lives and believe their unease or discontent stems from a certain situation or another. They blame themselves, other people, their past experiences, or their circumstances, such as their body issues, health issues, relationship issues, financial issues, or location issues. Most want change but often are not sure of how to go about it.

Unfortunately, in many instances, when people attempt to change, they go about it the wrong way. They pin down areas of their life that they feel is responsible for their suffering, and they get to work on fixing those specific issues. For example, if they are experiencing weight concerns, they try to go after 'Health Goals,' such as working out and eating healthy. If they have financial concerns, they try to go after 'Career and Financial Goals,' such as finding a better job or starting a savings plan. If they have relationship concerns, they try to go after 'Relationship Goals,' such as improving communication by seeing a counselor, or spicing things up by having a weekly date night.

Regrettably, because the attention is on the problem and not the source, they experience many obstacles and setbacks. These challenges lead them to either struggle or give up on their goals altogether before they see any tangible results. In either case they often end up still feeling angst, hopelessness, or frustration.

Does any of this sound familiar?
If it does, don't worry; for most of my life I was caught in the same cycle.

I created this program during a challenging time in my life. For years, I had been on a quest to improve myself and had invested a lot of time into personal development. The results had been slow coming; I was far from experiencing the outcomes I believed I should have. And then things took a turn for the worse. In the span of two years, I lost several people I cared for, faced serious hardships, and developed acute anxiety. Then, my family and I moved to a city where I felt completely isolated. All my projects were stalled. I was overwhelmed with panic attacks, plagued with health issues, and continually overcome with exhaustion. I spent most of my days in bed, and I was growing increasingly depressed. I had just spent close to a decade working on myself, or so I thought, and I didn't have much to show for it. What was wrong with me? Why did others get it and not me? Why couldn't I do better? Be better? And, amid all that despair and questioning, I suddenly realized how abusive I was being toward myself and thought, "Maybe what I need is a break."

It became clear to me that I needed nurturing and healing. So, I closed the books, stopped the teachings, took a sabbatical from anything relating to self-help, and decided to take some time to simply be good to myself. I didn't have a plan and wasn't sure what I was supposed to do. I just slowly reconnected with the wisdom of my heart, listened once again to the guidance of my intuition, and began heeding the needs of my whole being (physical, mental, emotional, and spiritual). I focused on self-compassion and took the time to care for myself. I refused to entertain anything that was stressful or negative. I gave myself permission to be who I was and where I was at the time, and I did things that felt good to my mind, my body, and my spirit. Back then I did not think about what I was doing in terms of self-love; I just wanted to feel better.

Soon, things began shifting within myself. In a matter of a few weeks, I was witnessing tangible changes, both within myself and in my reality. Changes like I had never seen in all the years I had solely focused on achieving specific goals through personal development. It dawned on me that these transformations were occurring because my relationship with myself had changed – for the first time in my life, I was beginning to genuinely love myself.

Of course, I had heard about self-love and self-care, but like most people, I just thought these terms were synonymous with fizzy bath bombs, mani-pedis, and clay masks – scheduled "me time." Amazingly enough, I never considered what self-love truly meant, and I had never imagined needing to develop a healthy relationship with myself. Even after years of trying to improve my circumstances and myself, it had completely escaped me.

How do we define self-love?

These days it seems everyone is speaking about self-love. It has thankfully become more mainstream, and people around the world are beginning to contemplate this concept. However, it also seems that most people are confused as to what it means. Loving the self in this book is not about doing nice things for yourself if and when you have time. It is not this romanticized idea of self-love that asks you to schedule some "me time" in order to honor and love yourself. At first, when you begin doing the daily exercises, it may seem like that is exactly what this program asks of you, but you will soon discover that it goes much deeper than that.

There is so much that could be said about what self-love truly means. Here I offer an abbreviated version of what I have in mind when I speak of self-love. Self-love is just as simple and incredibly complicated as what it implies – it suggests loving your "self," the wholeness of who you are. It means developing the inner knowing and conviction that you are a valuable and worthy being. It means adopting beliefs, habits, and thought patterns that benefit you. It means approving of yourself completely and being accepting and grateful for all that you have been, are, and will become. It means forgiving yourself and others for all real or perceived hurts. It means letting go of anything or anyone that doesn't serve you. It means stepping into your greatness and being unapologetically and authentically you.

It means saying yes when you mean yes, and no when you mean no. It means living on purpose and having the courage to reach for your dreams. It means stepping out the box and being adventurous. It means being kind and compassionate with yourself and being your own best friend. It means honoring and celebrating the fullness of your life. It means remembering that you are the most important person in your world. It means taking responsibility for your life and becoming mindful of your impact in the world. It means realizing that "ME TIME" is all the time because you are ALWAYS with yourself. Finally, it means loving yourself truly, profoundly, and unconditionally.

This is not a feat that can be achieved in 180 days – this is the journey of a lifetime, but this workbook can be a great beginning. Most of us are never taught about self-love, and the rest of us are all too often offered inaccurate teachings. In truth, from the moment we are born, we begin downloading, acquiring, and accepting certain thoughts, ideas, concepts, habits, and belief systems from our parents, our community, our teachers, our surroundings, and our experiences. Among the many false teachings we receive, we are led to believe that loving ourselves is selfish and egotistical. We are taught to see ourselves as a gender, an ethnicity, a type, a shape, and a number. We are compared, categorized, and classified. We are influenced to accept certain spiritual beliefs, values, traditions, and philosophies. We have been molded into a personality that we confuse with who we truly are. In the end, we become a disconnected persona, stuck in a reality that often does not fulfill us or live up to our dreams.

As I grasped all this, my eyes were opened in so many ways, and I came to the distressing conclusion that most of my life I had been my greatest enemy. I realized I had been treating myself in relentless abusive and harsh ways since I was just a little girl. And it horrified me. Furthermore, I found that I didn't even really know this self I disliked so much. It was a sobering moment. I understood the path would be long, but I was determined.

I would uncover the different parts of myself, and make peace with myself; I would heal, grow in love with myself, and learn to nurture myself.

Soon, I started to notice some extraordinary events begin to take place. I felt joyful and grateful. I appreciated myself. My body healed. I transitioned from chronic anxiety and daily panic attacks to occasional anxiety. I began functioning normally once again. New projects (including this one) were materializing. I received several unexpected windfalls, and amazing things started happening around me.

As the weeks turned into months, both my life and I were transformed in remarkable ways. I observed that most of the intentions and goals I had written down at the beginning of the year were all manifesting without me doing much of anything. This was the first time in my life that I was able to cross off most of my yearly goals that same year. Everything was coming about beautifully and easily. I finally understood what it meant to be in the flow and to see things come together. To finally overcome obstacles and let go of what no longer served me. To succeed where I had failed so many times before. To overcome areas of my life where I used to self-sabotage. To wake up smiling and grateful. To walk the world feeling joyful and light. It was amazing, and I realized I had found something special. I was intent on sharing my findings, but I wondered, was this just the result of years of self-help teachings, or was it something more? How could I be sure others would have similar results?

Erring on the side of caution, I decided that it would be prudent to test my hypothesis and see whether or not it worked for others. I wrote out the program based on my personal experience, and I invited people of different genders, backgrounds, socio-economic situations, ages, and familial circumstances to participate in a study on self-love. A group of people accepted, and these brilliant human beings embarked on a 180-day journey with me. I provided them with the exercises; they in turn gave me feedback and kept me abreast of their progress. The results were astonishing, and that's when I knew I had something truly extraordinary. My mind was made up; I had to make it available to the world.

Today, you are looking at the end product of all this research and experimenting. You hold in your hands a tool that I believe capable of transforming your life in the best of ways.

This program was designed to help you fall in love with yourself. It is about teaching you how to celebrate all of who you truly are, becoming aware of your innate brilliance, and appreciating the physical, mental, emotional, and energetic being that you are. It is about stepping down from the merry-go-round of your present life to enjoy being you, being alive, and loving life as a whole.

It is my heartfelt desire that this book will serve you as a powerful instrument on your own journey toward developing a loving relationship with yourself.

The intention here is to reawaken you to your own magnificence. Because once you intrinsically love yourself, everything will change. You will morph into the best you. You will emanate a completely different energy, and you will rise to a higher frequency, which will inevitably attract better situations, people, and things to you – resulting in a much better quality of life.

Does this mean self-love will prevent you from going through troubles? No. Life happens, and you will inevitably experience some obstacles and challenges. That being said, you will attract fewer unfortunate situations and encounters. And, whenever you do face difficult times, you will now tackle these life events in a completely new way. Being self-aware and self-loving, you will choose the meaning you want to attach to things and the perspectives you want to adopt. Your self-worth and newfound values will lead you to make better choices. Your confidence will help you raise your standards. You will attract the people and the teachers you need. You will detach from people, circumstances, or things that do not serve you. You will learn to be grateful for the lessons learned, and you will gain wisdom from all your experiences. You will embody the healthy aspects of surrender, forgiveness, and acceptance. You will function from a loving and compassionate perspective. Everything will be clearer and therefore easier. You will be a (s)hero and not a victim.

Think of this program as a bridge that will help you cross from where you are to a completely different reality. If you are diligent and you do all the exercises, within the next 180 days you will be transformed, and the world around you will have changed.

Like any transition there will be hills and valleys. Periods of introspection and periods of activity. Moments of planting, moments of weeding, and moments of reaping. You will experience wonderful emotions and not so wonderful emotions. You will be super motivated at times, and you will want to skip the exercises or simply give up at other times. Your mind will try to resist change, and it will relentlessly attempt to sabotage you by whispering words such as "do it tomorrow or later," "I don't feel like it," "this is foolish," or "I'm too tired for this!"

Don't give up on yourself. Envision the potential outcomes and stick to it. Keep the end in mind, the mental image of a self-loving, joyful, and happy you. In order to become the best you, it is essential that you contribute your greatest efforts.

A lot of the 'how' it will all go is going to depend on your efforts, your perspective and the meaning you attach to this process.

It is not going to be easy, but it can be a fun experience. Get excited about the changes you are about to go through. Have faith that there is an intelligence greater than you (call it God, Universal Intelligence, Guardian Angel, Source, Consciousness, Higher Self or Life – depending on your belief system), which orchestrated all of this, and that you are helped every step of the way. See it as an adventure. Most of all, see it as a great act of love toward yourself.

May you embark on this new journey with an open mind, a trusting heart, and the eagerness and curiosity of a child. Have fun, embrace the process, and give yourself the opportunity to make the best out of this program. I hope that you will complete each exercise intentionally, mindfully, and wholeheartedly, and that you will find the strength within yourself to persevere until the end. You are the most important person in your life, and as such you owe it to yourself to honor, cherish, and love yourself completely. For therein rest all your answers, your dreams, and your happiness.

Now, let's get started!

What can I expect from this workbook?

While this book specifically speaks to developing a loving relationship with yourself, it inevitably brushes upon other topics that impact the many facets of your life. Herein, among others, you will find exercises and activities that cover spirituality and universal principles, self-improvement and knowledge, health and fitness, relationships and connections, meaning and purpose, contributions and impact, fun and leisure, wishes and desires, fears and doubts.

For the next 180 days, you will be asked to see yourself with new eyes, to be more deliberate, and to embrace a holistic approach. Every day you will have to complete an activity and answer questions that will help incite new thinking patterns and develop a deeper connection with yourself. You will be asked to step out of your comfort zone, question your beliefs, change your habits, reevaluate your values and standards, shift your paradigm, and love yourself at every turn.

Here, I must forewarn that this book does not delve into topics such as the shadow self, trauma, inner demons, or any difficult subjects that could result in more harm than good.

In my personal experience, healing occurred organically only after I chose to stop focusing on the suffering, the hurts, and traumas I had endured, and I decided instead to fill my head, my heart, and my life with positivity, love, beauty, and potential. In other words, I am open to other schools of thought, but since I have not had personal success with procedures that focused on such topics, I do not offer activities related to them in this work.

I do, however, encourage you to observe and examine your negative beliefs and fears, and explore their root cause as they arise throughout this journey. I also recommend that, when painful memories from your past resurface, you do your best to make peace with them using the techniques I offer in the section titled 'When negativity attacks.' Still, I advise you to be easy and gentle about it. Do not force the process, as it would only result in misery and frustration. Healing inner wounds, forgiving abusers, letting go of heartbreak, and recovering from any form of suffering takes time. As you become aware of hurts or patterns that hold you back, find loving ways to remedy the current concern instead of focusing on anger, sadness, blame, resentment, guilt, shame, judgment, and fear. Take responsibility for your life by accepting that, no matter what has happened or will happen, you have the power and capability to turn things around. You are a powerful creator.

Having said that, if at any time you feel that you are dealing with persistent or recurring issues that are either debilitating, or preventing you from living a healthy life, please seek the help of a healthcare professional who will have the knowledge and experience to guide and assist you.

Why 180 Days?

I'm sure you didn't realize how long 180 days was until you looked at a calendar! Haha!
I understand six months seems like a long time, but this program is not a Band-Aid. It is not about temporary change; it is about changing your life. It took you this long to get to who you are and where you are. You can give yourself 180 days.

I put a lot of thinking into the timeframe a program like this one should take. I came up with this number conducting extensive research, experimenting, and observing others and myself. Researchers suggest that it takes between 30 to 70 days for someone to change a habit – that's only one habit! However, in my experience, people react to change in different ways, and while some changes are rapid, others take much longer than 30 to 70 days to stick. And that is without mentioning that for most, there are numerous painful setbacks. I compared these numbers with the usual time-period of rehab programs and saw that they lasted between 28 and 90 days. I know it can be surprising that I investigated information concerning rehab centers, but you must realize that whether you like it or not, you are addicted to your personality, your habits, your patterns of thinking, your relationships, your beliefs, your feelings, and many other things in your life. We think of addiction in terms of drugs, alcohol, or certain eccentric compulsive behaviors. In truth, addiction as defined by the Merriam-Webster dictionary is "a strong and harmful need to regularly have something or do something."

Looking at those numbers, I decided to take the longest suggested time and double it for a better chance at success. Then, I chose to take the shortest suggested time to divide the program into three phases, to mimic the process a gardener would go through while cultivating a new orchard: planting, growing, and blossoming. Finally, I loved that it coincided perfectly with doing a "180-turn-around" in your life.

What can I expect during each phase?

PHASE I: PLANT LOVE

During this phase, you will gently begin to transition from where you are and who you are, toward your ideal self and your best life. You will prepare your mind, body, and spirit to receive new thought and habit seeds; in the process, you will pull out some weeds and let others wither. From there, you will slowly begin to deliberately plant new seeds – more aligned with your intentions.

This is a phase of transition between releasing the old personality and starting to grow genuine self-love. You are introduced to, and become acquainted with, your three bodies (mind, body, and spirit).

You will begin adopting new patterns of thinking, feeling, and doing things. You will start becoming self-aware and conscious. You will also begin seeing some inner and outer shifts and changes.

PHASE II: GROW LOVE

Phase II will be a little more demanding as the roots grow and become stronger. You will need to move seedlings, remove certain pests, and continue to pull out weeds.

During this phase, you will continue to observe gradual shifts in your reality and within yourself. You will begin to understand how truly important it is for you to love yourself. You will begin raising your standards and upgrading your value system. Your confidence, self-respect, and appreciation will sprout.

You will develop a greater understanding regarding the power of your choices. You will become aware of how your energy affects your reality. You will act more mindfully. You are discovering how to balance and harmonize the three bodies (body, mind, and spirit).

PHASE III: LET LOVE BLOSSOM

This final phase will give birth to the first blossoms of true self-love. You will be asked to make additional efforts in the daily exercises.

At this stage, you will be more appreciative and loving toward your three bodies (body, mind, and spirit), and it will be easier for you to find a good balance between the three. Theories and philosophies become internalized – you will go beyond simply intellectually understanding certain concepts; you will embody them, or at least understand them in a more intrinsic and profound way.

You will know that, while at times some unexpected or unfortunate events may happen, you always have control over your perspective and choices. You will enjoy your own company and understand the value of being your number one priority. You will gain a newfound gratitude for your life. You will find joy in experiencing new things and stepping out of your comfort zone.

When should I begin the program?

You are welcome to begin this program anytime you want. Peruse through the book to get a general understanding of what the activities entail, and opt for a date that works for you. You may choose to embark on this journey according to your schedule, the first day of a month or year, in harmony with the moon's phase, or just by trusting your inner guidance and commencing when it feels right.

For the purpose of the study, I had arranged the exercises in a certain order to make it easier for the participants with more traditional Monday-through-Friday jobs. Therefore, they began their Day 1 activity on a Sunday. I have kept the same order.

I should add that you are free to reorganize the activities in whichever order you prefer. However, keep in mind that the exercises follow a certain progression, and I would suggest not shuffling activities beyond a week at a time.

Do I need to have prior knowledge of personal development to obtain results?

Absolutely not!

Personally, I am a lifelong learner. I am always eager to learn new things and discover new concepts and perspectives because life fascinates me, because I always want to expand my knowledge, and because I continually want to grow myself. This curiosity and passion lead me to study people and subjects that I find captivating (including personal development) – but that's me. As for you, I strongly believe that you should help yourself in any way you feel called to – trust your inner knowing and guidance to lead you where you need to go.

If you are interested in broadening your perspective or care about furthering your education, I have included a list of books and films that could be helpful with this program. It is far from being a definitive list, but it should give you a good head start.

Why will this process work?

Every day, as you turn to your daily exercise, you are reminded that you matter and immediately after, you are prompted to take actions that also remind you that you are significant. This, coupled with spending time daily focusing on your relationship with yourself, caring for yourself, and taking conscious steps toward growing genuine love for yourself, gives you no other choice but to embrace yourself.

This is not just a book filled with theories that give you the freedom to complete exercises when you choose. This book grabs your attention and focus by holding you to a daily schedule while simultaneously asking you to continually involve your mind, your body, and your spirit toward the specific intention and objective of loving yourself. It demands that you act over and over again until it becomes second nature.

As you complete the exercises, self-love will begin to grow, take root, and you will start feeling different. You will become more positive, and you will discover a new level of appreciation for yourself. This will result in you thinking differently and acting differently. From there, you will emanate a different energy, and things will not only change within yourself, but you will also notice changes outside of yourself.
A different you has no choice but to bring about a different reality.

I must yet again remind you that you will get what you put into it. The more diligent and persevering you are, the better your results.

What do I do if people around me are not supportive?

While some of you will enjoy the support of family and friends during this process, others may face quite the opposite from the people around them. This is the main reason I lost 20% of my study group in the first month of the program (the last 80% stayed until completion).

In the next pages, I will explain why and how to keep this program a secret from unsupportive and toxic people. But, here I want to be very forthcoming: whether you have supportive or unsupportive individuals in your circle, they will all have a difficult time adjusting to you changing – it is a threat to their own identities, habits and routines, and it can be scary or uncomfortable.

I could suggest a lot of tips and tricks, and you are welcome to do your own research, but in the end the only thing that will really work is standing up for yourself. This does not have to be done in a confrontational or offending way – a heartfelt conversation can be a fantastic equalizer. Simply let these individuals know that, at this moment in time, you are focusing on developing a loving relationship with yourself, and inform them that you would greatly appreciate it if they would kindly respect your choice. If this does not convince them, you want to consider distancing yourself from them.

It can be heartbreaking and distressing to have the people you care about be unsupportive toward your intentions, goals, and dreams, but in the end if they do not honor and respect you, the most loving thing you can do for yourself is to either ignore them or release them. Anyone worth being in your life should always encourage you in all your healthy endeavors.

What if I fall off the wagon?

If you miss or skip a day or two, just make sure that on those days you are still being loving toward yourself and doing things for yourself on purpose. Then, get right back into it.

If you miss a week or two, I suggest you restart the program from the beginning. I know it sounds a bit drastic, but again think in terms of patterns of habit and addiction. Being sporadic or discontinuing the program for such a long period of time will cancel out all your prior efforts.

Going into this, I must insist that you think of this program as the first step toward a new way of living your life – a life where you love and cherish yourself. After years of neglect or mistreatment, you will need to put in your best efforts. That means that for some time it will be something you have to do daily.

You will need to be strong as there are several factors that might try to deter you from pursuing the program to fruition. As much as you may think at this very moment that you are ready and want change, your mind will not take kindly to this and will unequivocally try to scare you or sabotage you. The best remedy is to remain conscious and present while persevering with the program.

Conversely, if you happen to "fall off the wagon" so to speak, it's okay. It happens to every one of us! Be loving and kind to yourself. Do not judge yourself; understand that change is hard work. Come back to it when you are ready. Sometimes it takes many attempts before we can successfully accomplish certain things, and that's perfectly fine because with each time we get better at it, and it gets easier.

How-to

Assessments

The first day and the last day of the study you will be asked to complete an assessment. Fill out your assessments as honestly and as thoroughly as possible. Once you are done with the first assessment, do not read it again for the remainder of the program. On the last day do not read your first assessment before answering the Day 180 Assessment. Only after you have successfully completed this last assessment can you compare the two. The objective is to get a truthful evaluation of the progress you will have made.

Exercises

The workbook offers daily exercises. Small steps that you can easily take to help you develop a relationship with your three bodies (body, mind, and spirit). You may wonder at first how these activities will help you, and sometimes you may even be confused as to how a certain exercise relates to self-love or can provide tangible results. Just trust the process, and keep in mind that those small steps taken regularly will create big changes.

If you pay close attention, you will notice that the weekly exercises fall under reoccurring categories:

- Self-Care activities
- Inner-Child and Fun activities
- Philanthropic activities
- Mindfulness activities
- Deeper Work and Journaling activities
- Mental and Physical Health activities
- Evaluation activities

These activities are all-encompassing and designed to care for your physical, mental, emotional, and spiritual well-being. They will help you connect and explore every level of your three bodies (mind, body, and spirit). They will create harmony between all the different parts of you and merge all these aspects into one self-loving and balanced being – your best you.

It is very important that you do the daily exercises consistently so that you can experience the desired results, and it goes without saying that you should do your very best to step out of your comfort zone. You must realize that your comfort zone got you where you are and cannot take you where you want to go. However, in the event that you cannot complete a certain exercise because of your circumstances, or because it really doesn't resonate with you, just swap it for another activity that you previously enjoyed, or create one of your own. Just make sure to highlight those specific exercises and try to complete them in due course, when your circumstances permit or when you feel more able to do so.

You can also choose to customize, improve, or optimize the daily activities any way you prefer to best suit your preferences, circumstances, moods, or intentions. Here, the objective is for you to enjoy the journey. The exercises in this book are just examples of what you can do, not strict guidelines. This is your journey! Make it as enjoyable and fun as you possibly can. Please consider sharing your adaptations on our **Loving Me 180** Facebook group to inspire and help others.

Finally, if there are exercises that you particularly enjoy, make sure to adopt them and implement them in your life.

Daily Journaling

I am a strong believer in the power of journaling; I feel that there are unlimited benefits to embracing this daily practice. I personally have been journaling since I was a child. There are many ways to keep a journal, but whichever way it is maintained, it is first and foremost a self-reflecting tool. It provides a stable support for us to become conscious of our day-to-day lives. Most of all it helps us become self-aware. For this reason, I have included some daily journaling prompts. The answers can be as long or as short as you want them to be; do what feels good.

Personally, I prefer answering in a detailed way as it helps me track my individual progress and make needed improvements or adjustments along the way.

Here are the daily prompts you will be asked to answer:

1. Today, I ...

The 'Today, I ...' should be filled out in the morning. It should be intuitively filled out with whatever comes to you. Close your eyes, take a few conscious breaths, and say "Today, I...' and write down what surfaces. It may be an affirmation, a feeling of gratitude, an intuitive feeling, a prayer, an intention, or an objective. Depending on your mood you can use this space in many different ways. It will set the tone for your entire day. When you are done, you can choose to hand over the words you have written to an intelligence greater than you (whatever that is for you) and go about your day, or you can use these words as an affirmation that you will repeat throughout your day.

- Today I am appreciating and loving myself more than yesterday.
- Today, I will have a beautiful and magical day!
- Today, I expect to see miracles.
- Today, I am grateful for being part of this program.
- Today, I feel like I'm about to receive a surprise.
- Today, I intend on having a fantastic meeting.
- Today, I love how much fun I'm having.
- Today, I plan on organizing my closet

2. Things that made me feel good today.

This prompt should be answered at the end of the day. This is about becoming aware of the good things that happened to you during the day instead of only focusing on the negative things. Look for the goodness in your days, and make sure to write down everything that pleased you or made you feel joyful: your accomplishments, the nice things people said to you or did for you, the fun things you experienced, the touching things you witnessed, every time something made you smile or laugh, the special moments, new encounters, etc.

3. Things I noticed about myself.

This prompt should be answered at the end of the day. This is about doing a little introspection and becoming more self-aware. Observe as objectively as possible the way you think, feel, act, and react during the day. At first this may be a hard pill to swallow because you will notice a lot of negative patterns, but do not let yourself be discouraged. On the contrary, feel proud of yourself for taking notice. Becoming aware is a great gift that will help you in all you do and in all your interactions. It will help you uncover triggers, dormant issues, and the root cause of certain fears or behaviors. It will likewise help you discover what brings you joy, what soothes you, and what makes you feel good. Make sure to write about certain recurring thought patterns, unconscious behaviors, strong reactions, feelings and emotions, attachments, fears, doubts, self-abuse, self-sabotage, habits, interactions, positive changes, etc. With time you will observe more and more positive shifts.

- Today, I noticed I got very angry when my boss reprimanded me in front of everyone. My body felt hot, and I experienced a prickly feeling throughout my arms and upper back. I felt embarrassed and humiliated. I notice that being confronted in front of people makes me feel inadequate. I'm still angry, six hours later!
- Today, I noticed that I didn't really feel like talking. I'm on hermit mode. I must be going through an introspective time. I've noticed everyone keeps asking me 'what's wrong?' That annoys me a little. Can't a person not feel like talking?

Examples

- Today, I noticed that the daily exercise really stretched me. It was easy, but for some reason I felt dumb doing it! I realized that I was completely disconnected from my inner-child! I promise I will take better care of you little one.
- Today, I noticed that everything felt so good! The sky was bluer than usual, the leaves on the trees were greener, the birds sang beautifully. I breathed deeper! Who knew taking deep breaths could feel this good! Note to self: Take deep conscious breaths daily.

4. Things I am grateful for.

This prompt should be answered at the end of the day. In my experience, aside from love, gratitude is the most powerful, healing, and transformative emotion you can feel. Adopting an attitude of gratitude is one of the fastest ways to change your life. Here, write about three to five things for which you are grateful. Do not get into the mind trap of feeling like you must feel grateful for your health, you family, etc. The objective here is for you to FEEL grateful. It is a feeling of "THANK YOU" that is accompanied with a smile, a sense of expansion, inner relief, and peace. It is a feeling you can experience during big events or at completely random times (e.g. the birth of a child, getting unexpected money and being able to pay a bill, healing from a serious illness, looking at someone you love, seeing something beautiful, having a fun time, etc.). It is not generally something we control, but here I want you to learn how to call upon this feeling whenever you want to. People often say that counting your daily blessings will change your life, but in my experience, it is the feeling of gratitude, and not counting the blessings, which radically changes things. At first, some of you will be horrified to realize that you cannot find something that makes you genuinely feel grateful. Do not worry, it is normal. Being disconnected from your true self means you are disconnected at some extent from everyone and everything else. With time it will get easier and easier. The important thing is to write about what really makes you feel deep appreciation. The first few weeks, you may want to close your eyes, take a few conscious breaths, put your hand over your heart (if you feel so inclined), and ask yourself "What am I grateful for today?" And see what comes up. Remember images are not enough; pay attention to the way you feel. Write down three to five things that make you feel the most grateful even if they seem superficial. Do that every day until this inner 'thank you' grows.

I assure you that doing this daily will strengthen your gratitude muscle, and with time you will find yourself spontaneously feeling more and more gratitude throughout the day.

5. Thoughts on the daily exercise

This prompt should be answered at the end of the day. This activity is self-explanatory: Write about your thoughts and feelings regarding the daily exercise. Did you like it? What did you do? Would you do it again? Did it make you feel good or bad? How did you or would you improve it? Did you have an easy or hard time understanding it? Do you think you will include it in your daily practices? Doing this will help you discover your inner resistance and blockages, as well as some of your qualities and shortcomings. It will help you explore your creativity, become aware of your likes and dislikes, and figure out what you truly want versus what you do not want.

6. Would you like to add anything?

This question is intended to give you a space to add anything you want. It can be used to record important events, celebrate happy news and accomplishments, note mistakes or setbacks, insert motivation or inspiration, repeat goals and/or intentions, document noteworthy insights or ideas, track your progress, create an action plan for the next day, or simply journal about your day.

Finally, I invite you to personalize this workbook as much as possible. Highlight what's important to you; write notes, doodle, make drawings; paste photos or mementos (ticket stubs, postcards, menus, pamphlets, letters, etc.), add stickers, and decorate it. Be creative and make it yours. I also suggest that you date your activities to keep a record of your progress, and to have a base of comparison in the event you choose to complete this program several times.

Bi-weekly Reports

These reports will ask you to answer certain questions to evaluate your progress. They are designed to help you become aware of the changes taking place within yourself and in your life. That said, they will also help you look back on past events in a more constructive way – to grow and make more positive choices for yourself. Too often people get trapped in endless memory loops that make them feel sad, mad, embarrassed, nostalgic, guilty, and other negative ways that are damaging to their inner well-being. The ability to look back can be a gift or a curse, it just depends on the way you use it.

Following the questions, you will be asked to repeat your favorite exercise of the past two weeks, or you will be given the option to create an exercise of your choice.

End-of-Phase Reports

The end-of-phase reports are designed to help you assess your progress for that entire phase as a transition into the next phase. You will be asked to answer a series of questions. Afterward you will be asked to reward yourself by giving yourself a gift or doing something you really want to do. **This is an essential step; do not skip it.**

It is a way for you to thank and celebrate yourself and acknowledge all your efforts. I highly recommend that, at the beginning of each phase, you decide how you will honor and reward yourself after successfully completing the entire phase. It will give you an incentive to look forward to, a vision, and a goal to motivate you when you are running out of steam or feeling a bit low. It will also give you time to save up or plan, if necessary.

It can be anything: a scrumptious dessert, a nice outfit, a delightful fragrance, a book, a camera, a class, a weekend getaway, a special outing, etc. Just make sure it's an indulgence, something that will really make you feel good.

It would be fantastic if you planned something BIG for the completion of the last phase – a real celebration of sorts: a get-together, a trip somewhere special or different, an experiential gift such as indoor skydiving or glamping, or better yet, throw yourself a party, and if people ask why, you can choose to explain, or smile and say, "Just because."

Extras

Facebook Group

For extra support, tips, and advice from people who have completed the program, or who are currently partaking in the program, you can join the **Loving Me 180** group on Facebook. I encourage you to actively participate by posting photos, sharing your experiences, suggesting tools and tips, and chatting with other members.

Notes

At the end of the workbook there is a section entitled "Notes." Use this space to record or include anything you would like: books you plan to read or have read, documentaries you have watched or want to watch, your favorite TED talks, special quotes, poems, lists of your current favorite songs or movies, photos, postcards, stickers, places you have visited or want to visit, drawings or doodles, recipes, your best ideas, etc.

Recommendations

Shhh..

When we begin something new and exciting, we often want to share our intentions with the people we care about. Some teachers and mentors approve of this strategy, and even profess that you should always share goals you are striving to achieve with family and friends to keep yourself accountable. It is supposed to shame you or motivate you to stick to your plans. In my experience, this can backfire and is not always as effective as silence.

You are free to share or not to share as you are your own best advisor, but I would guard against being too eager to tell your loved ones. I simply ask that you be very particular of whom you choose to invite on your journey.

In my opinion, silence is golden unless you have a person you are confident will never make you feel weird, awkward, or bad about what you are doing. Oftentimes, it's not that you don't have such a person around you, it's just that you are full of doubts about your own decisions. In any case, if you do not think or feel that you can trust people around you to encourage and support you regarding this new endeavor, or if you feel that sharing your process could negatively affect your journey, I would suggest not mentioning to anyone what you are up to. Frequently, the people closest to us have a way of pushing our buttons and making us feel insecure in ways that many outsiders can't.

Remember, this is something you are doing for yourself, and keeping it a secret may offer you the peace of mind you need during this process. At this stage you need a lot of inner will and strength to go through this transformation, and the judgments, the looks, the opinions, or even your fears of how others perceive you for completing this program can hurt your progress. Developing the ability to do something sacred for yourself without needing anyone's approval or opinion can be a great way to begin a relationship with yourself.

The exception here would be to complete the program with a loved one, or with a group of like-minded individuals (like on our Facebook group), who, like you, have chosen to embark on this journey determined to attain a healthy amount of self-love. Then, everyone would be able to share, encourage, inspire, support, and motivate one another authentically without fear of judgment. This can be a very powerful method to deepen relationships or develop new ones.

Be open to change

I know this seems like an obvious statement – if you are holding this book, chances are you are ready for change.

Conceptually, change can be very exciting when we want to see certain improvements in our lives. In reality, we do not actually understand what that implies until we are asked to change our habitual ways of thinking or doing things. Until we are asked to let go of certain relationships or certain things. Until we are asked to release certain patterns or stories. Until we are asked to step out of our comfort zones and make consistent efforts.

We are creatures of habit. Our various routines make us feel safe and secure. Stepping into the unknown and doing things differently is uncomfortable, and even the smallest of changes can fill us up with fear and doubt. That's why we often accept to endure or to stay in certain situations, abusive or toxic relationships, or the status quo. Why we make the same unhealthy choices and continually repeat our destructive habits. Preferring to remain in a chaos we know rather than face something new, for fear of ending up with something worse, and sometimes, believe it or not, for fear of ending up with something better.

In the next 180 days you will be asked to make some changes, and although I cannot force you to make any of these changes, I do hope that you will open yourself to the experience and trust your heart and intuition to guide you.

For things to change, you must be willing to change things, and you must allow change to occur.

We never really think in terms of life being short and unpredictable. Today you're here, tomorrow you have left this reality. Don't you deserve to live life on your terms? Don't you deserve joy and happiness? Don't you deserve to experience the best that life has to offer? Don't you deserve to really love yourself?
Be open, and trust that there is a sacred and infinite intelligence that will always help and guide you, as long as you allow it to do so. Let go of your need to control, listen to that inner voice, follow its guidance, act accordingly, and allow miracles to happen.

Look at the week ahead

Every week, make sure to scan through the entire week ahead for exercises that may need a bit more prep, and to schedule your time accordingly. It's a good idea to jot down the upcoming exercises in a planner or a calendar.

In the table of contents, you have probably noticed that there are one, two, or three asterisks (*) next to each exercise. Each asterisk represents a level of involvement:

- One asterisk: No prior planning needed.
- Two asterisks: Some planning may be required.
- Three asterisks: Planning required.

Remember your intention

It is very important that throughout this journey you always remember the intention that compelled you to start this program – the intention to embrace self-love. Keep it at the forefront of your mind and heart. Do not allow yourself to drift into your habitual patterns or fall into a routine of mechanically completing the exercises, as you will not attain the desired results.

To begin with, I suggest you schedule and plan for the daily exercise and any self-love activity you want to enjoy before anything else. Do not treat these exercises or any self-love activities as optional; see them as mandatory. Then, take time every day to discern how the activities relate to self-love, contemplate how they impact you, enjoy your own company, and appreciate caring for yourself. It is essential that you put as much attention and effort into you as you would if you were entering a relationship with someone you cared about.

Be mindful to always place your focus on the process of growing your relationship with yourself.

Be present

People spend most of their days in an unconscious state, lost in the ruckus of their mind, leaving much of their daily thoughts, activities, actions, and reactions up to their subconscious minds. You are sleeping through your own life.

Being present means to pause the "monkey mind" (the one that loves to swing from thought to thought) by becoming conscious of your inner world and the outer world. It means noticing your thoughts, paying attention to your emotions and feelings, observing your surroundings, remaining mindful of all your interactions, listening to others, thinking before reacting, staying aware of your impact, and remaining awake throughout your days. Living in the now promises to awaken you to a much richer, more peaceful, and more joyful life. It will allow you to live your life based on conscious intentions and decisions, and ultimately become a mindful and conscious creator.

This is not an easy undertaking, but like most things the more you will practice, the easier it will get. Throughout this program, try to be as present as possible. Most of all, be conscious and present while doing the exercises – this is about getting to know you and falling in love with yourself. To do that, you must become conscious of the now, of yourself, and of the world around you.

When negativity attacks

Negativity creeps in all the time. What's to blame? Some may point to our exposure to negative media outlets, our toxic relationships, or unfortunate circumstances. Others may place the guilt on our negative thought patterns and belief systems, a lack of faith and self-love, and various emotional triggers.

Please understand that it all comes down to the choices that we make. We give meaning to things and decide whether something is positive or negative. We decide whether to believe in our mind movies and thoughts. We decide whether we are going to take things personally. We decide whether certain things will affect us. We decide whether to believe or accept what people tell us; and so forth.

Furthermore, amazingly enough, we choose to simmer in our own negativity long after something has happened. For example, when someone says or does something that you find offensive, you will usually still feel upset about it days after the event. Why? It's finished. It's in the past. However, you have attached a meaning to their action; you may think, for instance, that they have disrespected you and so your mind goes to work proving you right, by feeding you a continual stream of negative flashbacks or possible negative scenarios. In fact, you agree to be sucked in by those thoughts, to make yourself sick, and to waste your energy over something that's long over. You probably gossip, complain, and invite everyone into your drama. You spread poison for days. For what? Who knows, maybe they did want to disrespect you but unless some part of you agrees with them, their behavior shouldn't bother you. Perhaps, they were experiencing some issue or personal problem and reacted poorly because of their own situation. Bottom line, you usually feed your fires or extinguish them by choice.

I am not trying to deny that we live in a world of contrast, or that there are not extremely negative circumstances or situations that happen to us and around us. I understand some things are upsetting, and some things need our attention. However, I believe that you always have the ultimate choice to entertain negativity or not.

Here are some ways to step away from negativity:

Observe your negative and fearful thoughts.
Become conscious. Observe the way your mind works – the negative patterns that arise, that follow you, that stick to you, and that repeatedly come back. Notice your triggers, what upsets you, your feelings, your emotions, and your reactions.
Becoming aware will create a healthy space between you and anything that causes an inner negative reaction. Becoming an observer will help you remain more objective and rational.

Decide to stop.
Whether you realize it or not, you are not your mind – you either use your mind, or it uses you. Your mind offers thoughts about things all the time, and you must decipher what is useful and what is not. This can be a difficult task: if you are like most people, you are likely addicted to your mind's melodrama – you love gossip, being a victim, pointing fingers, being sad, angry, and afraid – you may not realize it, but you do. Deciding to stop will not be easy, and it will take time, but in the end, it will be worth the effort. Pay attention to your negative impulses, and instead of automatically reacting, decide not to. Anytime your mind begins offering you ammunition to stir your inner pot, do your best not to give in to it. You can choose to distance yourself from the thoughts coming to you by simply observing them and deciding not to follow them down the rabbit hole. Alternatively, depending on the thought or your circumstances, you can choose a more proactive approach by saying a firm "STOP!" (silently or aloud) and moving your body in some way (stand up, clap your hands, jump, turn around, etc.). Afterward refocus your thinking toward something different. At first your mind will bombard you with more negative thoughts, and you'll experience increased emotional and physical reactions (e.g.: crying, feeling your inner temperature rising, feeling a knot in your throat, etc.). It's okay, with practice it will get easier. Remember that you are teaching yourself how to manage your mind instead of allowing your mind to control you. Keep it up, and with time you will see satisfying results.

Breathe consciously.
When a negative thought arises, you can deliberately slow down your breathing and relax your body, while paying attention to each inhale and each exhale – do this until you feel better. You can also take a few conscious breaths here and there throughout your day. A pleasant way of doing this is by breathing with your hands over your ears in order to hear yourself breathing – it is very soothing and will help a lot if you are suffering from acute stress or anxiety. Observing your respiration and listening to your breath is an amazing way to relax, and it helps bring your attention to the present moment.

Become present.

An easy way to do this is by simply bringing attention to your body, to the things around you, or to your environment. You are so often lost in your thinking that you do not take the time to appreciate physical sensations, such as the ground underneath your feet, the clothes against your skin, or how your inner body feels. You do not see the world around you, the colors, the shapes, and the textures. You do not taste the food you eat or listen to the sounds around you. Be present; observe the world around you without labels. Forget what you know about a chair, a tree, a bird's song, a mango, or your heart – simply become conscious and present, and really experience those things. Wherever you are, be there – not lost in your inner world.

Question your thoughts.

Instead of blindly accepting your thoughts, question their validity. There are several ways you can choose to do that. You can literally question the thoughts; for example, if you are thinking, "I'm going to be late for work and I will get fired," you can ask yourself, "Is it true that I'm going to be late for work and that I'm going to get fired? Can I be absolutely sure of that?" If you cannot be certain, then you have no need to stress. You could also ask yourself, "Is this thought useful to me? Does it help me right now?" The answer, of course, is "no." Therefore, you can follow up with "What can I do to improve the situation today? What can I do to improve things from now on?" Maybe the answer is to call the office and let them know that you're running late, and maybe from now on opt to place your alarm clock across the room, so that you actually have to get out of bed on time. Oftentimes questioning your thoughts will allow you to step out of your preconceived notions and automatisms (i.e. any reaction that occurs automatically without conscious thought or reflection).

Refocus or Reframe.

To refocus means to take your focus off something you do not want, or something that makes you feel bad, and putting all your attention on something completely different. You can refocus by consciously choosing to think in a more positive way – go for the best-case scenario instead of the worst-case scenario. Use distractions, such as uplifting music or funny movies. Listen to empowering messages or captivating audiobooks. Play some games that require your entire attention, such as crossword puzzles, Tetris, or do some mental math. Go swimming; spend some time in water or near water (water's negative ions are very helpful). Do something creative; write, sing, draw, paint, color, doodle, play music, or do a collage. Rearrange your surroundings – move furniture around, get rid of things, and organize other things. Do something nice for someone else or reach out to a loved one. Hug someone (touch is very soothing) or let it all out by venting – I didn't say complain because that would exacerbate the negative patterns, I'm merely talking about voicing facts in order to feel better.

To reframe means to consciously identify and change your negative beliefs or ideas. We all have a frame of reference based on our belief system and values. This frame determines how we see ourselves, the people around us, our stories, the world, and our life. Your new frame of reference is formed by changing your perspective or the meaning you have attached to things. It means identifying and disputing irrational or defective thoughts and finding new meanings – more positive alternatives. For instance, you can choose to reframe certain negative past events of your life and certain situations you are going through at the moment. The same goes for daily experiences and thoughts. So instead of thinking, "Growing up my parents were so strict and harsh with me," you could choose to think, "Things were different back then; my parents felt pressured by society and they did the best they could with the information they had." Or instead of "Nobody really cares about me, they never have time for me," you could think, "Everyone around me is pretty busy these days, I should attend this networking event or join this new cooking class to make new connections and friends!"

Move your body.

When you are in a negative frame of mind, the quickest way to snap out of it is to move your body. Straighten up, get up, move, dance, do some exercise, go for a walk, clap your hands, lift your arms, release those endorphins, and watch your thought patterns change on their own. You will feel more relaxed, calmer, and uplifted.

Write it down.

When you wake up in a bad mood, feel down or scared, or negativity is creeping in, write it down. Let it all out without editing or filtering your thoughts. Say what you feel, and allow yourself to ramble and rant for five or ten minutes. As the words pour out, your thoughts will calm down, and you will feel better. At times, you may even be surprised to see some pertinent and inspiring information transpire from your writings.

Affirmations or Power words.

People do not habitually give affirmations and power words the credit they deserve. An affirmation is a positive sentence said in the present tense that you say or write repetitively. A power word is just one word that symbolizes what you desire to achieve, e.g., peace, joy, love, compassion, etc. They help reprogram your subconscious mind. It is very important that your affirmations or power words produce spontaneous positive images and emotions within you. So, make sure that you believe your affirmations or power words are possible for you, and say them with matching emotions and images. So, for instance, if your word is "joy" or your affirmation is, "My life is full of joy," make sure that with every repetition, you feel as much joy as possible while visualizing people, animals, circumstances, and things that make you feel joyful. At first, this might feel a little awkward, or you may not feel strong emotions, but with time and practice it will get easier, and you will reap the benefits.

Stay away from your triggers as much as you can, and spend more time feeding your mind and heart the good stuff.

Stop watching five hours of news because it's all the same – if you feel you need to be informed, once a day is plenty. "Unfriend" the people that upset you on social media, and instead follow people or groups that inspire you and make you feel good. Stop watching violence on TV, your phone, or your computer, and watch funny movies or interesting documentaries. Stop getting over-informed about things that scare you, such as conspiracy theories or diseases, and learn new skills or read a good book. Stop hanging out with people that bring you down, and make new friendships with like-minded people. Try not to return to places that cause you emotional pain, and explore new spots. Release toxic relationships, if you can't, at least try to put a healthy distance between you and the person (or people) concerned. Finally, get rid of anything that reminds you of something painful, even if it was a gift or a high-priced item. Cut as many negative emotional cords as possible to allow much better things to enter your life.

Lastly, we are all unique individuals; therefore, you should explore and try different techniques that have the potential to help you step away from your negative patterns until you find the practices that best fit you.

Disclaimer: Here, I am speaking specifically about fearful and negative thoughts, which are completely useless most of the time. I am not talking about critical thinking, which is your ability to look at a situation, analyze it, and draw a conclusion that will benefit you.

For some, the techniques mentioned above will not be enough. While they can help, you may benefit from the additional assistance of a competent healthcare professional.

If you are experiencing uncontrollable panic or terror, suicidal thoughts, debilitating side effects, or compulsive and obsessive thought patterns, please help yourself by contacting a healthcare professional that can offer the help and support you need to heal. There may be underlying causes such as serious trauma, a mental or physical illness, a disorder, a chemical imbalance, or a deficiency that have been undiagnosed.

If at any time you or someone you know is distressed or is thinking about suicide and needs immediate assistance, please seek help, and contact a crisis center such as the National Suicide Prevention Lifeline at 1-800-273-TALK (8255). They are available 24/7 and offer free and confidential emotional support.

Get inspired

It's important that you find ways to get inspired daily. There are many ways to achieve this, and it will all depend on your own preferences. You could take walks in nature, listen to uplifting music, watch inspirational movies or documentaries, listen to motivational or spiritual teachers, read beautiful books or blogs, go to a place of worship or a seminar, join a class or a workshop, talk to close ones that make you feel good and encourage you, write in your journal, repeat affirmations, watch thought-provoking videos, or listen to interesting podcasts, etc.

Some days a song like "Happy" by Pharrell Williams is all you will need, while at other times you might need to watch two or three uplifting documentaries back to back. Just make sure to find ways to lift your spirit daily.

Practice a form of meditation

You can choose any form of meditation that suits you. Although people know the many benefits of meditation, many shy away from the practice because they feel that it is demanding or boring. There are countless forms of meditation. You can choose very short or very long meditations. You can choose guided meditations or meditations where you repeat a mantra. You can choose meditations where you attempt to focus on nothing, or meditations where you contemplate something specific. You will have to do a bit of research and exploration to figure out what works for you. I recommend that beginner meditators stick with simple and shorter meditations.

Sample meditations:

1. Sit or lay down comfortably, eyes closed, and practice conscious breathing. Place your attention on each inhale and each exhale – follow the breath inward and follow the breath outward. Feel the expansion with each inhale and the release with each exhale. When your mind wanders, gently bring your attention back to your breath. There is no right or wrong way of doing this, simply enjoy breathing consciously. Stop as soon as you've had enough. If two or three conscious breaths are all you can do for now, then do that.

2. Sit down comfortably, eyes closed, in silence. Do not do anything, do not listen to any music, do not move or fidget. Just be. Enjoy your own company. Feel your body. Observe your thoughts and emotions, with curiosity and compassion, not judgment. Do this for as long as it feels pleasant and stop when you've had enough. If all you can do is one minute, that's perfectly fine.

3. Practice walking meditation. Find a space where you can walk comfortably. You can keep your shoes on, but ideally you should be barefoot. Now relax your body; take a few conscious breaths. And begin walking very slowly, while focusing your attention on the movement of your feet, from heel to toe, and on every sensation that your feet feel as they lift and touch down. Stop as soon as you've had enough. If all you can take are five conscious steps, that's good enough.

The key to having a successful daily meditation practice is to be gentle with yourself. If at first all you have the patience for is one or two minutes every day, do that. Just go with your inner flow. Meditate until you feel like stopping, and stop when you've had enough. Any amount of time is better than no time at all, and you will still obtain positive results.

> Disclaimer: If you are curious about intermediate to advanced meditation practices, please make sure to contact a reputable teacher with great references. It can be unsafe to attempt certain meditations without the proper guidance.

Practice daily visualization

Visualization, also known as creative visualization or guided imagery, is a technique where you use your imagination to create specific mental scenarios of behaviors, experiences, or goals you would like to manifest in your life. It is a very popular technique among athletes, celebrities, influencers, and successful entrepreneurs.

Regardless of your opinions on the subject, it's undeniable that imagery has a significant impact on us. It is a well-known fact that certain images, colors, and shapes trigger emotions within you.

Every day, whether you realize it or not, you visualize detailed scenarios; these mind movies often spellbind you and ignite certain emotions that last long after you have stopped daydreaming. Unfortunately, the problem here, is that most people are in the habit of visualizing the worst-case scenarios instead of the best-case scenarios.

Use this know-how to create positive mind movies. Create detailed inner films depicting your life as it would be if you achieved all your present intentions and goals. Rehearse upcoming meetings or interviews. See yourself apologizing or forgiving people. Visualize healing a certain ailment or condition. Or create inner landscapes you can escape to when you need to relax or feel good. The trick here is to add emotions, sounds, smells, and as many details as you need to make it as real as possible for you. Of course, it will not be easy at first, but trust that if you can create horror movies, you are capable of creating beautiful ones.

To strengthen the process, you can also use vision boards or props; visit places that help you dream, meet people who inspire you, take part in guided visualizations, write out your visualizations (very powerful), and do anything that helps improve your visualization sessions. Optimally, to see rapid results you should practice daily.

If you want to manifest something, or feel emotionally involved in your inner movie, visualize things from a first-person point of view (associative). If you want to distance yourself emotionally, or heal from certain things, visualize from a third person point of view (dissociative).

Follow your intuition

Intuition has many labels: sixth sense, guardian angel, subconscious mind, gut feeling, God, higher self, inner voice, voice of the heart, etc. Whatever it may be, there is no refuting that it is real, that it seems to be all-knowing, and that it not only directly guides us, but also works harmoniously with life in order to communicate with us.

We all have different intuitive capabilities, and we are all more or less in-tune with our intuition. The more you connect, trust, and act upon your intuition's guidance, the easier and better things will become in your life. This intelligence will not only help you, but it will also direct you to assist others. It works for you and for the whole. It knows how to orchestrate everything in the best interest of all beings. The beautiful thing about intuition is that it helps us realize how unique and special we are, but it also helps us understand that we are all interconnected and interdependent.

At first, it can be a little tricky to differentiate the voice of your mind and the voice of your intuition. While your mind tries to reason, your intuition just offers information without any explanation. So, for instance, your mind will say, "Don't talk to him, he looks creepy," but your intuition will whisper, "Go home." The mind can be forceful and repetitive. The intuition is subtle and will simply offer gentle reminders if necessary. The mind continually calculates and analyzes how to survive and/or strive, while the intuition just continually tries to realign you with your highest calling.

In my opinion, they are both important but have different roles. The way I see it, the mind can foresee possibilities and deduce the best move based on acquired knowledge and past experiences, while the intuition can foresee every possibility and knows the best move. The mind helps us live within the parameters of this reality. Our intuition helps us fulfill our soul's purpose(s) and mission(s).

It is sometimes difficult for our minds to accept and follow our intuition, as it asks what could seem like awkward, puzzling, and/or perplexing things from us. "Don't board," as we have tickets in hand and are ready to get on the plane. "Don't eat that," as we are offered a meal at a dinner party. "Quit your job," as we have bills to pay. Of course, our intuition also gives us simple directives, such as "slow down," "listen," "smile," "relax," "breathe," or "trust," and offers comforting words such as "all is well" or "you are loved."

The more you connect to your intuition, listen to its wisdom, trust it, and act upon its guidance, the more you will experience phenomenal synchronicities, miracles, and most importantly, you will enjoy a magical life.

> Disclaimer: Your intuition will never pressure you, criticize, judge, or ask you to endanger someone's life or your own. If at any time you experience hallucinations, delusions, or believe that you are hearing voices, seeing people, or get "feelings" that are abusive and/or urge you to take dangerous and criminal actions, you could be experiencing a psychosis and should contact a healthcare professional immediately.
>
> A psychosis is a severe mental disorder wherein an individual loses contact or touch with reality. It impairs your ability to think, behave, communicate, and understand reality.
>
> Psychotic episodes can be the result of a number of different things, such as drug consumption, chemical imbalances, deficiencies, severe trauma, extreme events, emotional shock or distress, mental or physical illnesses, disorders, etc.

Move your body

People are becoming more and more sedentary and less motivated to move. Vehicles, machines, technology, our jobs, and pastimes all play a big part in this phenomenon. The less you move, the less you want to move, and the more fatigued and lethargic you feel. Often this leads to disorders, such as anxiety and depression, or feelings of boredom and dissatisfaction, which can result in undesirable outcomes such as overthinking, overeating, smoking, and other addictions. Our bodies, our minds, and our spirits need movement to remain as healthy as possible.

Exercising your body is important for your health and wellness. Here, I'm not asking you to join a gym or adopt a specific fitness routine; I am asking you to move your body.

Find methods to move your body every day in ways that feel good and fun. Dance, swim, walk, jog, stretch, skate, cycle, jump, hop, hike, play ball, windsurf, etc. Do what feels good, for however long it feels good. No strict regimen, or rules – just a good time.

If you feel up to it, invite others to join in on the fun. Ask a group of friends to join you on your evening walks; go to a salsa club with your sweetie on a Saturday night; try a yoga class with your favorite person, or yet again go swimming with your children.

And, if you want to kick it up a notch, join a gym or a fitness class (e.g. Pilates, yoga, water aerobics, Zumba, wall climbing, dance, cycle, martial arts, etc.).

Anything goes as long as you find a moment during your day to move your body in a fun and loving way. Sure, you will gain many benefits from being physically active, but the focus here is centered on caring for your physical body and creating a loving connection with it.

If you are limited in your mobility, do whatever is safe and feels comfortable. Water exercises or chair exercises can be good options, another great alternative is to get body massages. Getting regular massages are excellent to improve your overall physical and mental well-being.

Practice feeling good

I understand that asking you to practice feeling good can seem a bit strange or simplistic, but I assure you that it is a powerful tool that will undoubtedly challenge you at first but segue into miracles later.

If you are like most people, chances are you have no control over your moods and emotions. You may not realize it, but being a "victim" of your moods and emotions is actually a choice, one that you make repeatedly. Something happens, emotions surface, and you choose to entertain these feelings long enough that you end up in a mood. The problem here is that habitually, people do not choose to entertain positive emotions (those are often quickly dismissed), however they linger on anything that is even remotely upsetting to them. Ultimately, people often end up feeling miserable – this negatively affects them and the world around them. In conclusion, when I speak about practicing feeling good, I am talking about learning how to cultivate positive emotions instead of accepting to be led by emotions that do not support you.

Negative emotions, believe it or not, poison your mind, your body, and your spirit. You allow circumstances, people, places, and your thoughts to run your emotional life, and you wonder why you're a mess. If I ask you to make yourself mad or sad, very quickly you can call upon images or memories that will put you in those "moods." I suggest that you become as talented with the opposite spectrum of emotions. If you regularly practice feeling good for no reason, eventually you will be able to summon positive emotions at will.

This is a gradual process that will take time, but the payoff will be worth every minute you invest in the practice. To begin, whenever you experience a positive emotion, I want you to stay with that feeling and milk it for as long as you can. For instance, if someone offers a sweet compliment that makes you feel joyful, instead of quickly dismissing this positive sentiment, stay with that feeling for as long as possible. After you have done that for a few weeks, step it up. During times where you feel "okay," or during down times (before you fall asleep or when you wake up), try to deliberately feel certain positive emotions (e.g. love, joy, excitement, compassion, gratitude, peace, enthusiasm, etc.) – visualizing things that relate to these emotions will help. Once you are comfortable doing that, the next step will be to call upon good feelings throughout the day at completely random moments. And, finally, when you are proficient at carrying out all these steps, try cultivating positive feelings when unpleasant or upsetting things happen – start small and slowly progress to more important levels of discomfort. If you persistently practice all the above steps, eventually you will not only become skilled at managing your moods and emotions, but in fact you will also be able to feel exactly the way you choose to feel, instead of allowing moods and emotions to govern you.

Surprisingly enough, people are often conflicted about feeling good. It seems that we are continually reminded by our minds and the world why we shouldn't or can't feel good. You may believe that by feeling bad or negative, you are somehow helping a certain situation or showing compassion. You may think that if you dare choose to feel a more positive way, you are cruel, unrealistic, or irrational. But that's a lie. No matter how bad you feel, your negative feelings will not pay your bills, heal your friend, resuscitate your neighbor, feed the hungry, help the poor, etc. Don't misunderstand me; I am not proposing that you live in la-la land with unicorns and rainbows (well, maybe just part-time, haha!). Yes, there are upsetting things that happen in your life and in the world, and yes, it is normal to feel strong emotions or to stand up for your beliefs and convictions. What I am suggesting is that you refuse to stay trapped in negative states of being. A more positive emotional state naturally allows healthier answers and solutions to manifest and can prevent regrettable actions or reactions.

You owe it to yourself and to the world to feel good and emanate a more loving and positive energy.

Celebrate yourself for today

Self-love is first and foremost a choice that will reveal a new path to you. Like with any journey, you will have ups and downs. Remember to be kind, compassionate, patient, and loving with yourself. Listen to your needs and be as conscious as you can. Celebrate all your accomplishments. Think of objectives and goals you would like to achieve, but allow the road to unfold and your ideals to change. Most of all, regardless of the kind of day you've had, always remember to praise yourself every day for doing the best you could do for this day. Being human can be tricky, and it is important to celebrate yourself and your successes, no matter how small you may feel or they may seem.

Have fun

I know I have insisted on the difficulties you will be facing, and I have warned you of all the pitfalls you may encounter. I realize some may find this strategy somewhat counterintuitive, but in fact, I believe that knowing what to expect will be a great advantage to you. Change is not easy, and it does require heart and effort. To borrow a quote from the 80's cartoon G.I Joe, "Knowing is half the battle." If you know what to expect, you will know how to prepare, and you will have an easier time navigating through the program.

Still, your daily perspective and the way you choose to participate in this program will determine how well it all goes. My final recommendation is that you have as much fun as you can along this fantastic journey. A whole new world is about to open for you. Embrace the process, enjoy the ride, and delight in your new adventures.

Final Words

I want to congratulate you again for loving yourself enough to embark on this beautiful voyage. I admire your courage and willingness to step on this new path with this program in hand.

A lot of time and love have been poured into this project, and I know it has the capacity to transform your life for the better. My intention and greatest hope is that this book will assist you in finding self-love in the most joyful, exciting, gentle, and genuine way. That the seeds of love within your heart will grow and blossom, that you will carry out your unique purpose, and live your very best life.

Please remember that regardless of your past and present circumstances, the best is yet to come – your future is up to you. I know it sounds cliché and a bit corny, but it is the truth. Loving yourself will not only change the relationship you have with yourself, but it will also change your entire reality in the most incredible ways.

Now, go have fun!

Testimonials from a few participants

"I went into this journey craving to better myself and better my life. I wanted to stop looking so negatively at everything and the people around me. I wanted to not only change my circumstances but my perspective and outlook on things. In the beginning of this journey, I thought I had myself all figured out. I knew I was unhappy, and I knew I needed to work on myself, but I didn't understand just how lost I was. I cared about what people thought about me and let the words and actions of others affect my mood and how I behaved. I was very unhappy with where I was in my career (cashier) and the people I worked with, my grades were unsatisfactory, my study habits weren't the best, I had a challenging time standing up for myself and telling people how I felt. I was very self-conscious and barely posted pictures of myself, I had acne and hated my curly hair which resulted in me rarely leaving the house without makeup on or my hair straightened. I craved adventure and I wanted to travel but didn't know how to make it possible. This study forced me to form new, healthy habits and take much better care of myself. It caused me to step out of my comfort zone and experience new things. It made me dig deep and helped me see parts of myself I never knew existed and it helped me discover who I really am.

Now, I'm a pharmacy technician because I received a promotion from my job. I'm only getting A's and B's in school, it doesn't take me as long to study and retain information because I have a routine that works for me. I never let myself be unhappy or unsatisfied for someone else's comfort anymore. My face has cleared up tremendously and it is rare for me to get acne. I rarely put on make-up or straighten my hair, and I'm now comfortable in front of a camera. I've gone on multiple road trips, visited different states in this year alone, and discovered many cool new places and people.

After these 180 days, I can definitely say I've never been more different, and I've never been happier with myself as a person. Thank you for letting me be a part of this wonderful journey and for helping me truly learn what it means to love yourself first."

Marie B.

"I'm generally a pragmatic guy with a linear mindset focused on fairly traditional methods. I had recently completed my undergraduate degree (in my 40's). I have a decent job but no real growth potential in my current section – to advance, I would need to push outward and make changes. I was heavy, approximately 30 pounds overweight, poor muscle tone, and heading into the high blood pressure range. I was not communicating with my wife very well. After I finished my BS (and all of the evening work), I exchanged my school regimen into a lazy routine where I focused on mindless TV and not on my spouse.

In short:

- I was becoming a professional procrastinator
- I was not advancing professionally or receiving offers to interview
- I was overweight and unhealthy
- I was not communicating with my best buddy in the world
- I became a couch potato with no drive

Ok, great, so where am I at day 180? Does this stuff really work? It WILL work if you work it. If you are looking for magic, look in another section for the kids going to wizard school. Change takes effort and effort can be hard at first – how do you feel two days after you start going to the gym? Well, your mind and spirit are not immune to growing pains. Dig in and make it happen. Anyway – where am I?

- I am laser focused on my growth and began my MBA program
- I am highly motivated and open to radical career change. I am actively interviewing for positions that will facilitate professional growth and that will fulfil me personally. (Shortly after handing us this review, this participant contacted us to let us know he had been hired for a much better position.)
- I returned to the gym and radically altered my diet. I have lost 30 pounds and feel fantastic.
- My wife and I connect much better and have meaningful conversations about our fears, likes, dislikes, goals, and tomorrows. We support each other unconditionally.
- Lastly – I still like to watch TV but now it is an exception, not the rule.

In closing – there is zero risk in this program, only reward. How could learning how to love yourself be bad?"

Robert D.

"Ever had a feeling of being lost to the point you don't even recognize yourself anymore? That was me just before I was invited to take part in this study on self-love. I was afraid of being alone, afraid of failing, afraid to face reality, afraid of not being enough. I took care of everyone except me. I was unhappy in my relationship, I was unhappy with my body, I felt lonely, and had no idea what to do.

I was very excited to join this study! I was ready to invest time in myself. I was ready to love me again. I was ready to be happy. At the beginning I did not know what to expect, I just embarked on the journey. I loved that the exercises were always changing and they always seemed to come at the right time. For me this study covered everything (body, mind, emotions, etc.)

Today, I feel like a different woman. After a lot of work I have been able to face my fears and get down to the bottom of things. I am okay with being alone. I never used to feel grateful but now I count my blessings and say thank you for all that I have daily. I stopped saying thanks, I say thank you because it's more meaningful. I used to feel guilty for saying no to people, now I am able to say no easily. Before I thought having kids meant forgetting about myself and putting them first. Now, I know it is essential I put me first. I enjoy blasting my music, dancing, taking hot baths, going to the movies alone, and doing things for me. I never went out and would always decline invitations but now I am more open to have fun and do things with my family and my friends. I manage my time a lot better and I'm no longer stuck on my phone. Instead of wasting all my time on social media, I listen to audiobooks or read. I also spend time doing fun things with my girls like playing and coloring in coloring books. I was also able to declutter and let go of things I had emotional attachments to, I feel better knowing others will put them to great use. I am more in tune with myself and I listen to my emotions and gut feelings. I used to think I was too old to learn, I am proud to say I went back to school and I am now a CNA. I had stopped caring about the way I looked and was unhappy with my weight but I donated all my oversized shirts, began exercising and now I dress nicely again. I feel so much better about me and I continue to learn how to love myself more and more every day.

I know I'm going to need to continue practicing some of the things I've learned during the study to continue growing and I plan to. I was blessed to be a participant in this study. It turned my life around."

Annie V

"Before I started this study I was depressed. I had to quit dancing due to an injury, moved to a different apartment, not by choice, was heartbroken from my previous relationship, spent the majority of my time alone and felt like all my friends forgot about me. This book came to me at the time I needed and I am forever changed! You think as long as you aren't saying 'I hate myself!' or 'I'm ugly!' you love yourself, ya know? But loving yourself is so much more! I learned a lot about myself and those around me. I found a new perspective on life and how I want to live it! The past 180 days have been filled with love, knowledge, true happiness, new relationships and adventures. I got a job that I love, met a new group of friends that understand me, traveled to new places, and fell in love. Today, I feel like a new person and I love myself. I thank Melody for thinking to include me in this study."

Jadyn G

"Overall, I enjoyed the program. I thought the majority of the exercises were fun and I especially liked the outdoors one like hiking or walks in new places. I feel that it was a good learning experience that is well rounded towards finding peace and loving yourself.

I have experienced improvements in my work but also in my personal life. It has helped me create new rules for my life that are more helpful. Now I do not dwell on negativity and mainly focus on finding solutions. Since the program I have noticed that I have continued applying the different techniques that I learned to many aspects of my life which also helps me a lot.

One thing that I really liked from the program was that it makes you question yourself. I say this mostly due to the daily questions. At first I could not come up with good answers but in time it got easier and made me learn new things about myself that I found useful to know. Now, I believe it is very important to question everything, even yourself. I say this because there are a lot of things that we experience on a daily basis that we may store in our memory bank but don't consciously recognize and that was something I learned from those daily questions.

Looking back, the only thing I can say that I did not like was that I accepted to participate in the study at a time that was very busy at work and I didn't plan the daily exercises as I should have. It caused me to fall behind at times and I ended up rushing to catch up and it affected my results over time. I believe that I would have had even greater results if I had organized my time. If I were to do things differently, I would read the instructions carefully and I would make a plan. That would be perfect."

Kamaran W.

PART 2

Daily Love

Phase 1: Plant Love

Reminder: During this phase, you will gently begin to transition from where you are and who you are, toward your ideal self and your best life. You will prepare your mind, body, and spirit to receive new thought and habit seeds; in the process, you will pull out some weeds and let others wither. From there, you will slowly begin to deliberately plant new seeds – more aligned with your intentions.

This is a phase of transition between releasing the old personality and starting to grow genuine self-love. You are introduced to, and become acquainted with, your three bodies (mind, body, and spirit).

You will begin adopting new patterns of thinking, feeling, and doing things. You will start becoming self-aware and conscious. You will also begin seeing some inner and outer shifts and changes.

Today, I...

> ***"The beginning is the most important part of the work."***
> ***- Plato***

EXERCISE 1: Assess

In order to know where you're going, first you must assess where you are. Choose to complete this exercise when you can have at least an hour of undisturbed time. Make sure to make yourself as comfortable as possible by creating a soothing ambiance: get a warm drink, put on some relaxing music, or light a candle. Take a few deep breaths, relax and when you are ready, answer the following questions as honestly and thoroughly as possible.

1. As you begin this new journey, what are your expectations? What do you hope to accomplish in the next 180 days? Be as specific as possible.

2. On a scale of 1 to 10, with 10 being the most satisfied, how would you rate each area of your life? Circle the answer that best characterizes the way you feel at the moment.

Spiritual (connection with the Divine, mindfulness, meditation, etc.)	1	2	3	4	5	6	7	8	9	10
Relationship with yourself (self-love, self-care, self-awareness, etc.)	1	2	3	4	5	6	7	8	9	10
Family relationships	1	2	3	4	5	6	7	8	9	10
Romantic relationships	1	2	3	4	5	6	7	8	9	10
Friends and social relationships	1	2	3	4	5	6	7	8	9	10
Health	1	2	3	4	5	6	7	8	9	10
Fitness	1	2	3	4	5	6	7	8	9	10
Growth and learning (personal development, education, therapy, reading, etc.)	1	2	3	4	5	6	7	8	9	10
Career, business, occupation (student, stay at home parent, etc.)	1	2	3	4	5	6	7	8	9	10
Finances (income, savings, investments, etc.)	1	2	3	4	5	6	7	8	9	10
Philanthropy and community (volunteering, charity work, acts of random kindness, etc.)	1	2	3	4	5	6	7	8	9	10
Fun and recreation (hobbies, travel, entertainment, game nights, etc.)	1	2	3	4	5	6	7	8	9	10

3. On a scale of 1 to 10, with 10 being the happiest, how happy would you say you are? Circle the answer that best characterizes the way you feel at the moment.

Very Unhappy				Neutral					Very Happy
1	2	3	4	5	6	7	8	9	10

4. On a scale of 1 to 10 with 10 being the most positive, how would you rate the amount of love you feel for yourself presently?

I loathe myself				Neutral					I love myself completely
1	2	3	4	5	6	7	8	9	10

5. Write down words you would use to describe yourself (mentally, emotionally, physically, and spiritually).

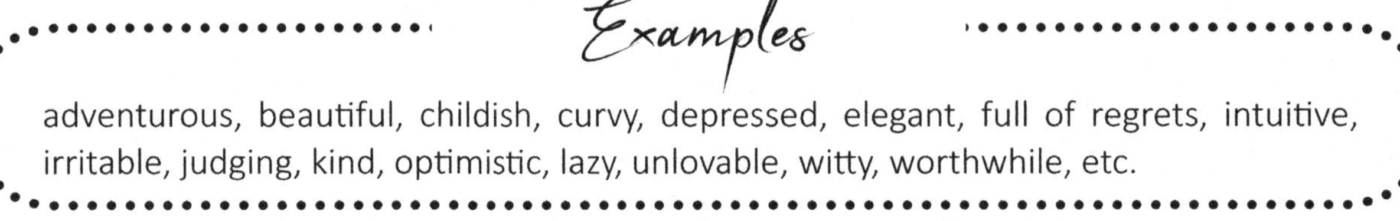

6. Are you able to spend time alone and enjoy your own company? Explain.

7. Do you think you are lovable and worthy of love? Explain.

8. Do you make time daily to do the things you love and enjoy? Explain.

9. When you look in the mirror, what do you see?

10. How do you feel about your body? Do you like or dislike it? Explain.

11. Do you allow circumstances and people to dictate whether you feel good or bad, or are you in control of your own well-being?

12. Do you rely on others to make you feel good about yourself, or do you have a good amount of self-esteem? Explain.

13. Do you feel you can be yourself around other people? Explain.

14. How are you unfair, hard, and abusive toward yourself?

15. How are you loving, kind, and gentle toward yourself?

16. Name your top five favorite things about yourself.

17. What are the most recurring thoughts and feelings you have about yourself?

18. If you continue treating yourself the way you do, what do you expect will happen in the long term? Explain.

19. Do you think things will be different in your life once you love yourself completely? Explain.

20. Do you connect to a higher intelligence and listen to your intuition daily? Explain.

Things that made me feel good today:

Things I noticed about myself:

Things I am grateful for:

Thoughts on the daily exercise:

Would you like to add anything else?

Today, I...

> ***"Keep your sunny side up, keep yourself beautiful, and indulge yourself!"***
> ***- Betsey Johnson***

EXERCISE 2: Indulge Yourself

Nowadays, most people lead very busy lives, continually feeling stretched between what they feel they need to do and what they feel they ought to do. Unfortunately, in the process, they neglect doing what they really want to do. Repeatedly pushing your needs and desires aside will inevitably result in anger, stress, resentment, and overwhelm.

Doing things that make you feel good should never be an afterthought – instead, they should be the first things you schedule when planning your day. To develop a healthy and loving relationship with yourself, you are going to have to step beyond your usual habits and start putting yourself at the top of your priority list.

Today, indulge yourself. Do something that makes you feel good. Be as present and conscious as possible during the process. Enjoy yourself, and be aware of the positive feelings and emotions that surface during this special time. Extend feeling good for as long as you can.

Examples

- Take a bubble bath.
- Buy yourself something nice.
- Get a massage.
- Take a nap.
- Go for a swim or a walk.
- Go to your favorite restaurant.
- Read a good book.
- Watch a documentary.

Things that made me feel good today:

Things I noticed about myself:

Things I am grateful for:

Thoughts on the daily exercise:

Would you like to add anything else?

Today, I...

> ***"Change happens through movement and movement heals."***
> ***- Joseph Pilates***

EXERCISE 3: *Neck Stretches*

Everyone, to an extent or another, deals with muscle tension that is uncomfortable or painful. An area of the body that commonly experiences stiffness, tightness, and pain is the neck – a lot of blocked energy and tension builds up in the neck because of different factors, such as stress, bad posture, being in a certain position for a prolonged amount of time, or sleeping on a bad mattress. Essentially, your neck is always holding your head; so understandably, it is always dealing with some degree of pressure. Taking measures to help prevent, ease, or relieve any discomfort in your neck area will assist your body significantly.

Today, you will alleviate the muscle tension in your neck by gently doing a few neck stretches throughout the day. While stretching, make sure to close your eyes, take a few deep breaths, relax your muscles, and enjoy the movements suggested in the examples below. Does your neck feel stiff? Does stretching feel good? Remain conscious of the way you feel, physically and emotionally, during each movement. Be gentle, remember to breathe, and do not force a stretch – you should never feel pain beyond a slight pulling. Always listen to your body and do what feels comfortable.

Remember, if you are experiencing severe or persistent neck pain, or other troubling symptoms, such as headaches, chest pain, vomiting, or numbness and tingling in your arms and legs, immediately contact a healthcare specialist for assistance.

Examples

- Gently move your head from side to side; bring your left ear toward your left shoulder and your right ear toward your right shoulder, making sure to go only as far as it feels comfortable for you.
- Gently tilt your head forward; bring your chin down toward your chest, and slowly bring it back up, going only as far as it feels comfortable for you.
- Turn your face gently toward your left shoulder, then toward your right shoulder, going only as far as it feels comfortable for you.

Avoid neck circles or any exercises involving your head going backward. Hyperextending the neck can be harmful and result in serious injuries.

Helpful Tips: Here are other ways to soothe your neck:

- Placing a warm or cool compress behind your neck is great for relieving tension.
- Allowing the back of your neck to get sun for a few minutes (about three to five minutes) can be very relaxing.
- Getting a massage from a reputable massage therapist, or a gentle neck massage from a loved one can be very soothing.

Things that made me feel good today:

Things I noticed about myself:

Things I am grateful for:

Thoughts on the daily exercise:

Would you like to add anything else?

Day 4

Today, I...

> ***"Your word is your wand. The words you speak create your own destiny."***
> ***- Florence Scovel Shinn***

EXERCISE 4: Affirmations That Make You Feel Good

Words are important, and they play an immense part in the way humans communicate, think, and feel. They are also significant when it comes to what you attract into your life or block out of your life. It is important to choose words that are positive and uplifting in your daily conversations, especially when talking to yourself and about yourself. Not only does putting yourself down or filling your dialogues with negativity upset you and the people around you, worst of all, it also impacts the way you program your mind; thus, your belief system. Your belief system determines a great deal of what happens to you; so be mindful.

Today, find or create five affirmations that make you feel good. Choose positive statements based on how they make you feel, not based on what you intellectually think you should affirm. Each statement should be written in the present tense, as in the examples below. Pay close attention to the feelings and emotions that arise with each statement you choose. Select statements that lift your spirit, and discard any statement that makes you feel unsure, negative, or triggers any inner resistance. Write them down and place them where you will see them daily. You can also choose to write them or repeat them every day. Each repetition will help reprogram your subconscious mind, change your thinking patterns, improve your belief system, and attract better circumstances into your life.

Examples

- "Every day, in every way, I'm getting better and better." – Émile Coué
- I am now open to receive all the good life has to offer me.
- I am now grateful for all my blessings.
- I expect miracles!
- Today, I choose joy.
- I love myself more and more every day.
- I am cool, calm, and at peace with life.
- "I love every cell of my body." – Louise Hay
- I value my well-being.
- I see opportunities everywhere.
- I make every day count!
- I welcome change; it's exciting!

Helpful Tips: You can write your statements on many medium

- Post-it notes you can stick to your desk
- Index cards you can read anywhere
- The cover of your journal or planner
- A dry erase board
- A bathroom mirror
- A vision board

Things that made me feel good today:

Things I noticed about myself:

Things I am grateful for:

Thoughts on the daily exercise:

Would you like to add anything else?

Today, I...

> ***"Attention pays attention to a lot of things, but when attention pays attention to attention, then there is a stillness, and that stillness introduces you to your Self."***
> ***- Mooji***

EXERCISE 5: Sit in Stillness

With busy schedules, busy pastimes, and busy minds, it is uncommon for people to make time for stillness. Becoming still and quieting down can feel uncomfortable and intimidating, as many of us are accustomed to continually having something to think about or something to do. It can even seem lazy or unproductive to those who believe that stillness is synonymous with procrastination.

There are several issues with never taking quiet alone-time for yourself. You end up feeling overwhelmed, exhausted, anxious, and often run into periods of burn-out. This in turn leads to confusion, depression, and sometimes illnesses and disorders. It is vital to disconnect from your busyness to restore a healthy balance, connect to yourself, and simply be.

Today, carve time out to sit in stillness, and quiet your whole being. Sit in a comfortable position, eyes closed, and embrace stillness by silently doing nothing. Be with the inflow and the outflow of your breath; be with your body; observe the thoughts that surface without losing yourself within them; be conscious of the emotions that arise without judgment; become aware of the sounds and the smells around you – enjoy being present. Do this for at least ten to fifteen minutes. When you are done, bring your hands over your heart, thank yourself for embracing this moment, and carry on with your day.

The more you practice stillness, the more you will benefit from stillness. Inviting and welcoming moments of stillness throughout your day will help you connect to yourself and find inner peace. As you become comfortable with this practice, you will be able to consciously bring more stillness into your days: in-between activities, during breaks, right after waking up in the morning, or right before falling asleep at night, etc.

Helpful Tips: To enjoy your moment(s) of stillness:

- Turn off all electronics (phone, television, radio, etc.).
- Make sure you will not be disturbed.
- Create a mood (light a candle, burn incense, etc.).
- Wear comfortable clothes.

Things that made me feel good today:

Things I noticed about myself:

Things I am grateful for:

Thoughts on the daily exercise:

Would you like to add anything else?

Today, I...

> *"In ancient China, the Taoists taught that a constant inner smile, a smile to oneself, insured health, happiness and longevity. Why? Smiling to yourself is like basking in love: you become your own best friend. Living with an inner smile is to live in harmony with yourself."*
>
> **- Mantak Chia**

EXERCISE 6: *List Your Smiles*

It is easy for people to spend an endless amount of time lost in negative thought patterns and scenarios. Allowing your mind to feed on negativity deeply affects your entire being in the worst ways. Many mental and physical symptoms, disorders, and illnesses are linked to negative patterns of thinking, as are many emotional and spiritual challenges and crises. Fortunately, to counter all of that, the list of benefits associated with positive and uplifting thought patterns is long: recovery from certain disorders and illnesses, better sleep, improved memory, healthier relationships, joy, well-being, etc. To enjoy more positive thought patterns, you must become conscious and choose better thoughts consistently. To do that successfully, it is imperative you feed your mind beautiful thoughts, and it is important to know what gives you an authentic inner smile. Knowing what makes you feel good is important in everyday life, but crucial during difficult times.

Today, list your smiles by creating a list of all the people, animals, places, and things that make you genuinely smile. Close your eyes, take a few deep breaths, relax, and ask yourself, "What makes me smile?" Observe what surfaces and write it down. Enjoy this process, and extend feeling good for as long as you can. Use this list as a daily reminder of what to focus on, or when you need to be uplifted during challenging times.

Examples

- Snails
- The color yellow
- Baby animals
- His Holiness the Dalai Lama
- Babies in tutus
- The ocean
- Dancing
- Seeing pictures of my children

My List of Smiles

Things that made me feel good today:

Things I noticed about myself:

Things I am grateful for:

Thoughts on the daily exercise:

Would you like to add anything else?

Today, I...

> ***"How do we change the world? One random act of kindness at a time"***
> ***- God (played by Morgan Freeman in Evan Almighty)***

EXERCISE 7: Do Something Kind

Although individuals often think of themselves in terms of dependent or independent, in truth we are all interdependent. I believe we all carry within ourselves the answers to each other's prayers, and true joy and happiness are found in answering those prayers – free of attachments or expectations. I am not suggesting you try pleasing everyone, or that you become a doormat incapable of saying "no." I am offering that you listen to your heart's guidance when it ushers you to do random acts of kindness.

Today, do something kind, thoughtful, or delightful for someone you care about – loved ones are too often overlooked. It is important you do this with no expectation of getting anything in return – no thank you, no reaction, nothing. The goal is to give joy freely to another without attachment or expectancy. That is true giving. If you already know what would please the person you want to surprise, do that. If you are not sure of what to do, close your eyes, take a few conscious breaths, relax, and think of the person. As you visualize that person, mentally ask them, "What can I do to make you smile today?" Wait and listen until an idea comes to you, and carry out whatever you feel inspired to do. Be present during the entire process, and act with a loving and giving heart. As soon as you have offered the gift or done the favor, let it go. Realize and appreciate that you are a powerful creator, capable of changing and affecting reality. Enjoy giving for the only purpose of giving.

Examples

- Do a chore your partner usually does.
- Make a special dinner or prepare a picnic.
- Send a greeting card.
- Give a thoughtful gift.
- Play a game with your children.
- Help a friend with a task.
- Write a cute note or send a cute text.
- Give a heartfelt compliment.

Things that made me feel good today:

Things I noticed about myself:

Things I am grateful for:

Thoughts on the daily exercise:

Would you like to add anything else?

Today, I...

> *"I take care of myself, because I learned early on that I am the only person in life who's responsible for me."*
> *- Halle Berry*

EXERCISE 8: Scalp Massage

The scalp is one of the most abused parts of the body, yet it is also one of the most neglected parts of the body. Caring for your scalp properly is vital, as a mistreated and unhealthy scalp can cause unpleasant outcomes, such as flakiness, itchiness, sores, and hair loss. Washing your hair regularly with gentle shampoo, avoiding the use of harsh styling products, eating properly, and staying hydrated are all ways of keeping your scalp healthy. However, another excellent way to maintain a healthy scalp is with massages. A scalp massage can provide many additional benefits, such as alleviating stress, improving sleep, stimulating blood flow, and even helping with hair growth.

Today, give yourself a well-deserved scalp massage. You can proceed in many ways. You can either move the tip of your fingers in a circular motion, or you can choose more of a kneading motion. Apply as much or as little pressure as you enjoy – just remember, no scratching and no use of nails, as this will irritate your scalp and break the hair. Make sure to massage all areas in a way that feels good and is relaxing to you. As always, the objective is to help you connect with yourself in a loving way, so do not rush the process. You can select to do a dry scalp massage, a massage while shampooing your hair, or use a medium, such as melted shea butter, or a warm oil, such as argan or coconut oil. Close your eyes, relax, and be conscious of the way you feel during the massage. Allow yourself to spend as much time as you need to delight in this moment.

Helpful Tips: Here are different ideas to enjoy your massage:

- Create a soothing atmosphere (candles, soft music, incense, etc.).
- Enjoy this massage while taking a bath.
- Massage your scalp while sitting down, elbows on a table, and head forward.
- Use all-natural oils or butters (olive, castor, jojoba, almond, sesame, cocoa, mango, etc.).
- Add essential oils to a carrier oil (peppermint, lavender, rosemary, lemon, etc.).

Professionals suggest scalp massages be performed, ideally, just before washing your hair.

Things that made me feel good today:

Things I noticed about myself:

Things I am grateful for:

Thoughts on the daily exercise:

Would you like to add anything else?

Day 9

Today, I...

> *"Too often we underestimate the power of a touch, a smile, a kind word, a listening ear, an honest compliment, or the smallest act of caring, all of which have the potential to turn a life around."*
>
> ***- Leo Buscaglia***

EXERCISE 9: Be Friendly

People's ability to ignore one another is quite mind-boggling and alarming. Constantly running from one activity to another, immersed in thoughts, or entranced by the screens of various electronic gadgets, it is easy to see how one would forget to notice the world around them. Conversely, since childhood we have been primed to fear others, with warnings such as "stranger danger," and we continue to be reminded of the perils of interacting with others through the incessant stream of news we receive from media outlets.

We live in a world populated by over seven billion humans, but sadly research shows a majority of people feel lonely. Sustained and chronic loneliness can have negative consequences in terms of our health and overall well-being. To be healthy, fulfilled, and happy, we need to interact with other human beings – to be touched, to be heard, and to be seen.

Today, take the time to be friendly and make small talk with someone you would usually overlook. Be conscious and present during your exchange, and really enjoy the other person with an open heart and mind. Recognize your capacity and ability to change someone's day or turn a life around. Appreciate that we are all capable of creating a better reality, not only with each other, but also for one another.

Examples

- Security guard
- Teacher
- Homeless person
- Janitor
- Cashier
- Neighbor
- Doorman
- Coworker
- Bus driver
- Crossing guard

Helpful Tip: Of course, safety first, pay attention to your gut feeling before talking with anyone. For added safety measures, you can choose to talk to people of the same gender or engage in public places.

Things that made me feel good today:

Things I noticed about myself:

Things I am grateful for:

Thoughts on the daily exercise:

Would you like to add anything else?

Today, I...

> *"The one thing that can solve most of our problems is dancing."*
> *- James Brown*

EXERCISE 10: Boogie Time

Dancing is an intrinsic part of cultures and traditions around the world – it has been a way for human beings to express themselves, communicate, exercise, worship, unwind, and celebrate for centuries. Have you ever seen someone dance and still be in a bad mood? Not likely.

There is something magical that happens when you allow your body to move and sway to music, it naturally uplifts you and transforms your frame of mind. While dancing feels good and is a lot of fun, it's also great for reducing stress levels, improving flexibility and balance, helping with weight loss and muscle tone, and supporting memory.

Today, turn on some of your favorite dancing music, and boogie. Let go of all your inhibitions, dance for as long as you feel like it, and anywhere you'd like. You can have a solo performance, or you can choose to invite family and friends to join the party. Really enjoy yourself – move your body, tap your feet, clap your hands, and simply allow your body and your inner child to have a splendid time. As your body moves to its own rhythm, remain present and pay attention to the way you feel physically and emotionally before, during, and after the process. Moving forward, try to dance a little every day and notice how it amplifies good feelings and enhances the quality of your life.

Examples

- In your shower (be careful not to fall)
- In your car (not when driving)
- In the street (look both ways)
- In a dance class
- At a club
- While doing chores

Things that made me feel good today:

Things I noticed about myself:

Things I am grateful for:

Thoughts on the daily exercise:

Would you like to add anything else?

Today, I...

> ***"Photography is simply a function of noticing things."***
> ***- Elliott Erwitt***

EXERCISE 11: Take Notice

Stop. Breathe. Look around. Observe all the things around you that you would usually ignore. There is an entire world out there that you are always too busy to see – people, animals, nature, and all sorts of things. Too often, lost in thinking, judging, and labeling, we forget to appreciate the life around us.

Today, as you go about your day, slow down, look around you, and take notice. Take photos of beings and/or things that captivate your attention. Do not overthink the process – just photograph whatever draws your awareness and speaks to you. The purpose of this exercise is to bring your attention back to the present moment, and to help you become an objective observer. For instance, do not look at a person in terms of woman or man, young or old, this or that – just do your best to observe the being without labels, judgments, or preset beliefs and opinions. Admire this fascinating reality – really look at it with a fresh perspective.

At the end of your day, before journaling, take a moment to look through all the photos you captured with the same unprejudiced and detached point of view. Appreciate seeing things with an open mind and a new point of view – find the beauty in everything you see. If you would like, share your favorite photo(s) on our Facebook group, share with others on social media, or print a few and paste them in your journal.

Remember, wherever you are, there are always a plethora of beautiful and interesting things to observe – even in the most devastated and desolate place, beauty can be found.

Examples

- People you love
- Flowers
- Insects
- Drops of rain
- Strangers
- Scenery
- Funny signs
- Murals

Helpful Tip: It would be wonderful if you took a selfie and really looked at yourself with the same unbiased and impartial mind. See yourself as you truly are, a beautiful and astonishing being. Your beliefs about your looks are learned labels and concepts. It is time to unlearn them and enjoy the truth – you are magnificent in all ways, and this shell, your body, is allowing you to enjoy this very existence. Appreciate it.

Things that made me feel good today:

Things I noticed about myself:

Things I am grateful for:

Thoughts on the daily exercise:

Would you like to add anything else?

Day 12

Today, I...

> ***"When I feel good about myself, things start happening for myself. When you look up, you go up."***
> ***- Herschel Walker***

EXERCISE 12: Feel Good Jar

On the journey to self-love, you will get down on yourself, have challenging days, and experience distressing emotions. During those tough times, it is valuable to have reminders to comfort you and help you remember that things will get better, that you are an amazing being, you are appreciated, you do great things, and that all in all, life can be really good.

Today, begin a "Feel Good Jar" – choose a nice container, or have fun, be crafty, and decorate a receptacle of your choice. Cut five small strips of paper, relax, and think about five things that genuinely make you feel good. You can write about something you are grateful for, a nice compliment someone gave you, an accomplishment you are proud of, a sweet memory, an uplifting quote you love, or anything that makes you happy. Fold the strips of paper and put them in the container. Take time to appreciate the present moment and bask in feeling good. From this moment on, try to add one strip of paper in the jar daily with something uplifting written on it. You can choose to wait until your container is full to read all your "feel good" mementos, or anytime you need a little pick-me-up, just grab yourself a few strips of paper. Make sure to place your jar somewhere you can always see it.

Examples

- Old pickle jar
- Empty box of Kleenex
- An empty water bottle
- A small basket
- A decorative bowl
- A papier-mâché box
- A mason jar
- A flower vase

Things that made me feel good today:

Things I noticed about myself:

Things I am grateful for:

Thoughts on the daily exercise:

Would you like to add anything else?

Day 13

Today, I...

> ***"Breathing in, I know I am breathing in. Breathing out, I know I am breathing out."***
> ***- Thich Nhat Hanh***

EXERCISE 13: *Mindful Breathing*

The physical body is so perfectly designed that it does most functions for our survival without us noticing or appreciating what truly takes place. Our breathing is one of those amazing natural phenomena that goes unnoticed and unappreciated – although without breath, we would not survive. Anyone having experienced breathing difficulties because of a disorder like anxiety, a reaction like anaphylactic shock, a disease like asthma, or any other issue, will tell you that breathing deeply and freely is an amazing gift.

Today, practice mindful breathing by taking several conscious breaths for one to three minutes. Repeat as often as you would like throughout the day. You can sit or lay down for this exercise – make yourself comfortable, close your eyes, and relax your entire body. Become aware of your breathing. Pay attention to the natural movement of your breath going in and going out. Follow each inhale into your nose and into your body. Follow each exhale out of your body and out of your nose. If your mind wanders, gently bring your attention back to your breath. Cease when you have had enough, but before returning to your activities, take a moment to appreciate that, with each precious breath, you are given the gift of life. Mindful breathing is a door into the present moment and allows you to expand your awareness. Consequently, it can be helpful in challenging and stressful times, as it will help you relax, find inner peace, and experience well-being.

Things that made me feel good today:

Things I noticed about myself:

Things I am grateful for:

Thoughts on the daily exercise:

Would you like to add anything else?

Today, I...

> ***"Nothing's better than a picnic."***
> ***- Zooey Deschanel***

EXERCISE 14: Picnic Time

For most of us, mealtime equates to a certain mechanical boring routine, so much so that ordinarily, the same repetitive meals are rushed and gobbled down between activities, or in front of some electronic device.

Today, skip the boring meals and the dreadful routine – it's time for a picnic! It doesn't have to be complicated. You can grab anything – a few sandwiches, some leftovers, a big salad, or a few pieces of fruit. The goal here is to eat differently. So, go have a fun adventure, and create a wonderful memory. You can enjoy a delightful picnic on your own, surprise that special someone, or organize a small outing with a few loved ones. If you have children, they will probably be very excited to partake in this activity. Whether you eat and enjoy the scenery, or plan a few activities, be as lighthearted as you can, enjoy stepping out of your routine, and let your inner child come out and play. Connect with your exuberance, relish the moment, forget the table manners, and have a blast. To truly be present and enjoy your picnic, take a few photos, then turn off your phone, and put away the gadgets.

Examples

- Lunch at the beach.
- Breakfast at the park.
- Dinner parked on a cliff overlooking the city.
- Brunch on a hilltop.
- Supper in your backyard.
- A poolside potluck.

Helpful Tips: To have a good time, keep these precautions in mind:

- Be aware of your surroundings; remember, safety first.
- Depending on where you are going and the time of day, remember bug repellent and sunscreen.
- A small first-aid kit can be valuable.
- Littering is not only bad for the wildlife and the planet, but can also result in a fine, so be mindful.

Things that made me feel good today:

Things I noticed about myself:

Things I am grateful for:

Thoughts on the daily exercise:

Would you like to add anything else?

Today, I...

> *"I've worked all my life on the subject of awareness, whether it's awareness of the body, awareness of the mind, awareness of your emotions, awareness of your relationships, or awareness of your environment.*
> *I think the key to transforming your life is to be aware of who you are."*
> ***- Deepak Chopra***

EXERCISE 15: *Bi-Weekly Report*

It is time to pause and reflect on the past two weeks. Complete this exercise when you can have at least one hour of undisturbed time. Make yourself comfortable by creating a soothing ambiance: get a warm drink, put on some music, or light a candle. Take a few deep breaths, relax, and when you are ready, answer the following questions honestly and thoroughly.

1. Summarize the past two weeks in a sentence.

2. Looking back, what are you most proud of?

3. What are some inner blocks and fears you noticed?

4. What important lessons did you learn?

5. What brought you the most joy?

6. What surprised you the most?

7. How are you doing in terms of loving yourself?

8. How has your relationship with yourself evolved?

9. How has your relationship with others evolved?

10. How has your attitude toward life evolved?

11. What tools, practices, or teachers have helped you the most?

13. What were your favorite and least favorite exercises? Explain.

14. What are you most grateful for at the moment?

15. What are things you would like to improve on in the upcoming two weeks?

Would you like to add anything else?

Today, as the daily exercise, either repeat your favorite exercise of the past two weeks or do an activity that feels good to your soul.

What did you do?

Today, I...

> ***"I've learned that every day you should reach out and touch someone. People love a warm hug or just a friendly pat on the back."***
>
> ***- Maya Angelou***

EXERCISE 16: *Hug, Hug, and Hug Some More*

It's not a secret that touch can be healing for the giver and the receiver. However, depending on the culture you live in, touch can be a "touchy" subject, where people feel uncomfortable embracing one another, or having any physical contact – this results in many people being touch-deprived.

It would be wise to reconsider the importance of touch as it offers unbelievable mental, physical, emotional, and spiritual healing benefits. Not only does hugging raise the production of happy hormones, such as oxytocin and dopamine, but it can also help prevent depression, relieve stress, and ease anxiety symptoms. Furthermore, it can assist with pain reduction, accelerating the healing process, and with the prevention of certain illnesses. Lastly, it helps us feel safe, connected, loved, and increases our sense of belonging. It is interesting to note that you do not need to touch another person to reap some of the many benefits of hugging. The small receptors under our skin are not choosy – therefore, you can hug your pet, a pillow, or yourself, and still benefit.

Today, hug, hug, and hug some more – cuddling and caressing are also excellent options. None of those side hugs or rushed hugs. Take the time to wrap your arms around yourself, your loved ones, your pets (remember to be mindful of their weight and size), or your pillow, and delight in big bear hugs.

I understand that for some of you, embracing yourself may feel strange at first, but that is all the more reason to do it – self-love and self-care include touching your own body in a loving way and letting go of those senseless taboos. As you hug, be conscious and present of how your body feels, the sensation on your skin, the feelings within your anatomy, and the emotions that rise. Let yourself relax into the warmth of the moment.

Remember, hugging a pillow, while thinking about someone you miss (e.g. during the grieving process, etc.) and allowing your emotions to come to the surface, can be cathartic and healing.

Things that made me feel good today:

Things I noticed about myself:

Things I am grateful for:

Thoughts on the daily exercise:

Would you like to add anything else?

Day 17

Today, I...

> ***"Beauty is really all about confidence. If you feel beautiful, then you are beautiful."***
> ***- Sofia Vergara***

EXERCISE 17: Hey, Good-looking

It is fascinating how wearing something that makes you feel attractive, something that makes you feel sexy, or getting all dressed up in a way that makes you feel beautiful or handsome can affect your confidence level. This program is not about inflating your ego or developing unhealthy narcissism, but a little vanity can be healthy.

Beautification of the body has had a significant place throughout history, and it means something different for each one of us. Depending on our backgrounds and our experiences, certain things make us feel attractive. Often it will be subtle things, such as a nice manicure, an exotic body butter, sexy lingerie, a blow-out, a new suit, jewelry, or a special fragrance. Each of us has very particular self-admiration standards.

Today, wear something that makes you feel attractive, or beautify your body in a way that makes you feel irresistible. If you have no idea what to do to feel beautiful, close your eyes, relax, smile, and ask yourself, "What makes me feel sexy and attractive?" Pay attention to the ideas that come to mind. You can also have fun and just experiment until you find your own formula. Take the time to pamper, groom, care, and dress yourself. You will know you have reached your goal when you begin to smile broadly, stand taller, and start feeling more confident. Enjoy the sensation of feeling attractive, versus trying to make yourself fit an inflexible idea or standard of beauty. Can you notice the difference? One makes you feel amazing – the other always makes you feel lousy.

Remember, this exercise is not about placing judgment upon your physical appearance, nor is it about improving it or perfecting it. This is about caring for yourself and feeling attractive without the need for a mirror.

Helpful Tip: If you are bound by a tight schedule, prepare your outfit the night before, go to bed earlier, and wake up an hour before you normally would.

Things that made me feel good today:

Things I noticed about myself:

Things I am grateful for:

Thoughts on the daily exercise:

Would you like to add anything else?

Today, I...

> ***"May your choices reflect your hopes, not your fears."***
> ***- Nelson Mandela***

EXERCISE 18: *Fearless*

Fear is a dominant emotion in people's lives, and unfortunately, it keeps many from accomplishing or realizing their dreams. The fear of failure, the fear of success, the fear of losing people you love, the fear of loneliness, the fear of change, the fear of ridicule, the fear of being different, the fear of getting hurt or dying – all fears that hold you back from being your best self and reaching your greatest potential. While some fears are apparent, other fears linger beneath the surface, subconsciously manipulating you.

Most fears have no roots in reality; still, they trap you, imprison you, and hold you back from living a joyful life. Nevertheless, there are some advantages to fear – the trick is in knowing how and when to use this emotion.

Fear is an emotional response to a real or perceived threat. Its purpose is to keep you safe and alive by triggering what is known as the "fight-or-flight response" (also referred to as "fight, flight, freeze response"). It warns you and protects you from certain dangers, and, in certain circumstances, it can help you do amazing feats, like lift cars, run at incredible speeds, or become hyper-focused (due to the release of certain hormones, such as cortisol, norepinephrine, and epinephrine (adrenaline)).

While fear is important for our survival and existence, it is also taxing and demanding. The physical, emotional, mental, and spiritual implications of allowing fear to incessantly run rampant are serious. Learning to differentiate a real threat from a perceived threat, and learning how to channel fear in helpful ways, is essential to live a balanced life.

In this exercise, we will only focus on one aspect of fear – the perceived fears that keep you from achieving your dreams. Being human means you can develop thoughts and estimate probabilities – situations that may come to pass and situations that would logically never happen, including your worst-case scenarios. When you allow certain fearful images and feelings to run amok within you, and entertain them endlessly instead of releasing them, rerouting them, or transforming them, you send the same signals to your brain you would if you were confronting a real threat.

Your brain cannot make the difference between what is real or imagined, so it releases the same cascade of hormones and triggers the same reactions it would if you were faced with real dangers. You react to your imaginings as you would in real-life situations – you fight, you run away, or you freeze.

You fear the unknown and what has yet to happen, based on your past experiences or data you have gathered from the world around you. You allow your worst-case scenarios to play in your mind over and over and believe them so much that you stop yourself from living. You do not allow yourself to have a beautiful love story for fear you might get hurt. You do not start that business for fear you might fail. You do not talk about your dreams for fear of being ridiculed. You do not want to be rich for fear it might change you. You do not want to appear overly happy for fear people will judge you. You do not want to leave an unhealthy relationship for fear you will end up alone.

Today, contemplate your recurring fears, and think about how your life would be different if you had none of these fears. Visualize a life where you do not allow your fears to dominate you and make you miserable. A life where the opinions of others do not matter. A life where you are authentically you, giving yourself permission to have fun, enjoy, try new things, and experience freely. A life where you understand that failure and rejection are only skewed point of views, that in reality all experiences help you grow and evolve. A life where you accept that joy, love, happiness, and abundance are your birth rights. A life where you follow your own heart and dreams regardless of what may or may not happen. A life where you are aware of the ephemerality of your time in this reality, and you purposefully and meaningfully live to your fullest and greatest potential. What does it look like? What would you be doing differently? Who would you be? What would you try? Who would you have in your life and who would no longer be part of your life? Now, on the space provided complete the statement with as many details as possible – be as descriptive as you can. Do not restrain yourself or think about what you deem possible or not for yourself. Allow yourself to give in to the experience, let yourself write as fast as you can and as freely as you can.

Helpful Tip: Your mind will attempt to make excuses or present a case for why certain things could never happen. It is fear speaking. Observe the fear, but instead of blindly believing it, do yourself a favor and question it, challenge it, or release it. Being fearless does not mean you will stop having fears; it means you will not be controlled by those fears any longer. It means you will consistently make more fulfilling choices for yourself, based on the possibilities you want to explore, the adventures you want to experience, and the dreams you want to actualize during your lifetime.

If I were fearless, I would

Now that you have allowed yourself to be fearless on paper, try to think of ways you could be fearless in your own life. Start with simple things, like saying "no" when you do not want to do something, or simply doing certain things, regardless of the sting of fear. Try to bring more fearlessness into your everyday life by remembering the mental images you created in this exercise. Remember, your life is worth living – be creative, have experiences, and allow your perspective of what is good or bad, acceptable and unacceptable, possible and impossible, to evolve and grow. Change your way of thinking in ways that support you and your aspirations. I find it helpful to keep the end in mind. I always ask myself the following questions: "If this was my last day, what would I say, do, try, or experience differently?" and "At the end, when I'm reviewing my entire life, what do I want to see?" From this perspective, nothing is a failure, and everything is an adventure.

Things that made me feel good today:

Things I noticed about myself:

Things I am grateful for:

Thoughts on the daily exercise:

Would you like to add anything else?

Today, I...

> ***"Let silence take you to the core of life."***
> ***- Rumi***

EXERCISE 19: *Silence*

When was the last time you enjoyed real peace and quiet? In this day and age, most people experience sensory overload brought on by noise, clutter, crowds, mass media, technology, and other modern stimuli. Whether we realize it or not, this overstimulation overwhelms us, is intensely stressful, and deeply affects our well-being.

People have become so accustomed to this chaotic lifestyle that silence has become unnerving, eerie, and scary. Interrupting or distracting ourselves from silence has become an automatism, and people have a real fear of sitting in silence with themselves. It makes them uncomfortable and uneasy, yet silence is a great healer and revealer.

To develop a more loving relationship with yourself, you must be able to spend quiet time in your own company. Practicing periods of silence will benefit your three bodies (body, mind, and spirit). It will relax your senses and your muscles. It will expand your intuition and offer clarity, inner peace, and bouts of creativity. You will feel energized and rejuvenated, present and aware. With that will come a reduced need to interject or interrupt, better listening skills, a deeper connection with yourself, and great wisdom.

Today, schedule at least 30 minutes of silence. Before you begin, make sure you will be undisturbed; turn off all electronic devices (yes, including your phone); make sure your surroundings are quiet from human or artificial noises, and begin your practice. Keep a notepad next to you in case you receive a great idea or insight, but do not journal. Do not partake in activities that would prompt you to talk or that would over-stimulate your mind, such as doing work or reading. Either relax or participate in light activities. Be present and listen to the silence. When your mind wanders, gently bring it back to the present. When done, place your hands over your heart, and feel gratitude for this precious moment. Slowly transition back to your activities.

If at any time you grow anxious or uncomfortable, be loving to yourself, and stop the practice for today.

Things that made me feel good today:

Things I noticed about myself:

Things I am grateful for:

Thoughts on the daily exercise:

Would you like to add anything else?

Day 20

Today, I...

> ***"Let food be thy medicine and medicine be thy food."***
> ***- Hippocrates***

EXERCISE 20: *Watch Your Diet*

In our fast-paced societies, eating is often a matter of opening a can, a box, or a carton. The convenience of these prepackaged and processed foods makes preparing meals so much easier and often a lot more affordable. While this could seem like a blessing, it has corrupted our instinctive wisdom and altered the way we eat, think, feel, and do things when it comes to nutrition. On one hand, the ease of grabbing a pack of chips and sitting in front of the television has pushed many to over-snack and overindulge. On the other hand, many of the ingredients, such as salt, sweeteners, colorants, preservatives, fats, additives, and chemicals in those foods, coerce our brains into ignoring the body's natural signals – which results in chemically-induced cravings. And to add insult to injury, these foods have disastrous consequences on our health. Our bodies are not designed to eat this way, so they slowly break down. A big part of self-love is developing a relationship with your body. While you might be in the habit of condemning and judging your body for everything you dislike, every cell that encompasses your anatomy works hard to keep you alive. Maybe it's time to appreciate it and offer it some tender loving care. The best way to begin this journey is to become aware of the way you nourish yourself.

Today, eat like you would on any other day, and write down everything you eat and drink during the entire day. Also, write down how you feel afterward – count around 20 minutes for a good estimate. Try to look up the list of ingredients of everything you consume. At the end of the day, look at your notes, and think about your everyday diet. Do not think in terms of body image because this is not the point of this exercise. Here, the goal is to awaken you to how you feed your body. To feel compassion for your body, and come up with a plan to adjust or improve your diet in a way that is healthy and healing for your body, so that you can enjoy a longer and fuller life.

Continuing this exercise for a week would give optimal results. In order to truly understand your patterns and how your diet affects your body and your mood, at least seven days are needed.

Time	Food / Beverage (and quantity)	**Body and mood aftermath** *(Bloated, sleepy, energized, sluggish, satisfied, heart burn, stuffed, etc.)*

Time	Food / Beverage (and quantity)	Body and mood aftermath *(Bloated, sleepy, energized, sluggish, satisfied, heart burn, stuffed, etc.)*

Things that made me feel good today:

Things I noticed about myself:

Things I am grateful for:

Thoughts on the daily exercise:

Would you like to add anything else?

Today, I...

> ***"Everything I learned I learned from the movies."***
> ***- Audrey Hepburn***

EXERCISE 21: *Flashback Movie*

As children, we all had movies and shows that shaped our beliefs and inspired wondrous dreams. Years later, as we look back on those films or series, we sometimes wonder what we found so funny or beautiful. Yet, there is a child who lives within us who might still smile and enjoy watching these older motion pictures.

During our early teens, we are told we can no longer be a child. We are pressured to grow up and act mature. So, with time, we associate acting like a child as being inappropriate and embarrassing. Sadly, this usually pushes us to become narrow-minded and self-important. Joy is a child's specialty – giggles, fun, adventure, and play are all synonymous with a jubilant heart – whereas taking yourself too seriously stunts your spirit, keeps you living a dull life, and prevents you from experiencing true delight. Recapturing this vibrant spirit and youth is essential for your happiness.

Connecting to your inner child, allowing this younger version of yourself to have a voice, to play, and have desires fulfilled, will help you heal childhood traumas and pains, as it will encourage you to give free rein to a more fun and more jovial you.

Today, go down memory lane and watch a movie or a show you watched and loved as a child. Enjoy watching from both your perspective and the perspective of that small child within. Do you still enjoy that film, show, or cartoon? Does it bring back good memories? Can you see why your inner child loved it so much?

What did you watch? How did it make you feel? Explain.

Things that made me feel good today:

Things I noticed about myself:

Things I am grateful for:

Thoughts on the daily exercise:

Would you like to add anything else?

Day 22

Today, I...

> ***"I love the magic of a hot bath, how time pauses and every grievance melts away."***
> ***- Richelle E. Goodrich***

EXERCISE 22: Bath Time

When looking into self-care practices, one of the first suggestions is always to take a bath, and for good reason. Not only does taking a warm bath help you unwind and feel good, but it also leads to many other benefits, such as muscle relaxation, relief of certain aches and pains, skin detoxification, and reduction of stress and anxiety. It is a great way to re-energize your three bodies (body, mind, and spirit).

Today, make time to slow down and take a soothing bath. Make sure you will be uninterrupted, then create an ambiance that makes you feel good: dim or turn off the lights, light candles, listen to gentle music or a guided meditation, or simply delight in a moment of deep mindfulness and silence. If you cannot take a bath, you could always soak in a hot tub, get a bath treatment at a spa, or just enjoy a warm shower. Bathe for as long as you want, and delight in this relaxing and peaceful moment.

Examples

- Add a tablespoon of a natural oil, such as coconut or olive oil to moisturize your skin.
- Add a few drops of essential oils, such as lavender or lemon.
- Use natural bath bombs or bath salts.
- Add oatmeal sachets to your bath water to enjoy all the anti-inflammatory benefits.
- Place a shower burst, a tablet, or a shower bomb in the shower to turn it into an aromatherapy experience (place away from the stream of water for slow release).
- If taking a shower, tie eucalyptus to your showerhead. The steam will release beneficial oils.

Helpful Tips: To enjoy your bath keep the following in mind:

- Take necessary precautions to prevent slipping, falling, and hurting yourself.
- Make sure the water is warm but not too hot, as it can strain your heart.
- Do not take a bath right after a meal, as it can provoke nausea and vomiting.
- If you experience any discomfort, slowly and safely get out of your bath.

Things that made me feel good today:

Things I noticed about myself:

Things I am grateful for:

Thoughts on the daily exercise:

Would you like to add anything else?

Today, I...

> ***"Every day I walk myself into a state of well-being and walk away from every illness; I have walked myself into my best thoughts."***
> ***- Soren Kierkegaard***

EXERCISE 23: Walk

Walking is often one of the most recommended physical activities because it is easy, it requires no equipment aside from tennis shoes, and most people can do it. Just thirty minutes a day can help with weight loss and digestive issues; it can even reduce the chance of heart disease and other chronic illnesses, such as diabetes. Finally, being low-impact, it is a very good option for people suffering from conditions such as arthritis, as it is easy enough on the joints.

Walking also offers other interesting advantages, such as reducing symptoms of anxiety and depression, uplifting your mood, and enhancing your creativity. It can help you see things from a different perspective and give you some needed inner peace. Even people with mobility issues who need a scooter or a wheelchair can gain from "going for a walk" in similar ways.

Today, go for a walk, and enjoy moving around in the world. Remember to remain present as much as possible and to connect to your body. Notice how the soles of your feet feel as they lift and fall back to the ground; feel your entire body as it moves forward; pay attention to your breathing and your heart rate. Take joy in opening your eyes and seeing your environment, smelling new scents, hearing different sounds, and observing yourself in the midst of it all.

Depending on the weather conditions in your area, remember to take precautions, and of course, make sure to stay hydrated.

Examples

- Go for a walk around the block with your human or furry babies.
- Go on a hike with friends or loved ones.
- Enjoy a walk in a natural setting, like the beach or a park.
- Walk around in a store or at the mall.
- Walk on a treadmill or in a pool.
- Mop your floors or go up and down the stairs.

Helpful Tips: Here are a few ideas to make your walk more interesting:

- Buy a pedometer, or download a tracking app, and have a fun challenge with yourself or with friends. Choose a number of steps to walk in a day and see if you can beat your own record.
- Plan a fun scavenger hunt for kids or adults (there are lots of ideas online).
- Nordic walking can be a fun choice that will also increase your upper body strength.
- Walk for charity. You can download an app like Charity Miles Walk & Run Tracker (http://www.charitymiles.org) and earn money for your favorite charities by walking, or visit websites like http://www.charitywalksblog.com/charity-walk-events or http://www.active.com and join a real walking event.
- Embark on a spiritual voyage and sign-up for a pilgrimage (e.g. Inca Trail to Machu Picchu, Kumano Kodo trail, El Camino de Santiago, Mount Kailash Trek, etc.).

Things that made me feel good today:

Things I noticed about myself:

Things I am grateful for:

Thoughts on the daily exercise:

Would you like to add anything else?

Day 24

Today, I...

> ***"Anytime you start a sentence with I AM, you are creating what you are and what you want to be."***
> ***- Wayne Dyer***

EXERCISE 24: I Am

The power of "I AM" has been talked about by spiritual teachers for centuries. The principle suggests people should choose wisely the words they utter after "I AM" because it is a creative power, a form of prayer, or an intention. You do not need to be a spiritual person to understand the authenticity of this philosophy. We witness the power of words in our lives every day; they make us smile, they make us happy, they inspire us, but they can also upset us, anger us, and sometimes break our hearts.

Your subconscious mind accepts whatever information you offer without question. Therefore, if you make negative or disempowering claims, such as "I am ugly," "I am stupid," and "I am always broke," or other self-sabotaging statements, such as "I try to be on time," "I should do my homework," and "I can't make up my mind," you are not only fusing certain patterns within your brain, but you are also continually programming your subconscious mind in ways that hurt and harm you. These declarations then affect your behavior, your actions, and your reactions. As you take steps toward self-love, it is important that you redefine yourself by changing the way you communicate with yourself and about yourself.

Today, complete the "I AM" mind map on the next page, and list all the qualities, the positive traits, and dreams you have, or wish to attract to you. Have fun, and do not stop to think whether something is possible for you; just make sure your words bring up powerful images that make you feel good, and allow the momentum to fill you with uplifting feelings and emotions. If you put your heart into this exercise, you will more than likely notice a shift in your energy and in your state of being. During the day, pay attention to the way you use the words "I AM" – be mindful and make sure your statements are aligned with who you currently desire to be or what you want to attract into your life.

Moving forward be mindful to use the words "I AM" in ways that are kind, supportive, and favorable.

Examples

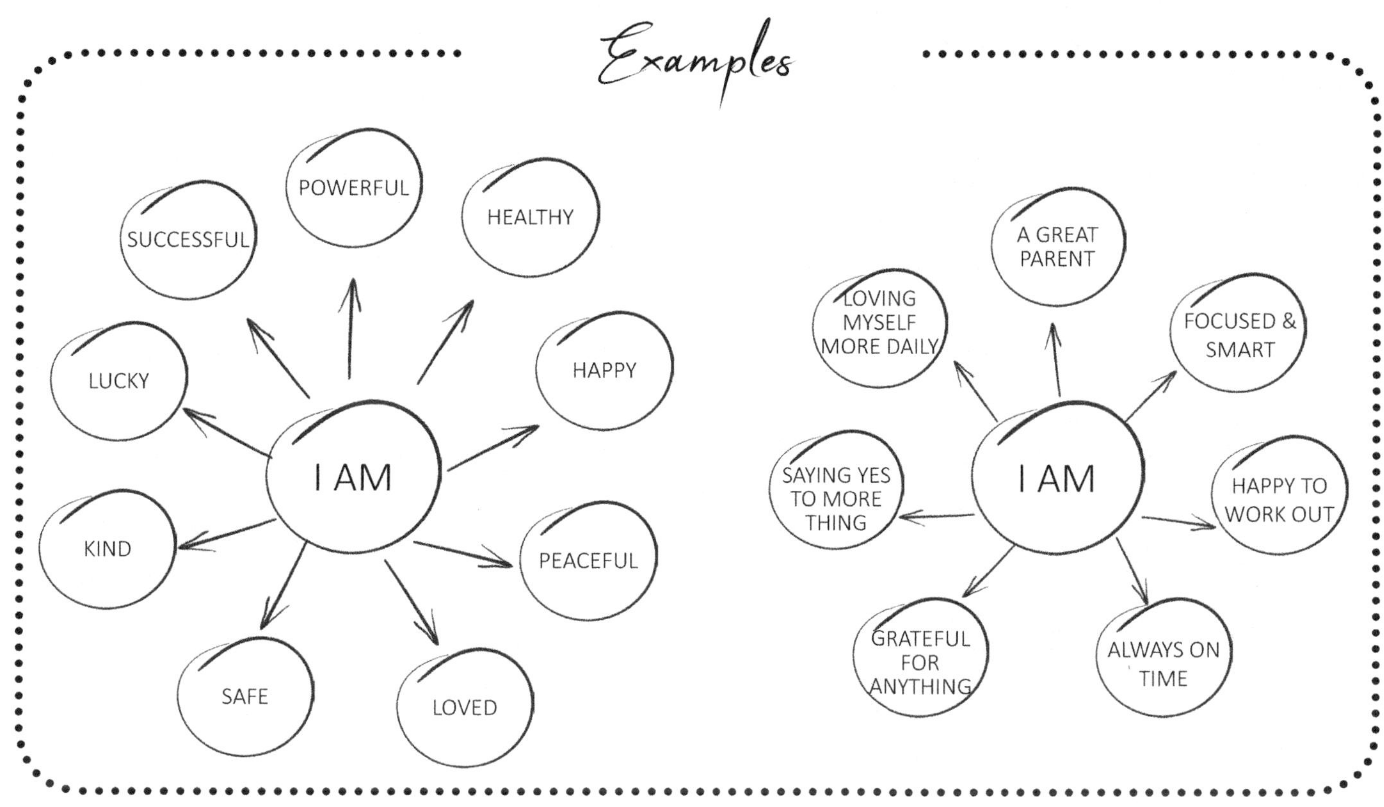
I AM
POWERFUL
HEALTHY
SUCCESSFUL
LUCKY
HAPPY
KIND
PEACEFUL
SAFE
LOVED
I AM
A GREAT PARENT
LOVING MYSELF MORE DAILY
FOCUSED & SMART
SAYING YES TO MORE THING
HAPPY TO WORK OUT
GRATEFUL FOR ANYTHING
ALWAYS ON TIME

I AM

Things that made me feel good today:

Things I noticed about myself:

Things I am grateful for:

Thoughts on the daily exercise:

Would you like to add anything else?

Today, I...

> ***"The body is consuming energy when tense, and restoring energy when it is relaxed."***
> ***- Ronnie Lott***

EXERCISE 25: Relax Your Muscles

The body is such a beautiful piece of organic machinery, yet it is continually mistreated and abused. It tries to perform all the functions it was designed to carry out relentlessly, and it will always do its best, given its unique set of issues and circumstances, to keep us alive, regardless of the stress and the abuse.

As we go through our daily lives, we take this magical phenomenon for granted and rarely pay attention to the needs of our body. Many inner and outer stimuli deeply affect the body: the thoughts we think, the emotions we feel, the long hours sitting or standing on our feet, the different sounds around us, the harsh lighting, the fluctuating temperatures, the allergens and chemicals in our environment, dehydration, etc. This all leads to muscle tension, which inevitably burns through the body's energy and slowly breaks it down, resulting in fatigue, various ailments, and diseases.

You may not realize it, but your body is probably tense as you are reading these words. Perform a quick body scan, and try to notice if your jaw is clenched, if you feel tension behind your neck or in your shoulders, if your hands are in a tight fist, or if you are frowning. When one body is stressed (in this case the physical body), it affects the other two bodies (mind and spirit) as they are deeply interconnected; therefore, it is important to maintain harmony and balance within each one.

Today, help your physical body unwind by consciously relaxing your muscles each time you notice they tense up. Pay close attention to the neck and shoulder area, and your jaw and brow area, as they tighten up more noticeably than other muscle groups. Reduce the tension by closing your eyes, taking a few conscious breaths, and deliberately relaxing the stressed area(s).

Visualizing the color blue, a body of water, or sending loving energy to the affected area(s) can also be very helpful.

Helpful Tips: Here are other ways you can ease muscle tension:

- Get a professional massage.
- Take a warm bath or shower.
- Do some light stretching exercises or yoga.
- Massage your muscles using a foam roller.
- Enjoy a sauna session.
- Practice meditation or take a nap.

Things that made me feel good today:

Things I noticed about myself:

Things I am grateful for:

Thoughts on the daily exercise:

Would you like to add anything else?

Today, I...

> *"We all possess more power and greater possibilities than we realize, and visualizing is one of the greatest of these powers."*
> *- Genevieve Behrendt*

EXERCISE 26: *Let Yourself Be Guided*

Visualization and meditation are two of the most misunderstood practices, yet both are powerful and can transform your life. People often confuse one for the other, and although meditation sometimes includes visualization, they are different and offer different results.

The objective of meditation is either to help the mind focus, or to quiet the mind. It involves relaxing the body and breathing slowly and deeply. Meditation generally encompasses focus, breathing, inner peace, healing, deep relaxation, and spiritual connection.

Creative visualization (also known as guided imagery) is proactive and helps attain a certain goal or desire. It uses our ability to envision images, our senses, and our emotions to form a mental movie in line with the desired results. It is used for relaxation and healing, achieving physical and material goals, changing certain patterns and habits, connecting to various aspects of ourselves, or developing spiritual connections. Visualization includes, but is not limited to, reprogramming your subconscious mind, creating new connections in your brain, developing new habits, accomplishing goals, and attracting desires.

Sometimes, whether you are a novice or a seasoned practitioner, it is nice to open yourself to some external guidance. Guided visualization or meditation will help the beginner become acquainted and comfortable with the practice, and help the more experienced student discover new techniques, or enjoy new adventures.

Today, decide whether you want to visualize or meditate, and choose material in line with your desired outcome. Would you like to relax, cleanse your chakras, or sleep better? Then, perhaps a guided meditation is the perfect practice for you. Or would you prefer to talk with your inner child, heal from a certain disease, or experience success in a certain area of your life? In that case, a guided visualization may be better for you.

When you have found a recording, try to listen to it entirely, or at least to the first few minutes, to verify that the voice of your guide, the pace of their speech, the music, and all the sounds resonate positively with you. Once you are ready to begin, make sure you will not be disturbed; dim the lights or turn them off, get comfortable, and listen to the audio material you have chosen. I recommend using headphones; they will help you focus and feel immersed in the experience. At the end of the day, share your insights in the space provided.

Remember, regularly practicing both meditation and visualization will be valuable to you and will offer amazing results, inwardly and outwardly.

Helpful Tips: Here are a few ideas that can be helpful:

- Listen to material from popular teachers, such as Deepak Chopra (http://www.chopra.com).
- Listen to free recordings on YouTube (https://www.youtube.com).
- Download an app, such as Headspace (https://www.headspace.com) or Calm (https://www.calm.com).
- Find a script you like online, record it on your phone, and play it for yourself.

What did you practice? How did it make you feel?

Things that made me feel good today:

Things I noticed about myself:

Things I am grateful for:

Thoughts on the daily exercise:

Would you like to add anything else?

Today, I...

> *"Think of something new you've actually learned in the past week; if you can't think of anything, get comfortable where you're at because you're not going anywhere. To stop learning is to stop living."*
>
> **- Robert Kiyosaki**

EXERCISE 27: *Learn Something New*

Being the product of boring and daunting educational systems, learning can be associated with negative, even painful memories, and make people reluctant or unwilling to learn anything new. So, ordinarily, unless someone is forced to learn something different due to life circumstances, educational or professional requirements, most individuals become complacent and embrace routines that leave no room for acquiring new knowledge. This can have detrimental consequences and deeply affect someone. Depression, anxiety, precocious aging, boredom, and isolation are potential side effects of staying in a mundane and non-changing reality.

Learning is a lot of fun once you open yourself up to enjoying new experiences, new adventures, and new knowledge. There are many benefits to learning new things; you will feel happier, and you will connect with new people. You will have more confidence, and your purpose will become clearer. You will develop more skills. You will broaden your perspective, become more creative, and more interesting. Finally, it can also help reduce your risk of developing dementia.

Regularly learning new things will be transformative for you.

Today, learn something new. If you are perplexed or unsure of what to learn, sit down and make a quick list of all the things you would like to learn, or are interested in learning. Begin with the one you can start today. Go into this activity with enthusiasm and make sure to have a lot of fun during the process. To successfully integrate this new exercise more consistently and become a lifelong learner, frequently switch between simple subject matters and more challenging ones.

Examples

- Learn how to code or play a new game.
- Learn a new hack or magic trick.
- Listen to a new audiobook or album.
- Learn how to play an instrument or play golf.
- Go to a workshop or a seminar.
- Begin a new exercise program or a university course.
- Read a book on gardening or investing.
- Join a book club or a knitting club.
- Learn how to swim or ride a skate board.
- Take a cooking class or an art class.

What did you learn? Did you have a good time? Explain.

Things that made me feel good today:

Things I noticed about myself:

Things I am grateful for:

Thoughts on the daily exercise:

Would you like to add anything else?

Day 28

Today, I...

> *"I want to give some positive messages and to empower some people."*
> *- Chaka Khan*

EXERCISE 28: Positive Messages

Occasionally, we all need to be pleasantly surprised out of the humdrum of our routines. Getting an unexpected call from an old friend, finding money on the street, being given a spontaneous compliment, or finding a sweet surprise on our desk can change our days from ordinary to extraordinary.

Today, leave positive messages of hope, love, encouragement, and kindness wherever you go. You can do this exercise alone, or invite friends and loved ones to partake in this fun activity. You will need to gather a deck of post-it notes, index cards, or small pieces of paper, and write uplifting, inspiring, comforting, and friendly messages on each note. Think of writing things you would love to read, or simply share some heartfelt messages; it can be a few words or a few sentences. Now, go out into the world, and have an awesome time leaving them around, or hiding them in different, obvious and less obvious places. Be discreet about it and leave before anyone can see you. Do not stay to witness the reactions of the recipients – the joy is in the doing. Delight in imagining the joy in the hearts and the smiles on the faces of those who will receive your gifts.

Allow your intuition to guide you through the entire process.

Helpful Tips: Here are a few ideas of where you could place your notes:

- In the pockets of garments at a boutique.
- In books at a library or a bookstore.
- Taped to products at a grocery store.
- In the stall of a public restroom.
- On the desk of a teacher or coworker.
- On the seat of a bus or the subway.
- On your neighbor's door.
- In pots, pans, or cookie jars at a retail store.

Things that made me feel good today:

Things I noticed about myself:

Things I am grateful for:

Thoughts on the daily exercise:

Would you like to add anything else?

Day 29

Today, I...

> ***"We don't stop playing because we grow old; we grow old because we stop playing."***
> ***- George Bernard Shaw***

EXERCISE 29: *Play A Little*

The idea that play is only reserved for small children and that we should stop engaging in play as we grow up is senseless and actually quite detrimental to our well-being. To remain healthy and well-balanced, play is essential.

It is unfortunate that most people feel that participating in games and fun is juvenile and irresponsible. Who wrote the silly rule, implying leisure and fun are reserved for small children, and engaging in play as an adult is embarrassing, foolish, and unproductive? Women and men should be able to enjoy video games, dolls, sports, role-playing, coloring, and taking part in other playful and fun activities. Engaging in play at any age offers amazing results. It can help lower stress levels, connect with others, enhance creativity, decrease depression and anxiety, manage pain, improve brain function, keep you young, and even help reduce chances of developing dementia. Most of all, it will make you happy and joyful.

Today, allow your inner child to come out and play! Play means something different to each one of us, and unless you regularly partake in playtime, you will need to figure out what that means for you. Have a good time connecting with your inner child with no negative predispositions. Let loose and open yourself up to having a wonderful experience by yourself, or with family and friends. Try anything that sounds enjoyable and exciting to you.

Examples

- Video games or computer games.
- Chess or Checkers.
- Brain puzzles or jigsaw puzzles.
- Ping-Pong or tennis.
- Karaoke or arcade.
- Cards or dominoes.
- Tabletop role-playing games or live action role-playing games (LARP).
- Letter games or number games.
- Board games or stacking games.
- Quizzes or trivia.
- Frisbee or bocce.
- Marco Polo or parasailing.
- Kids toys or grown-up toys.
- Scavenger hunt or I Spy.

Things that made me feel good today:

Things I noticed about myself:

Things I am grateful for:

Thoughts on the daily exercise:

Would you like to add anything else?

Day 30

Today, I...

> *"Life doesn't actually knock you down. It does, however, provide you with many opportunities to evaluate your standing in life: what you stand on, what you stand for, how you stand within yourself and for yourself."*
>
> ***- Iyanla Vanzant***

EXERCISE 30: Bi-Weekly Report

It is time to pause and reflect on the past two weeks. Complete this exercise when you can have at least one hour of undisturbed time. Make yourself comfortable by creating a soothing ambiance: get a warm drink, put on some music, or light a candle. Take a few deep breaths, relax, and when you are ready, answer the following questions honestly and thoroughly.

1. Summarize the past two weeks in a sentence.

2. Looking back, what are you most proud of?

3. What are some inner blocks and fears you noticed?

4. What important lessons did you learn?

5. What brought you the most joy?

6. What surprised you the most?

7. How are you doing in terms of loving yourself?

8. How has your relationship with yourself evolved?

9. How has your relationship with others evolved?

10. How has your attitude toward life evolved?

11. What tools, practices, or teachers have helped you the most?

13. What were your favorite and least favorite exercises? Explain.

14. What are you most grateful for at the moment?

15. What are things you would like to improve on in the upcoming two weeks?

Would you like to add anything else?

Today, as the daily exercise, either repeat your favorite exercise of the past two weeks or do an activity that feels good to your soul.

What did you do?

Day 31

Today, I...

> *"Nobody else knows your reason for being. You do. Your bliss guides you to it. When you follow your bliss, when you follow your path to joy, your conversation is of joy, your feelings are of joy - you're right on the path of that which you intended when you came forth into this physical body."*
>
> **- Esther Hicks**

EXERCISE 31: Follow Your Bliss

Tick-Tock, Tick-Tock goes the clock. That is a reality every human being, regardless of his or her age, gender, nationality, creed, or social status, must deal with. We like to think we will all benefit from a long timeline, but tomorrow is a gamble for each one of us.

We all have different obligations and responsibilities we must answer to, and we all have a future we are working toward. Those are important things to consider in our daily lives. Still, there is so much more to life than always doing what we feel we must or need to do. Those "musts" and "needs" should be counterbalanced by leisure and pleasure to have a good, enjoyable, and harmonious life. The pressure and stress of continually doing things that weigh you down or deplete your energy are harmful to you at all levels of your being; the more you follow your joy and bliss, the lighter and brighter you will feel and become.

Being in a state of joy as much as possible is essential for your well-being and for you to have a happy life.

Today, follow your bliss as much as you can throughout the day. Begin your morning by taking a few minutes to close your eyes and relax. Put your hands over your heart and ask it to guide you during the day. It can go something like this: "I am sorry for neglecting you too often. I want to reconnect with you; please help me. Show me the way to joy, love, happiness, and bliss. Thank you... So, what should we do?" Be like a curious and eager child, and let yourself do all the things that feel good to your soul, heart, mind, and body. Be conscious and present all day long, and keep your bliss and well-being your top priorities. On your journey to self-love, this should be an exercise you practice daily. As you follow your bliss more and more, you will discover more answers and attract more miracles, but best of all, you will give yourself the gift of joy.

Things that made me feel good today:

Things I noticed about myself:

Things I am grateful for:

Thoughts on the daily exercise:

Would you like to add anything else?

Today, I...

> *"Decide what you want. Believe you can have it. Believe you deserve it and believe it's possible for you. And then close your eyes and every day for several minutes, and visualize having what you already want, feeling the feelings of already having it. Come out of that and focus on what you're grateful for already, and really enjoy it. Then go into your day and release it to the Universe and trust that the Universe will figure out how to manifest it."*
>
> **- Jack Canfield**

EXERCISE 32: Dream Big

If you are like many people, you have a tough time answering the question: "What do you want?" Most individuals spend an incredible amount of time thinking about what they do not want and how miserable they are. However, they spend almost no time at all thinking about what they do want. Of course, when asked most people will say: "Well, I want to be happy!" But, what does that mean? What is happiness to you? Wouldn't you say that happiness means something different to each one of us? Thinking about what you want – your dreams – is a little like inputting a destination in your GPS when you want to get to a certain location. It will help Universal Intelligence, your heart, and your mind lead you toward your best life. Anytime you are looking at changing, transforming, or improving your circumstances, you must take the time to contemplate what you want.

Today, create a rough draft of your dream life – along the way, this draft will change many times; that's normal, and you should never feel bad about changing your mind or your direction. First, it is important to create a vision for yourself that makes you happy, hopeful, and enthusiastic. This will serve as a new point of reference and focus, instead of your habitual negative scenarios. As you begin forming a vision, working on its details, and spending time contemplating it, things will begin to shift because you will begin to shift.

Take a moment during the day to envision your best life. Make sure you will not be interrupted, make yourself comfortable, and imagine that you have accomplished your biggest dreams. You look the way you want. You are doing exactly what you want to be doing; you have everything you desire. You are happy, grateful, and you love yourself; life is amazing! What do you look like? What does a day in this ideal life look like? Where do you live? Are you in another country? What work do you do? How are you contributing? Who is around you? What do you do differently? Where do you vacation? How is your health? Do you work out? Are your standards different? Is this all happening one year, three years, or five years from now? The more questions you ask yourself, the clearer your vision will become.

Let your intuition and your emotions be your guide. Let go of images that feel forced, stress you, or make you tense up, and follow what feels wonderful and makes you smile.

Write out your draft in the present tense as if it were all happening now, and put in as many details as possible, using wording that triggers highly positive emotions and images within you. Spend little time (if any) on loved ones, as they have their own free will, and this is essentially about you. Trust that the Universe knows how to choreograph all things and will arrange everything in the best interest of everyone involved. Have fun during this process, and remember to think about all the different areas of your life. It is perfectly fine if you take a week or two to create your first draft; just please, love yourself enough to do it.

This draft should be revised weekly until you feel you are satisfied and content with your creation. Following this step, I highly recommend reading it daily, or recording it on your phone and listening to the recording once a day, while visualizing yourself living your ideal life (remember that feeling positive emotions during your visualizations is essential to the process – feel the way you would if all your dreams had materialized).

This is a lengthy process; you will need time to discover what you truly want, and afterward, you will need time to create a mental movie that vibes with you. Regrettably, most people do not feel like investing the time, the energy, or the effort for this fundamental step, so their lives never change. Again, as I have said many times, change is work and it takes effort.

Dream Big Draft

Things that made me feel good today:

Things I noticed about myself:

Things I am grateful for:

Thoughts on the daily exercise:

Would you like to add anything else?

Day 33

Today, I...

> ***"You can have all the potential in the world, but unless you have confidence, you have nothing."***
> ***- Tyra Banks***

EXERCISE 33: Walk with Confidence

We can all agree that self-confidence is something most humans struggle developing or achieving. Self-confidence comes from having faith in our own aptitude to be great and to do great things. As self-love takes root and grows, the fruits of self-confidence will naturally grow.

To take a first step toward feeling more confident, we will address your posture and your walk, as they play a huge role in how you feel and how the world perceives you. Think about people you know that are very confident. Do they slouch? Do they drag their feet? Do they stare at the floor? Absolutely not!

Today, stand tall and walk with confidence. Hold yourself straight, shoulders back, head high, arms at your sides, and walk taking nice long strides – make sure not to drag your feet. Look straight ahead, smile at people along the way, and remember to breathe. Move at a decent pace, not too fast, but not too slothful either. Feel your body, and pay attention to the shift in your energy, your mood, and your attitude as you walk more gracefully and elegantly. From that improved state of being, look around, and watch how the world responds to you.

Helpful Tips: Here are two tricks to help you get in character:

- Before stepping out into the world, take a moment to visualize yourself as an important figure, a famous model, a celebrity, an important CEO, or simply the greatest version of yourself. Really embody that personality, and when you feel ready, start walking – you will be amazed.
- Before going out, relax and remember a time when you won something, were celebrated for something, or were victorious. Recall the feelings you felt: the joy, the pride, and the confidence. Sit with those feelings for a while, and when you are ready, simply stand up. Your body will do the rest.

Things that made me feel good today:

Things I noticed about myself:

Things I am grateful for:

Thoughts on the daily exercise:

Would you like to add anything else?

Today, I...

> ***"If you believe in the power of words, you can bring about physical changes in the universe."***
> ***- N. Scott Momaday***

EXERCISE 34: Power Words

Words are powerful. Every individual develops a personal and intimate relationship with words, each one conjuring images and feelings capable of lifting us toward the heavens or overwhelming us with sorrow. Collectively, certain words can produce great discomfort or immense joy, but at an individual level, most of our reactions to words are unique, depending on culture, tradition, beliefs, and experiences.

Power words are emotionally charged words that trigger certain images or emotions on their own. We all interpret words differently, we all have a unique list of power words that inspire us, motivate us, and make us feel great, or discourage us, hurt us, and upset us. Knowing these words, especially the positive ones, is significant to feel good, to reprogram your subconscious mind, or to attract certain things to you.

Today, take a moment in the morning to discover your own power words. Watch for words that awaken strong emotions within you, and make a list of your favorite and least favorite. The objective of this exercise is for you to find words that make you feel great as well as help you become aware of words that negatively trigger you. Once you have found the power words you want to focus on, repeat them, silently or aloud, throughout the day. Be mindful to eliminate the words which negatively affect you and try to replace them with more pleasant ones. In the future, remember to add power words you discover to your list, and use them wisely for your own benefit.

Examples

- Hope
- Beautiful
- Abundance
- Powerful
- Health
- Life

- Failure
- Idiot
- Hate
- Shame
- Discrimination
- Disease

My Power Words

Things that made me feel good today:

Things I noticed about myself:

Things I am grateful for:

Thoughts on the daily exercise:

Would you like to add anything else?

Day 35

Today, I...

> *"We are all animals of this planet. We are all creatures. And nonhuman animals experience pain sensations just like we do. They too are strong, intelligent, industrious, mobile, and evolutional. They too are capable of growth and adaptation. Like us, first and foremost, they are earthlings. And like us, they are surviving. Like us they also seek their own comfort rather than discomfort. And like us they express degrees of emotion. In short like us, they are alive."*
>
> **- Joaquin Phoenix**

EXERCISE 35: Be Kind to Animals

To have a compassionate heart toward others also means reaching out to our extended nonhuman family. All life is important and majestic. Many animals could benefit from our kindness.

Too often, people forget this planet is not exclusively ours; we share it with billions of other sentient beings who deserve to live a happy and healthy life as much as we do.

Today, do something kind for critters that are not your pet babies. You can become vegan, bring food to a shelter, volunteer at a wildlife rehabilitation center, build a small protective habitat, do some naturescaping, or provide water and food to the wildlife around you – just make sure to feed them food that is safe and gentle on their digestive systems. If you are in a position where you are incapable of doing any of these things, you can always donate to an organization, such as The Humane Society (http://www.humanesociety.org), PETA (http://www.peta.org), The Gentle Barn (http://www.gentlebarn.org), or any one of your favorite organizations.

Always take precautions and stay at a safe distance from animals that could present a danger. Remember that some animals could carry rabies or more serious diseases.

Examples

- Eat a plant-based diet.
- Build a bat house or a birdhouse.
- Feed lettuce to bunnies.
- Feed (defrosted) frozen peas to ducks.
- Plant native flowers for butterflies.
- Put water in a birdbath.
- Pick up litter.
- Mark windows with vertical or horizontal stripes for birds.

Things that made me feel good today:

Things I noticed about myself:

Things I am grateful for:

Thoughts on the daily exercise:

Would you like to add anything else?

Day 36

Today, I...

> *"We lift ourselves by our thought, we climb upon our vision of ourselves. If you want to enlarge your life, you must first enlarge your thought of it and of yourself. Hold the ideal of yourself as you long to be, always, everywhere - your ideal of what you long to attain - the ideal of health, efficiency, success."*
>
> **- Orison Swett Marden**

EXERCISE 36: Create a Vision Board

Vision boards (also known as dream boards or soul boards) are mediums that help individuals visualize their dreams. It is a collage of images that ignite positive feelings within you, or that represent the intentions and objectives you wish to reach.

Whether you believe in the potential power of a vision board or not, creating one that makes you feel exactly the way you want to feel or the way you would expect to feel once you have acquired your desired results, will have a positive effect on you. It will uplift you and incite you to visualize regardless of your belief system and that will inevitably have a positive impact on your life. Many people report attracting incredible relationships, opportunities, and material things into their lives thanks to vision boards. Crediting the law of attraction, or calling it luck are personal preferences; still, the fact remains, being continually exposed to inspiring and empowering images will create shifts within you and in your reality.

Today, create a vision board. To accomplish this activity, you will need several hours of spare time. Begin by thinking of the feelings you would like to feel daily. Do you want to feel joyful, healthy, abundant, or even peaceful? Think of images, words, and quotes that could assist in generating such feelings. Finally, gather the needed supplies, and piece your vision together. Look at the examples below, and choose a technique that resonates with you. When creating your vision board, take care to choose images that produce genuine positive feelings. Placing an image of a mansion or the "perfect" body is fine if seeing these images motivates and uplifts you – if not, it is defeating the purpose of putting together this board. Your feelings and emotions let you know what you truly believe is possible for you at this moment. Allow that information to guide you in creating the perfect "feeling" board for you. So maybe, instead of putting the image of a perfect body, you could choose an image of fresh fruit and veggies, or instead of a mansion, choose an image of the word "luxury" or "abundance."

Remember, if you are around people that tend to be unsupportive, you might want to keep this board to yourself. On your journey to self-love, you must give yourself the time and space to grow at your own rate, and as things shift within yourself, it might be a sensitive time for you – do not create space for any added discomfort and insecurities by inviting comments or judgments from others.

Make sure to put images that inspire self-love and self-care on your vision board.

The following pages were left blank in order for you to create a vision board within this workbook.

Examples

- Glue images to a foam board.
- Save pictures to a folder on your computer.
- Use a vision board app.
- Tape printed images on a page in your journal.
- Create an entire notebook dedicated to your vision.
- Create a slideshow of images.
- Create different boards on Pinterest (https://www.pinterest.com/).
- Cover an entire wall with images and posters.

Helpful Tips:

- EXERCISE 32: Dream Big can serve as a guide for your board.
- Place photos of you among the other images, unless seeing yourself triggers negative feelings and emotions.
- Look online for inspiration, but, most importantly, allow your intuition to guide you, and have fun.
- If you only find a few images that inspire you, that's perfectly fine. You can build your vision board over several days or weeks.

Vision Board

Things that made me feel good today:

Things I noticed about myself:

Things I am grateful for:

Thoughts on the daily exercise:

Would you like to add anything else?

Today, I...

> ***"Don't ever save anything for a special occasion. Being alive is the special occasion."***
> ***- Author Unknown***

EXERCISE 37: Wear It, Use It

Unless you are a devoted minimalist, you probably have something laying around that you are saving for that special occasion. Sadly, people hold off from wearing, using, and enjoying their favorite things (e.g. clothes, fine china set, good perfume or cologne, a pricey tea, etc.) to either impress another human being or to celebrate a specific event. This is not a good formula for true joy.

Every breath you take, and every minute spent on this earth are gifts; the future is always uncertain, therefore it's important that you seize the present moment as much as possible. Keep in mind that enjoying something through the eyes of another can never bring you true satisfaction. Each moment you are alive is a special occasion, a glorious gift, and you deserve to celebrate and enjoy things for yourself.

Today, wear or use those exceptional things you've set aside for so long and enjoy them. Do not put off celebrating your life or yourself. From now on, do not wait for the perfect venue, person, time, or place to enjoy your belongings. Use them, cherish them, and appreciate them whenever you feel like it.

Examples

- Wear that outfit for the first time.
- Spray some of that expensive perfume or cologne.
- Eat on your fine china.
- Wear that piece of jewelry.
- Light those candles.
- Put those sheets on your bed.
- Wear that delicate lingerie.
- Drink that special tea.

Things that made me feel good today:

Things I noticed about myself:

Things I am grateful for:

Thoughts on the daily exercise:

Would you like to add anything else?

Today, I...

> *"I'm a world-class people watcher. I like to watch people's body movements, their expressions. It says so much about them."*
> *- Jill Scott*

EXERCISE 38: *Observe People*

It is important to develop self-awareness and to notice our place in the world. Likewise, it is important to observe the world around us to connect emotionally and develop empathy toward others. Combining self-awareness and awareness of the "other" is essential to develop both emotional intelligence and social intelligence. However, continually being lost in the world of thoughts and in various electronics makes it easy to forget the world around us, dehumanize others, and be dismissive or reactive.

Bringing in more mindfulness in our everyday lives by observing others helps us remember that we all have feelings and emotions, good days and bad days, doubts and fears; simply put, we are all in this together, interconnected to each other, and part of a whole.

It also helps us become aware of our own personality, our own qualities and shortcomings, as people often mirror us in some way or another.

Through this process, we can emerge more understanding, empathetic, and compassionate toward others and ourselves. Being human does not come with a special manual for you or anyone else – most people, like you, are trying their best.

Today, be present, and observe people around you. Pay attention to their facial expressions, their mannerisms, and their body language. What emotions do you think they are experiencing? Do they look confident, insecure, or fearful? Do they look happy, angry, or sad? Do they talk loudly, mumble, or whisper? Pay attention to them and their place in the world at this present moment. Do this with passersby, but also do this with people close to you, such as family members and friends. Are they much different from you?

Please, be mindful to observe in a gentle and noninvasive way. Do not stare or make people uncomfortable. This exercise is about objectively observing people and not gathering material to criticize, make fun, or judge others.

Things that made me feel good today:

Things I noticed about myself:

Things I am grateful for:

Thoughts on the daily exercise:

Would you like to add anything else?

Today, I...

"I finally realized that being grateful to my body was key to giving more love to myself."
- Oprah Winfrey

EXERCISE 39: *Dear Body...*

Chances are, if you are like the vast majority of people, you are likely to have a strained relationship with your body. It is easy to focus on all the things that upset us or distress us: the illnesses, the disabilities, the weight issues, the wrinkles, the hair type, the cellulite, the acne, the scars, our looks, etc. However, it's important to remember that the body is an envelope that allows us to experience life, it is not who we are. Some call it a home, others a vehicle – regardless of how you prefer to define it, this fantastic organic machine is the reason you have a name, the reason you are breathing, the reason you are alive.

So yes, at times there are factors, such as genetics, diseases, circumstances, and environment, which can play a role regarding our body's health and well-being, but for the most part, your thinking and your actions have been the biggest adversaries of your physical body. Take a moment to reflect and answer this question: When did your body become your enemy?

Today, switch things around, instead of judging or criticizing your body, think of all the wonderful things your body allows you to experience: the kiss of a loved one, dancing to some music, laughing to a funny joke, crying to a good movie, typing at your computer, seeing your child's face, tasting delicious fruit, and so many other amazing things. When you are done, write a love letter to your body, thanking it for all the incredible things it allows you to experience and, if need be, apologizing for how you have been treating it. To some, this might sound corny and feel a little uncomfortable – do it anyway. Loving yourself means loving every part of who you are, and to do that, you must reconnect to all aspects of your being.

During this exercise, you may experience some difficult emotions. Allow yourself to feel vulnerable, and cry if you need to. From this moment forward, learn to love your body by seeing it more objectively, and appreciating it more wholly. As you treat your physical body in a gentler and kinder way, your other bodies (mind and spirit) will greatly benefit.

Dear Body,

Things that made me feel good today:

Things I noticed about myself:

Things I am grateful for:

Thoughts on the daily exercise:

Would you like to add anything else?

Today, I...

> ***"Change your plate. Change your fate."***
> ***- Kris Carr***

EXERCISE 40: Say No To Junk

As I explained on Day 20 (Exercise 20: Watch Your Diet), you don't need to be a doctor to understand that consuming chemically processed foods is harmful. These foods, engineered to create cravings and addictions, have changed our natural eating patterns, our relationship with food, and our inner chemistry. Worst of all, these nutrient-poor, highly acidic foods, and their long list of additives disrupt our health and well-being. Consumption of such foods have high consequences on your mental and physical welfare and can cause serious damage, such as chronic diseases, inflammation, digestive problems, hormonal imbalances, weight issues, spikes in insulin levels, allergies, depression, anxiety, etc.

If you are like most people, you are probably oblivious to the fact that you are highly addicted to these foods psychologically, emotionally, and physically – with each generation, the problem worsens, and the health issues grow.

To recover from the negative effects of these junk foods (pun intended), and lower the chances of possible long-term health risks, individuals must revert to a more alkaline, natural, and whole diet, composed of unprocessed products, such as fresh fruits and vegetables, whole grains, legumes, natural juices, teas, and plenty of water.

Today, say no to junk! No to packaged foods, fast foods, bottled juices, or soft drinks, and commit to clean eating by enjoying simple, healthy foods. Taking good care of your body is essential on the road to self-love, and it is important to nurture this connection with your body by learning how to nourish it properly – feeding it healthy, nutrient-rich foods.

Be advised, you may feel discomforts, such as cravings, headaches, moodiness, and some lightheadedness – those are part of the withdrawal symptoms from your involuntary addiction to a diet high in salt, sugar, and fat. Said symptoms will take about a week to dissipate if you continue eating a clean and whole diet, which I highly encourage.

Examples

- Smoothie
- Soup
- Grains such as brown rice or quinoa with veggies
- Bean stew
- Salad (Fruit or veggies)
- Fresh juice (Fruit or veggies)
- Nuts and dried fruits
- Baked root vegetables
- Ratatouille
- Buddha Bowl
- Vegetable stir fry
- Natural nut butter and bananas
- Nice cream
- Veggie platter with hummus

Helpful Tips: Here are some informative documentaries you might be interested in watching:

- Hungry for Change (http://www.hungryforchange.tv)
- Fat, Sick & Nearly Dead 1 (http://www.fatsickandnearlydead.com)
- Fat, Sick & Nearly Dead 2 (http://fatsickandnearlydead2.com)
- Super Size Me (http://morganspurlock.com/work/super-size-me)
- Forks Over Knives (https://www.forksoverknives.com/the-film)
- Food, Inc. (http://www.takepart.com/foodinc/film)

**Most of these documentaries are available on Netflix, Amazon, YouTube, or Vudu.*

My No Junk Day

Breakfast

Lunch

Dinner

Snacks

Drinks

Things that made me feel good today:

Things I noticed about myself:

Things I am grateful for:

Thoughts on the daily exercise:

Would you like to add anything else?

Today, I...

> ***"There is no life that does not contribute to history."***
> ***- Dorothy West***

EXERCISE 41: Honoring Angels

As the cycle of life on this plane of existence will have it, many inspirational souls have crossed over into the non-physical. Their legacy remains with us through their works, their gifts, and our memories of them.

Most of us have gone through the painful grieving process of letting people go, and although we continue to carry them within us, we still reminisce and miss their physical presence in our everyday lives. Honoring the memories of people who have directly and indirectly affected our existence is a beautiful way of acknowledging their impact in our lives and their contributions to history. It is also a tribute to their time spent on this earth and a celebration of their footprint in our world.

Many societies remember and honor their departed through different acts, celebrations, gatherings, and prayers – believing the souls of their ancestors and loved ones watch over these homages with delight. Whether you share the same beliefs or hold a more skeptical point of view, performing a simple ritual or an action of grace can still soothe, heal, and uplift those of us who remain among the living.

Today, honor angels. Take the time to remember and celebrate the lives of people who have passed by doing something special in their name. You can honor a loved one, one of your heroes, people who have died in wars and conflicts, or do a universal honoring of all lives passed.

Remember, this is not meant to be a sad event, but an event of commemoration and appreciation – a celebration of life, therefore keep your spirit light.

Examples

- Burn a candle in their name.
- Make a donation in their name.
- Have a mass in their name.
- Have an inner conversation with them.
- Say a prayer in their name.
- Plant a tree in their name
- Post a picture with kind words on social media.
- Do an activity you loved doing with them.
- Write them a letter of gratitude.
- Make a scrapbook of their life.
- Create an altar or shrine with some incense, candles, flowers, and photos.
- Place a nice plant at their resting place.

Who did you honor and how did you honor them?

Things that made me feel good today:

Things I noticed about myself:

Things I am grateful for:

Thoughts on the daily exercise:

Would you like to add anything else?

Today, I...

> ***"Just play. Have fun. Enjoy the game."***
> ***- Michael Jordan***

EXERCISE 42: Game Night

In most technologically advanced countries, people are now largely dependent on their devices, and story time, game night, and fun activities have been replaced with spending one-on-one time with electronic gadgets, isolated from others.

Having electricity, television, tablets, cell phones, and a Wi-Fi connection are some of the great privileges many of us can enjoy. Still, making time for play and connecting with others should not be an archaic form of entertainment and should not be retired. There are some fantastic benefits to having an "old school" game night! Game nights are an incredible opportunity to bond with the people in your life, prevent loneliness, improve motor skills or mental faculties, and have a great time.

Today, organize a family game night, or host a game night with friends, coworkers, or peers. Plan a fun night for your entire brood, free your inner child, and have an amazing time.

Examples

- Play cards or dominoes with older relatives or friends at a retirement home.
- Play a board game with your partner and children.
- Host a friendly video game competition.
- Enjoy the arcade or the bowling alley with peers.
- Enjoy a game of pool volleyball or basketball with friends.
- Join a game of golf or darts with coworkers.
- Complete a puzzle with your siblings.
- Go to a bingo game with your family.
- Play giant chess or battleship with your child.
- Play ring toss or croquet with your parents.

What game did you play?

Things that made me feel good today:

Things I noticed about myself:

Things I am grateful for:

Thoughts on the daily exercise:

Would you like to add anything else?

Day 43

Today, I...

> ***"Be good to your skin. You'll wear it every day for the rest of your life."***
>
> ***- Renée Rouleau***

EXERCISE 43: Exfoliate Your Skin

It often eludes the mind, but skin is the largest organ on the body, and, as such, it deserves special care and attention. It may be resilient, but with the elements, our environment, and our lifestyles, our skin is too often mistreated and disregarded.

One of the easiest and best ways to help your skin, aside from hydration and moisturizing, is exfoliation – the removal of dead skin cells and debris that clog your pores.

Notice I am talking about your skin, as opposed to exclusively talking about your face. That's because all the skin on your body needs the same treatment to be healthy and glowing. Exfoliating will help remove dead skin cells, prevent ingrown hairs, clear impurities, smooth, and improve the surface of your skin.

Today, gently exfoliate the skin of your entire body. Take a moment during the day to create a nice and soothing ambiance, and then proceed by carefully scrubbing or brushing your epidermis. Be conscious during this process, and remember to be loving and kind to your body. Pay close attention to the way your skin feels as you exfoliate, and enjoy taking care of yourself. When you are done, wash your body with a gentle cleanser and apply a nourishing oil, a body butter, or a good moisturizer.

Examples

- Store bought face and body scrub
- All-natural face scrub and body scrub (baking soda or sugar scrubs are good options)
- Dry body brush
- Bath sponge
- Exfoliating loofah pads or mitts
- Mud bath spa treatment

Things that made me feel good today:

Things I noticed about myself:

Things I am grateful for:

Thoughts on the daily exercise:

Would you like to add anything else?

Today, I...

> *"Be impeccable with your word. Speak with integrity. Say only what you mean. Avoid using the word to speak against yourself or to gossip about others. Use the power of your word in the direction of truth and love."*
>
> **- Don Miguel Ruiz**

EXERCISE 44: No Gossip

Most humans are addicted to gossip. Just look at the popularity of gossip-media and magazines. In most societies, gossip is considered a common part of conversation and is often the only conversation. While many people love gossiping, seldom do they enjoy being the reason for gossip.

Spreading rumors or talking about someone's behavior or affairs in a negative way, is harmful and unimaginative. It's a technique people use to make themselves feel better or superior for a moment, but it does more damage than anything. Participating in such an activity has negative consequences for the person you are talking about, but it also affects the way people see and feel about you. Can you trust someone who enjoys belittling others? Can you trust someone who gossips about others, to not gossip about you? To make matters worse, gossiping about others produces negative emotions and feelings within your own mind and body, which negatively affect your health and well-being. No one gains from destroying or hurting another.

Today, do not gossip or participate in gossip. Do not allow yourself to speak or think ill of anyone, including yourself. Find other subjects of conversation, be creative, and if people around you give in to gossip, walk away, steer the conversation away from the subject, or simply remain quiet. Slip-ups will happen, and that's okay. Just stop when you realize what is happening. Initially it may be difficult for you and your gossip buddies, you may even lose a "friend" or two, but by using your words in a more constructive, kind, and loving way, you will gain self-respect and feel amazing.

Throughout the day, pay attention to this impulse to talk or think poorly about others, and see how it makes you feel emotionally, mentally, and physically to not give in to it.

Remember, you can talk about the way things affect you and share your experiences without gossiping. To share facts is one thing. To go on and on about someone intending to hurt them, making them look bad, or under the guise of helping them is a completely different story.

Helpful Tips: Here are a few ideas of interesting topics you can talk about:

- Talk about a project you are working on.
- Share helpful information or tips.
- Talk about something you are learning, or a new activity you are enjoying.
- Talk about your dreams and aspirations.
- Talk about the latest books you have read, movies you have watched, or music you have listened to.
- Share philosophical ideas and opinions.
- Talk about fun and exciting upcoming events.
- Share meaningful memories or future goals.

Things that made me feel good today:

Things I noticed about myself:

Things I am grateful for:

Thoughts on the daily exercise:

Would you like to add anything else?

Today, I...

> *"The key to our transformation is simply this: the better we know ourselves the better equipped we will be to make our choices wisely."*
> *- Gregg Braden*

EXERCISE 45: *Bi-Weekly Report*

It is time to pause and reflect on the past two weeks. Complete this exercise when you can have at least one hour of undisturbed time. Make yourself comfortable by creating a soothing ambiance: get a warm drink, put on some music, or light a candle. Take a few deep breaths, relax, and when you are ready, answer the following questions honestly and thoroughly.

1. Summarize the past two weeks in a sentence.

2. Looking back, what are you most proud of?

3. What are some inner blocks and fears you noticed?

4. What important lessons did you learn?

5. What brought you the most joy?

6. What surprised you the most?

7. How are you doing in terms of loving yourself?

8. How has your relationship with yourself evolved?

9. How has your relationship with others evolved?

10. How has your attitude toward life evolved?

11. What tools, practices, or teachers have helped you the most?

13. What were your favorite and least favorite exercises? Explain.

14. What are you most grateful for at the moment?

15. What are things you would like to improve on in the upcoming two weeks?

Would you like to add anything else?

Today, as the daily exercise, either repeat your favorite exercise of the past two weeks or do an activity that feels good to your soul.

What did you do?

Day 46

Today, I...

> ***"The human spirit lives on creativity and dies in conformity and routine."***
> ***- Vilayat Inayat Khan***

EXERCISE 46: *Morning Routine*

It is common for people to be attached to certain routines, especially morning routines. Wake up, get up, brush your teeth, exercise, shower, kiss your loved ones, eat breakfast, etc.

While some routines are enjoyable and make people feel safe, others can become boring and dull. It's healthy to change things around every now and then, but it is particularly important if your morning routine and rituals are not conducive to having a positive day or a positive outcome in terms of your aspirations. Take a moment to think about your early morning patterns, and contemplate whether they are beneficial to you. Do you get out of bed looking forward to your routine? Does it uplift you? Are your early morning habits a good match for what you want to realize? Your morning routines set the tone for your entire day and in essence shape your life. You are what you do repeatedly.

Today, shake things up, and change your morning routine. Read up on some ideas, or think from the perspective of what you would consider your ideal morning scenario. You can find a lot of fascinating information online regarding the morning routine of famous people, past and present, which can inspire you and help you be more creative. Play around and try different approaches until you find a routine that uplifts you, energizes you, and brings positive long-term results.

Examples

- Wake up an hour earlier than you usually would.
- Drink water as soon as you wake up.
- Drink a green juice, have a smoothie, or enjoy a healthy breakfast.
- Go for a walk or a jog.
- Do yoga or some other exercise.
- Journal or practice free writing.
- Meditate, contemplate, or pray.
- Read or listen to something motivational.
- Make your bed.
- Read an inspirational book or listen to some music.
- Take a (cold) shower.
- Watch the sunrise or observe nature.
- Do not look at your phone or watch television for the first hour.
- Set intentions or repeat affirmations.

Things that made me feel good today:

Things I noticed about myself:

Things I am grateful for:

Thoughts on the daily exercise:

Would you like to add anything else?

Day 47

Today, I...

> ***"I'm always learning new things."***
> ***- Serena Williams***

EXERCISE 47: Try a New Sport

The human body must move regularly to be healthy and function properly. It is essential to practice some kind of sport to maintain an optimal level of health and well-being. Exercising the body is not only good for our anatomy, it also supports our mental and emotional wellness. Some of the many benefits of exercise are better mobility, confidence, energy, stamina, reduction of certain health risks or issues (e.g. high blood pressure, osteoporosis, depression, anxiety, etc.), and improved mood and brain function.

Adopting a good exercise routine by choosing sports and practices that are fun or engaging will ensure that you do not get bored or frustrated and give-up. Another valuable tip to keep you from hitting a plateau or to maintain a healthy level of motivation and interest is to change your exercise routine periodically, as it teaches your body and mind new tricks and abilities.

Today, try a new sport. This will challenge your body and stimulate your mind. You can try something you have always wanted to experience, or sign-up for something new and exciting. Be mindful about your body before participating in any activity – you want to challenge but not hurt, as doing so will have negative consequences. Most people do not partake in regular physical activities because they either attribute the process to physical pain or to mental misery. To prevent similar outcomes, listen to the needs of your body and your mind. Try to take on a sport or practice that is appealing to you – start slowly, enjoy yourself as much as you can, and gradually challenge yourself to raise the bar. The goal here is to learn something new while having a great time.

Examples

- Belly dancing or the Hula dance
- Tai Chi or Qigong
- Rebounding or rope jumping
- Skateboarding or biking
- Calisthenics or aerial fitness
- Swimming or water aerobics
- Kickboxing or boxing
- Pilates or yoga
- Stepping or tap dancing
- Hula-hoop exercises or resistance band exercises

What sport did you try? Did you enjoy it?

Things that made me feel good today:

Things I noticed about myself:

Things I am grateful for:

Thoughts on the daily exercise:

Would you like to add anything else?

Day 48

Today, I...

> *"Make a list of your current wants and desires. Next to each, put down what benefit or payoff there would be when you achieve it. Look at this list often throughout the day and before retiring at night."*
>
> ***- Denis Waitley***

EXERCISE 48: Your Bucket List

A bucket list is a list of all the things you dream about doing, experiencing, or accomplishing during your lifetime. There are mixed feelings and reviews about whether a person should create a bucket list. Some suggest it's a way to deny death, fill a void, compete with others, or set expectations that are too high. Meanwhile, others think it is a must if you want to live life to the fullest.

I would guard against creating a superficial bucket list made up of other bucket lists found on the internet, or a list that causes inner stress. However, in a world where the day-to-day absorbs all your attention, it's easy to forget you have dreams, desires, and things you would like to do or experience during your lifetime. Most people have never even really thought about what they want, and creating a bucket list is a great way to discover those hidden wishes. It can range from very simple things, like trying a specific exotic fruit, to bigger objectives, such as visiting a certain place in the world.

Today, make a bucket list of the things you wish to experience. Get yourself a beverage, make yourself comfortable, and take a few conscious breaths. When you are ready, write your list. If at any time you feel you have nothing else to add, breathe deeply and ask yourself, "What do I want to experience during this lifetime?" Wait patiently until ideas come to mind. Please make sure each item on your list is something you really want to experience, and not something that "sounds good," or something you think you should want. Once you are done making your list, read it often, and cross out or add things as time passes.

Examples

- Taste rambutan.
- Sing at a karaoke club.
- Be part of a flash mob.
- Visit the Citadel Laferrière (Haiti).
- Go to a silent retreat.
- Save an animal.
- Join a march.
- Surprise someone.
- Go scuba diving.
- Fly in a helicopter.
- Get a tattoo.
- Sleep in an igloo.

My Bucket List

Things that made me feel good today:

Things I noticed about myself:

Things I am grateful for:

Thoughts on the daily exercise:

Would you like to add anything else?

Today, I...

> ***"I found I could say things with colors that I couldn't say in any other way – things that I had no words for."***
>
> ***- Georgia O'Keeffe***

EXERCISE 49: Color

Unless you are an artist or a painter, playing with color is usually reserved for children. Adults can feel a little uncomfortable or embarrassed partaking in activities that involve coloring of any kind. Thankfully, nowadays, more people are letting go of their inhibitions; they are allowing their inner child to come out, and they are picking up different coloring mediums.

Many therapists advocate coloring to their patients, as there are many valuable benefits to gain, such as stress reduction, emotional well-being, creativity, personal expression, connection with others, meditative states, and mood improvement. Color is so important that there is an actual form of healing, called color therapy, which helps people heal using colors and light. On a more intuitive note, different colors affect and influence us in various ways; for instance, blue relaxes us, yellow makes us happy, and red energizes us.

Today, play with color! Have a good time and let your inner child lead the way. You can do this activity with your children, family, friends, or all by yourself. Whatever process you decide to indulge in, make sure to connect with the different colors you are using, and see how they affect your mood and behavior. This is a great opportunity to connect with deeper parts of yourself.

Examples

- Color in an adult coloring book.
- Take an art class.
- Spray paint a beautiful graffiti on a piece of plywood.
- Make tie-dye shirts.
- Paint a mural.
- Paint a wall in your house.
- Have fun with body paint.
- Print and color a mandala.
- Paint rocks.
- Paint your emotions on canvas using colors that reflect the way you feel.

How did you play with color?

Things that made me feel good today:

Things I noticed about myself:

Things I am grateful for:

Thoughts on the daily exercise:

Would you like to add anything else?

Day 50

Today, I...

> *"The key to being confident is taking care of yourself and feeling like you're the best you can be."*
>
> ***- Dania Ramirez***

EXERCISE 50: Personal Care and Grooming

Beyond personal hygiene, which is incredibly important for your body's health, grooming adds personal touches, in terms of small details.

A body that is clean and well-groomed influences how the world perceives us and will react to us. Some would argue it should not matter, but the fact remains that people notice those seemingly small details, and a majority attach a great deal of importance to someone being clean, neat, and well put together.

The way you maintain your body says a lot about the way you feel about yourself and your life. Past all that, simply taking the time to care for your body in a mindful and loving way is fantastic for your self-esteem, your self-confidence, and your overall relationship with yourself. It's a beautiful way to connect with yourself and grow your feelings of self-worth and self-love.

Today, take some time to enjoy a bit of personal care and grooming. Make a point to have a good time, whether you choose to consult a professional or do it on your own. If you decide to do it yourself, make sure to create a nice ambiance that makes you feel good and relaxed. If you choose to visit a professional, ensure you go to a specialist that you like or that has good referrals and/or reviews. Remain conscious and present throughout the process and enjoy treating your body with all the love and respect it deserves.

Examples

- Remove chipping nail polish and give yourself a "mani-pedi."
- Clean your ears.
- Brush your hair and style it.
- Get a trim or a shave at a hair salon or barbershop.
- Moisturize your face and body.
- Get a facial at a spa.
- Cut and clean your nails.
- Wear clean and wrinkle free clothes.
- Trim your ears and nose hairs.
- Care for the heels of your feet.
- Floss your teeth.
- Tweeze or wax your eyebrows.
- Scrub your lips and moisturize.
- Exfoliate your face and body.

Things that made me feel good today:

Things I noticed about myself:

Things I am grateful for:

Thoughts on the daily exercise:

Would you like to add anything else?

Today, I...

> *"The struggle comes when we sense a gap between the clock and the compass - when what we do doesn't contribute to what is most important in our lives."*
>
> *- Stephen Covey*

EXERCISE 51: Time Management

Time is a valuable commodity, and regardless of who we are, we all have the same amount of time during a typical day to accomplish our long to-do lists.

While some people are better at managing their time than others, most will agree they regularly feel overwhelmed when it comes to scheduling their days. Managing our time can feel like a gift or a curse, depending on whether we can find the right balance between what we feel we need to do versus what we want to do.

Instead of scheduling our time in a way that is sensible, productive, and pleasurable, we ordinarily spend and waste our time on mundane and repetitive tasks or distractions that offer no real personal benefits.

It's easy to forget our time here is a real gift, and using this time in ways that correspond to our heart's calling and desires is of the utmost importance.

Today, track the amount of time you spend on each of your activities. To make adequate changes to the way you manage your time, first you must know exactly how you spend your time. This will allow you to evaluate whether your time is spent wisely or mindlessly. At the end of the day, reflect on your list, and contemplate how you occupy your time in contrast to your dreams and goals. Do not be self-judging or harsh. Evaluating how you regularly allocate your time will help you become aware of whether you are moving toward your objectives or not. This will allow you to organize your timetable deliberately and focus on putting your energy and time toward what is truly important to you. Make every day count. Take charge of your schedule –shift and change your daily plans to reflect your desires. This process will be hit-or-miss for a while, as you will need to transform certain habits, find solutions, and possibly even delegate some responsibilities. Be patient and enjoy experimenting until you find the time management solution that best fits you.

Time	Activities

Things that made me feel good today:

Things I noticed about myself:

Things I am grateful for:

Thoughts on the daily exercise:

Would you like to add anything else?

Day 52

Today, I...

> ***"Growing old is mandatory; growing up is optional."***
> ***- Chili Davis***

EXERCISE 52: Forbidden No More

Being a child is said to be the easiest thing in the world, but it must be quite challenging to be a young human being. Being so eager and excited to discover the world, but continually hearing an incessant stream of "Noes" must be quite frustrating.

Can you remember times during your childhood when you were denied certain things you wanted to do? The irritation? The anguish? Don't you think it's time you gave your inner child the freedom to finally experience some of those things?

Many of your fears, inner blocks, and repressed emotions date from the first few years of your childhood – anytime you deny that inner child, additional suffering is caused. To heal certain aspects of yourself, and find inner balance and well-being, you must give that young child a voice, and listen.

Today, have some fun, and do one or more things you were forbidden to do as a child. Enjoy the process, even if it feels a little awkward or silly. Before beginning the exercise, it can help to sit comfortably, close your eyes, relax, and take a few conscious breaths. Visualize your younger self; see that little one giggling, playing, and enjoying life. Feel the innocence, the curiosity, and the eagerness you felt during those early years. As you look at that younger version of yourself, ask, "What is something you were forbidden to do that you would really love to do today? We'll do whatever you want; it's your choice." Listen for an answer. Remember to thank your inner child after receiving a reply and tell them you love them. When you are ready, slowly transition back to the present moment, and go enjoy yourself.

Examples

- Write on the walls of your house.
- Paint your body.
- Dance in the rain.
- Have dessert for breakfast.
- Play with your food.
- Double dip.
- Watch a show or movie you were not allowed to watch.
- Eat sweets before noon.
- Have a sleepover.
- Jump in puddles.
- Play video games.
- Write or highlight in a book.

What childhood rule did you break? How did it feel?

Things that made me feel good today:

Things I noticed about myself:

Things I am grateful for:

Thoughts on the daily exercise:

Would you like to add anything else?

Today, I...

> *"You must look for the good in people to have more of it appear. As you look only for the good things in a person, you will be amazed at what your new focus reveals."*
>
> **- Rhonda Byrne**

EXERCISE 53: Look for the Good

On a day-to-day basis, we typically interact with our family, our friends, and our immediate circle or acquaintances. That said, we also socialize with others in person, through electronic mail, or on various social media platforms. These brief interactions often give way to negative impressions and opinions that remain silent judgements or evolve into flagrant unkindness. Unfortunately, this impacts the way people feel and perceive us, but worse, this impacts the way we feel about ourselves, the world around us, and our place in it.

If all you look for and focus on is the negativity, chances are you are not a very hopeful individual, you do not feel very safe, and you do not believe in a better tomorrow.

Of course, there are people who do harmful and unspeakable things, but they represent a very small percentage in contrast to the majority of people, who are decent human beings, with great qualities and many positive traits.

Today, look for the good in people. Come up with five to ten positive qualities or traits for individuals you come across – they can be complete strangers, famous people, coworkers, or even friends and family. Give people the benefit of the doubt and the same chance you would like to receive from anyone. Deliberately looking for the good in people will help your energy shift in a positive way, and as a result you will be uplifted, feel more hopeful, and optimistic. As life would have it, whether you believe in it or not, by feeling good and emanating positive energy, you will attract better people and situations to you.

Examples

- The Lyft driver: She is punctual, cordial, friendly, has a pleasant voice, good conversationalist, smooth driver, great listener, curious, funny, and smart.
- The YouTuber: He makes great videos; he is captivating, engaging, creative, adventurous, and hilarious. Nice haircut!
- Your coworker: She is friendly and has the kindest smile. She always dresses nice and is super helpful. She is great at organizing and planning!
- The janitor: He is so kind and has such a positive attitude; he always has a nice word for everyone he meets. He does such a wonderful job at keeping this space nice and clean. He has a lot of patience. What an admirable hard-working man!

Helpful Tip: Everyone appreciates a heartfelt compliment, so do not hesitate to offer some praise.

Things that made me feel good today:

Things I noticed about myself:

Things I am grateful for:

Thoughts on the daily exercise:

Would you like to add anything else?

Today, I...

> *"The key to making healthy decisions is to respect your future self. Honor him or her. Treat him or her like you would treat a friend or a loved one."*
>
> **- A. J. Jacobs**

EXERCISE 54: *Your Future Self*

Who will you be in the coming years? Where will you live? What will you do? Who will be around you? It is human nature to look back at who we used to be, in contrast to who we are, who we wish we were and who we hope to become. However, few people take the time to examine the differences between their ideal future self and the future self they will inevitably evolve into if they continue making the same choices and living life as they are.

Envisioning that preferred future version of yourself will help you change course and make decisions more aligned with your desired scenario.

Today, you will meet and converse with your future self to gain some needed guidance and perspective. You will get a glimpse of your future life and bring back some new advice and information to help you make new and improved choices.

Please do not underestimate this exercise, as it can be a life-changing experience. You will need 20 minutes to an hour of uninterrupted time for this activity.

Steps:

1. Make sure to create a pleasant atmosphere and make yourself comfortable.

2. Close your eyes, relax, and take a few conscious breaths until you feel calm and completely peaceful.

3. Visualize yourself slowly walking into a beautiful and tranquil place. As you walk, pay attention to the details of this perfect setting – the sounds, the colors, the smells.

4. At a distance, you see your future self, sitting down. As you slowly approach, you discover a serene, older, and wiser version of yourself smiling at you. That future version of yourself has accomplished all your dreams and has lived your best life.

5. Sit next to that gentle, powerful, and sage being. For some, your older self will begin the conversation, whereas for others, you will be the one greeting your older self first.

6. When you feel ready, ask, "What is the most important advice you have for me today?" Listen carefully, try not to force an "answer," and allow the knowledge to come spontaneously and naturally. Ask as many questions as you would like, and carry on a chat as long as you would like. I must warn against asking for specific details about anything, as such questions often come from a space of worry and fear and will close the connection with your intuition.

7. When you are ready to stop, thank your future self, stand up, and slowly walk away.

8. Take a few conscious breaths and open your eyes. You may want to journal the advice you were given below and begin thinking about how to start applying this wisdom today.

Things that made me feel good today:

Things I noticed about myself:

Things I am grateful for:

Thoughts on the daily exercise:

Would you like to add anything else?

Today, I...

> *"You should aspire to a level of personal excellence - to be the best you can be. You should aspire to have the richest life you can get in terms of fulfillment, happiness and peace."*
>
> **- Kimora Lee Simmons**

EXERCISE 55: *One Step Closer*

In yesterday's exercise, you were prompted to gather wisdom from a future version of yourself, but every day, your higher self (i.e. the all-knowing part of yourself) tries to guide you and direct you according to your wishes and desires. The problem is that, ordinarily, people choose to ignore that inner voice. For example, if I were to ask you, right now, "What is the one thing you can do to improve your circumstances?" chances are you would get an immediate insight, but instead of acting upon it, you would probably rely on an excuse (e.g. time, relationships, fears, gender, age, etc.) and postpone doing anything.

It is crucial for you to understand that, in order to love yourself and move positively toward your dreams, you cannot continue doing what you habitually do, and you cannot continue being the person you are today. Everything that you are, in this present moment, is a result of your past and current thoughts, feelings and emotions, relationships, habits, and experiences. Nothing will improve until you make some changes.

Today, do something that will take you one step closer to where you want to be in life. Take a moment during the day to think about your current reality and envision the one you wish for yourself. Then, take a closer look at the person you are in comparison to the person you wish to become. Note the differences, and take some alone time to think about small changes that could bring you closer to your ideals. When you are done, evaluate which one you wish to implement right away, and make the decision to embrace this new change.

Remember, it is better to implement a small change and apply it consistently, than to attempt taking on big things and giving up.

What small change have you decided to implement?

Things that made me feel good today:

Things I noticed about myself:

Things I am grateful for:

Thoughts on the daily exercise:

Would you like to add anything else?

Day 56

Today, I...

> ***"The replenishing thing that comes with a nap - you end up with two mornings in a day."***
>
> ***- Pete Hamill***

EXERCISE 56: Nap

While some cultures around the world embrace naptime, unfortunately, others snub this practice, either dismissing it as something only for children and seniors, or as something unproductive and borderline lazy. It's sad that, for many, it has become a competition as to who can sleep less and be more productive. In truth, great women and men have extolled the benefits of napping; many have even suggested their inventions, their creativity, and answers to their inquiries came during a siesta.

Additionally, taking a nap offers incredible health benefits, while exhausting yourself can have severe consequences. Sleep deprivation and overexertion can affect your physical, mental, and emotional health in undesirable and sometimes dangerous ways. However, a nap boosts alertness and creativity, improves mood, increases productivity, helps clear the mind, and lowers stress. Even corporations are beginning to recognize the advantages of napping, and avant-garde companies such as the Huffington Post, Google, and Nike now have nap pods and quiet rooms – spaces where their employees can recharge their batteries by taking time for a snooze.

Today, indulge in a nap. Take a moment, ideally between 1:00 PM and 3:00 PM to get some quality shut-eye. If possible, darken the room, make yourself as comfortable as you can, and silence your electronics. Enjoy any sleep time you can gift yourself.

In the event you are unable to nap, just close your eyes for a few minutes, and consciously breathe while completely relaxing your body.

Examples

- Enjoy a 2- to 5-minute micro-nap for a boost of energy.
- Take a 15- to 20-minute catnap to increase alertness, stamina, and relieve stress.
- Take a 30- to 60-minute power nap to boost memory, improve problem solving and productivity.
- Take a long, relaxing 60- to 90-minute nap to enjoy a full sleep cycle, rejuvenate, make new connections in the brain, and boost creativity.

Things that made me feel good today:

Things I noticed about myself:

Things I am grateful for:

Thoughts on the daily exercise:

Would you like to add anything else?

Day 57

Today, I...

> ***"Everybody needs a place they can go to rest, sheltered from the past and the future. A place you can live one moment at a time."***
>
> **- Carol Orsborn**

EXERCISE 57: Recharge Your Batteries

Hectic schedules, daily obligations, noise pollution, and electronic devices are all reasons people experience feeling drained, exhausted, and run down. How often do you hear yourself complain, "I have no energy," or "I'm tired"? If you are like most, you probably refer to your low energy levels several times throughout the day.

The strain of feeling worn out is often accompanied with unpleasant mental and emotional side effects, such as moodiness, stress, lack of motivation or focus, and irritability. Sometimes, all it takes to feel better is taking a nap, meditating, or spending time in a special place.

Today, take a moment during the day to recharge your batteries. Spend some quality time in a place that makes you feel good and reenergizes you. Take all the time you need, and enjoy replenishing your energy – breathe calmly and consciously, be present, and feel gratitude for giving yourself this privileged moment. If you cannot go anywhere, close your eyes, relax, take a few conscious breaths, and visit that special place in your mind for as long as it feels good.

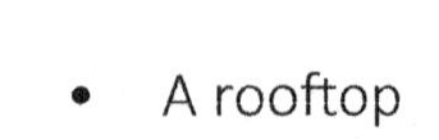

Examples

- A rooftop
- The beach
- The forest
- A mountain peak
- A park
- A place of worship
- Your garden
- On a boat

Where did you recharge your batteries?

Things that made me feel good today:

Things I noticed about myself:

Things I am grateful for:

Thoughts on the daily exercise:

Would you like to add anything else?

Day 58

Today, I...

> *"Keep only those things that speak to your heart. Then take the plunge and discard all the rest. By doing this, you can reset your life and embark on a new lifestyle."*
>
> ***- Marie Kondo***

EXERCISE 58: Declutter Your Phone

Whether a person has a hoarding disorder, is a pack rat, or is simply disorganized – amassing things in a closet, on a desk, in a home, or on a phone – negatively impacts them. Clutter of any kind can cause you to feel overwhelmed, stressed, fatigued, and can affect your overall well-being.

On average, people spend a remarkable amount of time on phones that are (typically) cluttered with different apps, pictures, videos, etc. This clutter can cause issues with your phone's performance, but more importantly, it can lead to undue stress at conscious and unconscious levels. Therefore, making time to declutter is essential to regain inner balance and peace of mind.

Today, take a moment to declutter and organize your phone. Delete old pictures, apps, and videos that are irrelevant, do not make you feel good, or are not in line with your goals and aspirations. Once you are done deleting and/or transferring all the extra data, create folders to organize and categorize. Make sure to update your screen saver to an image that inspires or motivates you. Finally, remember to clean your phone properly, as it is a haven for germs and bacteria. Do not use harsh products or cleaners; instead use antibacterial phone wipes, a screen cleaner, or use a UV sanitizer. Enjoy the process and notice how much lighter you feel once it's all done.

Helpful Tips:

- If you question whether you should delete something, you probably should.
- If you have 20 photos of the same sunset, you probably have 19 too many.
- Any photos of your ex or people who upset you probably are not great images to keep on your phone. They will continually trigger you and prevent you from moving forward.
- You do not need 100 videos of your pet doing the same trick over and over.
- If you want to be productive, you probably shouldn't have a collection of gaming apps or other apps that will distract you.
- You do not need ten apps that do the exact same thing – limit to one.
- Delete anything you do not use.
- Push all your apps to the secondary screens and keep your home screen simple, clean, and clutter free.

Things that made me feel good today:

Things I noticed about myself:

Things I am grateful for:

Thoughts on the daily exercise:

Would you like to add anything else?

Day 59

Today, I...

> ***"Learn to be thankful to everyone, to the entire creation, even to your enemy and also to those who insult, because they all help you to grow."***
>
> ***- Amma***
> ***(Mata Amritanandamayi)***

EXERCISE 59: Send Positive Energy

Every day, people have experiences that trigger certain emotions and feelings. For the sake of this exercise, we will by-pass good feelings and emotions, and we will solely focus on the negative ones, as they are responsible for all your suffering.

It is natural for emotions or feelings to spontaneously surface, however being reactive or holding on to these states of being is a matter of choice. Anger, frustration, sorrow, jealousy, and resentment can all surface in an instant, but only you have the power to keep them alive. The more you simmer in negativity, the more darkness you experience, and the more suffering you endure. To live a happier and more peaceful life, it is essential that you learn how to handle and release these lower energies.

To begin, you must acknowledge that no other being, environment, or circumstance has the power to make you feel a certain way – you are always responsible for the way you choose to feel. Then, it's important to understand that in order to transcend these negative states, you must consciously choose to take ownership of your emotions and feelings. This involves being present and understanding the difference between what you are witnessing and the story your mind is creating. Doing this will favor forgiveness, benevolence, gratitude, love, hope, joy, and other higher energies.

This process requires time, patience, and awareness. An effective way to begin this journey is to purposefully send positive energy toward anyone (including yourself) about whom you feel negatively.

Today, anytime you think or feel negative emotions toward yourself or anyone, pause, take a few conscious breaths, relax your body, and send a prayer, a kind thought, or positive energy in their direction or yours. When you are done, focus your attention on something else. If you have a hard time doing this, go through the entire process again (breathing consciously, relaxing the body, sending positive energy, etc.) until you feel lighter and are able to move on. At first, you will probably be surprised to notice that you apply this exercise toward yourself more than others. It is perfectly fine. The more love you send yourself, the more you will grow to love yourself, and the less the world outside of you will have any power over you.

If you live with a mental illness or disorder (e.g. bipolar disorder, OCD, depression, PTSD, anxiety, etc.) the views and opinions expressed above don't necessarily apply to you. Do the best that you can with this activity. Remember to honor your healing process and be patient, loving, and gentle with yourself.

Things that made me feel good today:

Things I noticed about myself:

Things I am grateful for:

Thoughts on the daily exercise:

Would you like to add anything else?

Today, I...

> *"The only way you can sustain a permanent change is to create a new way of thinking, acting, and being."*
>
> ***- Jennifer Hudson***

EXERCISE 60: *End-of-Phase Report*

Congratulations! You have successfully completed PHASE I and will now begin PHASE II. As you end one phase and get ready to enter another, it is time to pause and reflect on the past 60 days. Complete this exercise when you can have at least one hour of undisturbed time. Make yourself comfortable by creating a soothing ambiance: get a warm drink, put on some music, or light a candle. Take a few deep breaths, relax, and when you are ready, answer these questions honestly and thoroughly.

1. What were your greatest successes and/or achievements during this phase?

2. What brought you the most joy during this phase?

3. What are fears and challenges you are still facing?

4. What are the biggest changes you have noticed about yourself?

5. What are the biggest changes you have noticed in your relationships?

6. What are the biggest changes you have noticed in your life?

7. What has become easier for you since beginning this journey?

8. What are you the most grateful for at the moment?

9. What are the things you still must work on or improve?

10. What teacher(s) or tools (practices, documentaries, exercises, etc.) have helped you the most during this phase?

11. What are the greatest lessons you have learned during this phase?

12. On a scale of 1 to 10, with 10 being the most positive, how satisfied are you with your progress so far? Explain.

Completely dissatisfied				Neutral					Completely satisfied
1	2	3	4	5	6	7	8	9	10

13. On a scale of 1 to 10, with 10 being the most positive, how comfortable are you with trying new things? Explain.

Very uncomfortable				Neutral					Very comfortable
1	2	3	4	5	6	7	8	9	10

14. On a scale of 1 to 10, with 10 being the most positive, are you satisfied with the amount of commitment you have put into Phase I? How can you improve?

Completely dissatisfied				Neutral					Completely satisfied
1	2	3	4	5	6	7	8	9	10

15. On a scale of 1 to 10, with 10 being the most positive, how much do you love yourself now? Explain.

I loathe myself				Neutral					I love myself completely
1	2	3	4	5	6	7	8	9	10

Would you like to add anything else?

You did it! Now, it's time to celebrate by doing something special or giving yourself a gift. Please do not skip this step, as it is significant for your present and future progress. Positive reinforcement will assure future success in changing certain behaviors, certain patterns, and achieving your dreams and goals.

Today, I celebrated completing ***PHASE I*** by

Phase 2: Grow Love

Reminder: Phase II will be a little more demanding as the roots grow and become stronger. You will need to move seedlings, remove certain pests, and continue to pull out weeds.

During this phase, you will continue to observe gradual shifts in your reality and within yourself. You will begin to understand how truly important it is for you to love yourself. You will begin raising your standards and upgrading your value system. Your confidence, self-respect, and appreciation will sprout.

You will develop a greater understanding regarding the power of your choices. You will become aware of how your energy affects your reality. You will act more mindfully. You are discovering how to balance and harmonize the three bodies (body, mind, and spirit).

Today, I...

> ***"Follow your bliss and the universe will open doors where there were only walls."***
> ***- Joseph Campbell***

EXERCISE 61: Follow Your Bliss (Yes, again)

If you sit and think about all the things you are tasked with, or the things you feel compelled to do in a day, you will, more than likely, experience some inner turmoil. Clearly, we all have responsibilities we must answer to, but it should not constitute the better part of your days.

Being in a constant state of unhappiness disconnects you from your inner guidance system, drains you of your energy, and causes you to feel upset, which effectively blocks any good trying to come your way (i.e. opportunities, new relationships, happy circumstances, gifts, etc.).

For things to flow positively in your life, you must feel lighthearted, inspired, and relaxed. The surest and fastest way to feel positive emotions and feelings is to follow your bliss. Following your bliss means making your joy a priority, not a happenstance – it's about taking responsibility for your happiness and not counting on mere luck.

Today, if you can, take the day off, reschedule appointments, cancel obligations, and follow your bliss. Plan nothing in particular; just follow your heart. Give in to any activity that makes you feel joyful, blissful, and serene. Stay away from any activity that frustrates, stresses, or upsets you. If you cannot take the entire day off, or if you have certain obligations you can't reschedule, still make sure to enjoy yourself as much as possible. To help, ask yourself questions such as "How can I have fun right now?" "What do I really feel like doing at the moment?" or "What could I do to feel joyful here and now?" Be conscious of the positive feelings that surface, enjoy following your heart, and have a beautiful day.

Things that made me feel good today:

Things I noticed about myself:

Things I am grateful for:

Thoughts on the daily exercise:

Would you like to add anything else?

Today, I...

> ***"Be a storehouse of happy memories."***
> ***- Gretchen Rubin***

EXERCISE 62: Joyful Memories

People spend a senseless amount of time living in their past; they revisit the pain, the hurt, the aggravation, the suffering, the loss, and all the most negative memories their minds can reach and pull out. It goes something like this; an unpleasant memory surfaces, and instead of releasing it, you choose to get lost in this biased inner movie and allow it to wreak havoc on your heart and mind. Even when you happen to reminisce about something beautiful and positive, you often transform it into a nostalgic and painful experience by convincing yourself that nothing could ever surpass those "good old days".

It's mental, but you regularly give in to this heartbreaking pastime. You would heal from so many grievances if only you learned to use your memory file as the helpful tool that it is, and not as a torture device.

Choose to learn from yesterday's mistakes, hurts, and trauma, hold on to the wisdom, but heal by deciding to move on. Choose to remember happy memories with gratitude and delight. Live for today, but if you must relive yesterday, at least make sure to come back with something to smile about.

Today, go down memory lane, but only revisit joyful memories. Feel grateful for all the fun, the love, the opportunities, and all the beautiful memories you are fortunate to have. This is a great occasion to look at old photos, or watch videos and home movies you haven't looked at or watched in a long time. Now, record your five favorite memories below, and revisit them whenever you need a mood boost.

Food for thought: Your past experiences make up the story of your life, you can choose a great one or a disempowering one, which one will you choose?

Some of My Favorite Memories

Things that made me feel good today:

Things I noticed about myself:

Things I am grateful for:

Thoughts on the daily exercise:

Would you like to add anything else?

Today, I...

> *"A lot of times when I buy a lot of toys, I get a little jealous and keep one or two for myself. So I've got a couple of drones. I've got a couple of remote-control cars. I like to have fun."*
>
> ***- Shaquille O'Neal***

EXERCISE 63: Buy a Toy

Toys play an important role in our lives and are a fundamental part of our personal development. We can all think about our childhood toys, reminisce about our favorite playthings, and even remember that special toy or game we wanted but never got. Still today, most of us can look at toys or games with a childlike cheerfulness and lightheartedness.

Your inner child never grows up and regardless of your age, it still loves to play and have fun.

To live a balanced and happy life, it's important to embrace and indulge this childlike part of yourself.

Today, have some fun and buy a toy. Choose to purchase something you would have loved as a child, or follow your inner child's current desires and buy something that resonates with you. Once you have made your purchase, you have several options: you can keep it and play with it yourself; you can give it to a child you know and either play with them or simply let them have fun, or you can donate it. Regardless of your decision, enjoy yourself, stay present, and pay close attention to your feelings and emotions; you will probably notice a deep sense of relief, gratitude, and inner satisfaction.

It's always a good idea to buy age appropriate toys for children, and before offering a gift, check with their parents to verify it's okay with them. Be mindful to ask the caretaker discreetly, so as not to distress the child or place the guardian in an awkward and uncomfortable position.

Examples

- Play-Doh or slime
- Telescope or microscope
- Remote controlled helicopters, planes, or cars
- Cabbage Patch Kids or Care Bears
- Lego or K'NEX
- A Tamagotchi or a retro game system
- Mancala, Jenga, or pick-up-sticks
- Action figures or stuffed animals
- Barbie dolls or My Little Pony
- Trampoline or Water Slide
- Race Tracks or train sets
- Monopoly, Uno, or Life
- Electric scooter or drone
- Bike or Skateboard

What toy did you buy and what did you do with it?

Things that made me feel good today:

Things I noticed about myself:

Things I am grateful for:

Thoughts on the daily exercise:

Would you like to add anything else?

Today, I...

> ***"Sweat is an ancient and universal form of self-healing, whether done in the gym, the sauna, or the sweat lodge."***
> ***- Gabrielle Roth***

EXERCISE 64: *Work Up a Sweat*

While many people associate sweating with being dirty, stinky, and sticky, perspiration actually offers many benefits.

The primary function of sweat is to help cool down your body's temperature, but it also detoxifies your body, unclogs and cleans your pores, releases "feel good" hormones (endorphins), and helps boost your immune system.

Today, work up a good sweat. Have fun sweating on purpose without any negative judgments or feelings. Give your body the opportunity to perspire like never before while doing an activity that makes you feel happy and energized. Be present, enjoy your body, and delight in the process. Once you're done, make sure to give your body time to cool down (20 to 40 minutes) before taking a nice shower.

Examples

- Exercise at the gym or at home.
- Spend some time at a sauna.
- Go for a run or a walk.
- Redecorate and move furniture around.
- Play fitness video games.
- Enjoy a nice steam bath.
- Do some gardening or start a home project.
- Go cycling or skateboarding.
- Play a game or a sport with your children.
- Go up and down the stairs.
- Parkour or do some rock climbing.
- Do some cleaning or dance while cooking.

Helpful Tips:

- Make sure to keep yourself hydrated to replenish the lost fluids. Opinions diverge regarding whether it is better to drink water at room temperature or ice cold. I believe shocking the body is never a positive option, therefore I would suggest drinking slightly chilled water (a little colder than room temperature) at a slower pace. As always, use your best judgment.
- It is important not to let sweat linger too long (i.e. past the cool down period) in order to avoid unwelcomed side effects, such as breakouts, rashes, chafing, bacterial infections, fungal infections, and body odor. Make sure to shower with hot water to relax your muscles and get rid of the oils and grime, lather up, and rinse your body well. Ending your shower with cool or cold water can be helpful with muscle recovery.

What did you do to work up a sweat?

Things that made me feel good today:

Things I noticed about myself:

Things I am grateful for:

Thoughts on the daily exercise:

Would you like to add anything else?

Today, I...

> *"I always encourage people to get out there, travel the world, see new things, experience new people, experience new food, experience new culture. What happens is that helps you to grow and be your best self."*
>
> **- Karamo Brown**

EXERCISE 65: Surprise Your Palate

By now, you are probably beginning to understand the importance of trying and experiencing new things. Still, most people are reluctant to attempt the unfamiliar. For instance, this world is filled with delicious and diverse food options, originating from an abundance of places and cultures, however most individuals still find a way to eat the same predictable meals.

Stepping away from habitual food choices is actually one of the hardest things to do for many of us. To be fair, venturing and tasting different foods is not easy, and it's a natural reflex to pull away or talk yourself out of the experience. Yet, if you allow yourself to be a tad more adventurous, tasting and savoring new dishes can be thrilling and exulting.

What if instead of fearing the taste of something, you decided to be excited about trying something different? If you do not like something, you do not have to eat it, but if you never try, you may waste a great opportunity to discover new delicious foods.

Today, get out of your food rut, and surprise your palate by eating something you have never tried before. It can be anything, a simple piece of fruit you are intrigued about, a three-course meal at a restaurant serving an unexplored type of cuisine, or a recipe you are curious to try. You can have fun doing this on your own, or invite family and friends to partake in the adventure. Be as mindful as possible and savor every bite. Take the time to contemplate the reasons you like or dislike this new food. Is it the taste? Is it the texture? Is it the aroma? Regardless of your experience, moving forward make sure to try new foods regularly.

How did you surprise your palate? What did you try? Did you enjoy it?

Things that made me feel good today:

Things I noticed about myself:

Things I am grateful for:

Thoughts on the daily exercise:

Would you like to add anything else?

Day 66

Today, I...

> ***"Do your little bit of good where you are; it's those little bits of good put together that overwhelm the world."***
>
> ***- Desmond Tutu***

EXERCISE 66: Share Something You Love

At one point or another, everyone needs a bit of inspiration, motivation, or just a reason to smile. If you take a moment to think about it, you will realize that many of your favorite books, movies, mentors, music, etc., were all passed down to you by people or "lucky coincidences." Keeping in mind how much you have benefited from all these outside sources, you must realize that it's equally important that you share worthy information that could assist others. While some of you may believe you have nothing special to share, I assure you that there is always someone out there in need of exactly what you know or have to offer.

Today, share something you love with whomever you choose. Let it be something that really uplifts your spirit and makes you feel really good. Do it with the heartfelt intention of brightening someone's day, and make sure not to impose on anyone. Kindly offer your gift without insistence or expectations.

Examples

- A favorite song
- A great movie
- An inspiring book
- An informative documentary
- An interesting article
- A funny meme
- A motivational quote
- A beautiful piece of art
- An encouraging video
- A motivational speaker
- Cute animal pictures
- An uplifting blog

Helpful Tips:

- Share a beautiful poem on social media.
- Leave your favorite book on a restaurant table.
- Forward a quote you love to your coworker.
- Send an article that inspired you to a friend.
- Talk to someone about a favorite teacher or mentor.
- Watch your favorite children's movie with your students.

What did you share and who did you share it with?

Things that made me feel good today:

Things I noticed about myself:

Things I am grateful for:

Thoughts on the daily exercise:

Would you like to add anything else?

Today, I...

> *"I'm more interested in the idea of role-playing in general than the idea of role-playing in art. I like the childlike quality of making pretend or the optimistic idea of pretending something's happening when it's not."*
>
> ***- Laurel Nakadate***

EXERCISE 67: Role-Play

On the path of change, it's easy for people to get confused as to what should be done, transformed, or improved. The answers are not always apparent because of the lack of perspective and guidance; this can make the entire process frustrating and disconcerting.

To gain some clarity, you must step out of your box and analyze the situation from a different point of view. Begin by thinking of a role model or a person you admire who embodies certain traits, attitudes, values, or behaviors you would like to emulate. Take a moment to visualize that inspiring figure; looking at a photo or watching a video where they appear may be helpful.

What does their life look like? What are their habits and routines? How do they walk and talk in different situations? Try to imagine as many details as you can. Now, pull back and imagine what they would do if they were in your shoes. How would they tackle your challenges? How would they interact with your friends and family members? What would they change or improve? How would they behave and act? How would they care for their body, their mind, and their soul? Try to imagine how they would live your life and what they would do differently. You can choose to go through the same process with different people you admire to gain various perspectives.

Today, role-play and go through your day as you believe your role model(s) would. Remain in character throughout the entire day in order to make a sound assessment at the end of the exercise – this means embodying that inspirational figure by doing everything you imagine they would do if they were in your shoes.

At the end of the day, look back and notice how differently you cared for yourself, held yourself, thought, behaved, reacted, and interacted with others. Did you notice any improvements? How did you feel? Did you enjoy yourself? Are there any changes you plan on adopting? Below write a quick summary detailing your observations, what you gained from this experience, and the adjustments you plan to implement.

Please understand that, in reality, this technique helps you connect with what you subconsciously believe to be the "best" you. Pretending to be an ideal helps you embody that highest version of yourself without the usual resistance. People we admire are only reflections of our greatest potential. This process will help you realize how much you hold yourself back, and it will give you some insight into your deep-rooted belief system.

Things that made me feel good today:

Things I noticed about myself:

Things I am grateful for:

Thoughts on the daily exercise:

Would you like to add anything else?

Day 68

Today, I...

> **"You learn a lot when you're barefoot. The first thing is every step you take is different."**
>
> **- Michael Franti**

EXERCISE 68: Mindful Walking

Being more conscious and inviting more and more mindfulness into your everyday life is a sure way of relaxing, letting go of stress, and broadening your awareness. There are many different ways to practice mindfulness, but one of the easiest ways is to bring your complete attention to the act of walking. Walking comes so naturally to most people that it is generally an unconscious happening and process. Becoming conscious, connecting to your body and to your environment, awakens you to the present moment, and grounds you.

Today, invite presence and calmness into your life through the practice of mindful walking. You can practice this exercise in several different ways, but for today, find a space where you can comfortably walk barefoot. Turn off any electronics that may distract you, and relax your body. Take a few conscious breaths and begin walking very slowly. Keep your attention on the movement of your feet from heel to toe as they lift up and step down; be aware of the way your body feels as it moves, and feel the different sensations in your feet (textures, pressure, temperature, movement, etc.). When your mind becomes distracted by the scenery or a thought, gently bring your attention back to your walking. Continue mindfully and silently walking until you feel like stopping. Pause, stand straight, take a few conscious breaths, feel gratitude for the ability to walk, and slowly resume your activities.

In the event that you cannot practice mindful walking because of a mobility issue or a disability, simply do your best to adapt this exercise in a way that is possible for you, or just choose to practice being as mindful and as present as you can throughout the day.

Helpful Tip: If you decide to do this exercise outdoors, please be mindful not to step on anything sharp, any surface that might be too hot, or tiny critters.

Where did you choose to enjoy this practice?

Things that made me feel good today:

Things I noticed about myself:

Things I am grateful for:

Thoughts on the daily exercise:

Would you like to add anything else?

Today, I...

> *"Don't judge or analyze what you observe. Watch the thought, feel the emotion, observe the reaction. Don't make a personal problem out of them. You will then feel something more powerful than any of those things that you observe: the still, observing presence itself behind the content of your mind, the silent watcher."*
>
> **- Eckhart Tolle**

EXERCISE 69: Observe Your Emotions

With each external or internal trigger, be it something we see, something we think about, or something someone says, an emotion is born. That emotion then gives birth to positive or negative thoughts and reactions. Those in turn exacerbate the initial emotion, triggering more thoughts and reactions, and the cycle repeats. That is the process that runs your life.

The more you get mentally and physically accustomed to an emotion, the more it will grow roots and direct your life. This is great news if you spend most of your time feeling positive emotions; however, if you spend your time succumbing to negative ones, it can have terrible consequences.

Today, observe your emotions. Pay close attention to them. What provokes them? How do they make you feel physically? What thoughts do they fuel? What reactions do they incite? This will probably not be a very comfortable experience, as you become aware of an unpleasant truth: you deliberately choose to spend a lot of time simmering in negativity, while you usually dismiss or move on from your positive emotions quite rapidly.

Please do not be harsh on yourself and do not take it all too personally. You have been oblivious for a very long time. Realize that, like thoughts, emotions are addictive, and in order for things to improve, it is imperative that you take healthier decisions when it comes to what you think or feel repeatedly. The more mindful you become, the better things will get. By becoming aware of your inner workings, with practice, you will have an easier time both releasing the negative and generating the positive. Meanwhile, deliberately do things that ignite positive feelings and emotions in you; be mindful to enjoy and nurture pleasant and happy states of being for as long as you can. Do your best to stay away from negative triggers and be as present as possible. Do not entertain your negative thoughts and emotions. Whenever they surface, acknowledge them, if need be (for more persistent or painful emotions) try to understand their root cause, and let them fly away like balloons by relaxing the body and taking nice deep breaths.

At the end of the day share your experience on the spaces provided.

What are your most recurring feelings and emotions?

Moving forward what feelings and emotions do you intend to nurture? How do you plan to do that?

Things that made me feel good today:

Things I noticed about myself:

Things I am grateful for:

Thoughts on the daily exercise:

Would you like to add anything else?

Day 70

Today, I...

> ***"A hobby a day keeps the doldrums away."***
> ***- Phyllis McGinley***

EXERCISE 70: Something You Enjoy

Living a fast-paced life in a fast-paced world sometimes forces us to jump from one thing to the next. It's not uncommon to hear people complain about never having a moment to themselves to do the things they really love and enjoy.

Not creating time for favorite activities, past-times, or hobbies can have dire consequences on the psyche, the heart, the spirit, and the body. It's important to set aside some time to do things you love every single day.

Having schedules crammed with obligations and responsibilities without space for your own passions is unacceptable and completely unloving towards yourself. Remember, time on this earth is precious. Taking care of your joy and well-being must be your top priority if you are to love yourself and live a fulfilled life.

Today, think of a hobby or something you enjoy doing that you haven't had the opportunity to do in a long time. Schedule a block of time to indulge in that cherished activity. You can choose to do this activity alone or with family members and friends. Have a great time, enjoy yourself without pressure or guilt, and remain as conscious as possible throughout this activity. Moving forward, make sure to plan time for the things that bring you happiness.

Examples

- Perform at a comedy club.
- Do yoga outdoors.
- Read a good book.
- Go dance at a club.
- Draw Zentangles.
- Surf with some friends.
- Play chess at the park.
- Volunteer to cuddle babies.
- Go to the movies.
- Create a collage.
- Stargaze.
- Play ping-pong.
- Write poetry.
- Go to an amusement park.
- Keep a nature journal.

What did you do?

Things that made me feel good today:

Things I noticed about myself:

Things I am grateful for:

Thoughts on the daily exercise:

Would you like to add anything else?

Today, I...

> *"A diet rich in fruits and vegetables plays a role in reducing the risk of all the major causes of illness and death."*
>
> ***- Walter Willett***

EXERCISE 71: Eat the Rainbow (no, not Skittles)

It's not a secret that eating a diet rich in fruits and vegetables offers many health benefits and helps in preventing certain diseases and conditions. Nature's foods are rich in vitamins and minerals, phytonutrients, fibers, and antioxidants. Not only is it important to eat plenty of fruits and vegetables with each meal, but it is also vital that you eat a wide variety of them. Mother Earth bestows us with colorful foods, each color containing specific nutritional health benefits – knowing the advantages that can be gained from each particular color will help you care more effectively for your health and body.

Today, color your plate and eat the rainbow. Eat as many different fruits and vegetables as you can, and try to eat some from each color group. Have fun, enjoy what you eat, and record in the table below what you consume during the day in the appropriate color group. Pay attention to the way you physically feel while eating the different fruits and veggies and to the way you feel afterward. Remember to follow the wisdom of your body and allow it to guide you toward the fresh produce it craves or desires. Also note that if you are not used to eating large quantities of fresh produce daily, you may experience some bloating and increased visits to the restroom. In order to prevent bloating and discomfort, eat smaller portions throughout the day, as opposed to large portions in one sitting.

Here is a table to help you understand the benefits of each color.

Colors	Examples	Benefits
Green	Avocado, kale, broccoli, asparagus, green apples, chard, parsley, green peppers, collards, green peas, spinach, etc.	Reduces the risk of certain types of cancers, boosts the immune system, improves energy, supports eyesight, improves digestion, powerful antioxidants, protects body from viruses, etc.
Yellow	Pineapple, yellow peppers, lemon, yellow pears, yellow apples, gold kiwis, corn, etc.	Reduces the risk of certain types of cancers, lowers cholesterol and blood pressure, boosts the immune system, supports joints and tissues, keeps skin healthy, etc.
Orange	Mango, orange, pumpkin, squash, sweet potato, carrot, apricot, cantaloupe, orange peppers, nectarines, etc.	Reduces the risk of certain types of cancers, reduces heart disease, improves immune function, anti-inflammatory, antioxidant, protects the skin, promotes collagen growth, etc.
Blue/Purple	Blueberry, beet, blackberry, eggplant, figs, purple potato, purple cabbage, purple grapes, plums, etc.	Reduces the risk of certain types of cancers, helps memory function, promotes heart health, supports healthy skin, anti-inflammatory, reduces risk of Alzheimer's, slows the aging process, etc.
Red	Strawberry, pink grapefruit, raspberry, tomato, cherry, watermelon, pomegranate, red peppers, papaya, red potatoes, red apples, etc.	Reduces the risk of certain types of cancers, protects skin, helps skin regeneration, reduces risk of diabetes, reduces the risk of stroke, promotes heart health, etc.
White	Banana, garlic, potato, cauliflower, jicama, ginger, mushroom, onion, coconut, etc.	Reduces the risk of certain types of cancers, reduces free radicals damage, lowers risk of cardiovascular diseases, prevents ulcers, supports healthy bones, etc.

Your turn! What foods did you eat today?

Colors	Food I Ate Today
Green	
Yellow	
Orange	
Blue/Purple	
Red	
White	

Things that made me feel good today:

Things I noticed about myself:

Things I am grateful for:

Thoughts on the daily exercise:

Would you like to add anything else?

Today, I...

> *"Music, at its essence, is what gives us memories. And the longer a song has existed in our lives, the more memories we have of it."*
>
> ***- Stevie Wonder***

EXERCISE 72: Old School Music

Who doesn't appreciate a good melody? It goes without saying that for many of us, if not all of us, music plays or has played an important role in our lives. Everyone has experienced their body being moved by certain beats, their emotions touched by a certain song, or a blast from the past listening to a special tune.

Beyond the personal pleasures we can gain from music, it also provides many wonderful benefits, such as uplifting people's moods, reducing stress and pain, decreasing road rage, and helping with sleep. There are even accounts of people suffering from Alzheimer's disease or dementia that can at times remember their identity and recall old memories when listening to a beautiful composition or a certain piece of music they enjoyed during earlier years. Furthermore, music is so powerful that it is often used as a therapeutic medium to help individuals of all ages.

Music has been around for all recorded history and will probably always have an important place in our world. Nowadays, with the internet and access to various melodies from many different cultures, it's easy to go from one favorite song to another in the blink of an eye. However, we can all still remember special tunes that have marked significant times in our lives – they remind us of certain people or events, rekindle certain emotions, or reconnect us with younger versions of ourselves. Can you think of a few?

Today, travel back in time and listen to some old school music – here, old school implies music or songs that take you back to another time; they can be songs you used to love in middle school or high school, or songs you used to listen to ten years or fifty years ago. Just make sure they are melodies that reawaken positive emotions and put a smile on your face. Enjoy some old favorites, visit with some good memories, and be as carefree as possible; sing, dance, and have a good time.

What did you listen to?

Things that made me feel good today:

Things I noticed about myself:

Things I am grateful for:

Thoughts on the daily exercise:

Would you like to add anything else?

Day 73

Today, I...

> ***"Flexibility comes from having multiple choices; wisdom comes from having multiple perspectives."***
>
> ***- Robert Dilts***

EXERCISE 73: Change Your Perspective

You are probably familiar with the adage, "Before you judge a man, walk a mile in his shoes," which means that before judging someone you should see things from their point of view, understand their experiences, their motivations and thought patterns. This is excellent advice; however, if a person isn't skilled at being present and conscious, they can find it hard to implement in moments of stress, duress, or while having any ego-based reactions.

Stepping away from your "me, myself and I" point of view and choosing to grow your perspective is essential if you want to develop understanding and compassion. It can also help you make better decisions for yourself, gather new ideas, and assess situations in a more balanced and realistic way. The best way to begin this process is by consciously choosing to see things through the eyes of others in non-confrontational or negatively charged moments – choosing to experience their viewpoint during random moments in their presence or absence.

Today, change your perspective; choose to put yourself in other people's shoes and see the world through their eyes. In order to be as successful as possible, do your best not to let your judgments and opinions get in the way. Sometimes to better understand someone's point of view, it helps to ask questions. Just make sure that when asking, you do it with a real willingness to understand them without letting your own views or sensitivities interfere. Start easy and choose to glance through the perspective of people you appreciate and enjoy, as it will feel more comfortable and pleasant. With time and practice, you will be able to become more objective and capable of taking on the perspective of individuals who directly or indirectly provoke a negative reaction within you. You can do this with your children, your friends, your significant other, your parents, your pets, your business partners, a flight attendant, a favorite celebrity, a politician, etc. At the end of the day, observe what you have learned and gained from doing this exercise, and write a short summary about your experience below.

Things that made me feel good today:

Things I noticed about myself:

Things I am grateful for:

Thoughts on the daily exercise:

Would you like to add anything else?

Day 74

Today, I...

> ***"When we clear the physical clutter from our lives, we literally make way for inspiration and 'good, orderly direction' to enter."***
>
> ***- Julia Cameron***

EXERCISE 74: *Let Go of Something*

Unless you adhere to minimalism, chances are you collect things that gather dust in a closet, your bathroom, your drawers, your garage, your bookshelves, or even your wallet. There is nothing wrong with having things and enjoying things; conversely, it's your emotional attachment to these things that cripple you and clutter your space and mind.

To be attached to certain belongings means that you have identified with those belongings to the point that they have become an extension of you. Letting go of personal possessions can be quite scary for some people. For example, parents can have a hard time giving up their children's baby clothes, brides their wedding gowns, and others can fuss over letting go of clothes that no longer fit, treasured tools, timeworn furniture, or family heirlooms. The prospect of separating from their possessions jeopardizes their sense of identity and their cherished memories – this can be destabilizing, induce meltdowns, and create anguish.

Things are things – appreciate that you are a whole being and that you are the carrier of your memories; let go of the illusory belief that you are incomplete or broken without certain possessions to remind you of who you are and your life story. Decluttering your space will clear your mind, revitalize your spirit, release stagnant energy, and remove reminders of an outdated identity.

Today, let go of something. Go through a small area of your living space and let go of certain belongings. Beginning with clothes is always a great idea. Yes, getting rid of your clothes can be one of the most difficult things to do, but it can also be one of the most rewarding and most satisfying experiences. That being said, the choice is yours. When you are finished, throw away what is considered junk (e.g. undergarments, holey socks, ripped pants, stained shirts, broken electronics or furniture, rusted tools, etc.), and donate your gently worn clothes or used items to family and friends, people going through hard times, or a charity of your choice. Do not dwell on what you are seemingly "losing;" instead, be grateful for the opportunity to do good. Celebrate yourself for accomplishing this activity and enjoy paying it forward.

What did you release? How did it feel?

Things that made me feel good today:

Things I noticed about myself:

Things I am grateful for:

Thoughts on the daily exercise:

Would you like to add anything else?

Today, I...

> *"The more you know yourself, the more clarity there is. Self-knowledge has no end - you don't come to an achievement, you don't come to a conclusion. It is an endless river."*
> ***- Jiddu Krishnamurti***

EXERCISE 75: *Bi-Weekly Report*

It is time to pause and reflect on the past two weeks. Complete this exercise when you can have at least one hour of undisturbed time. Make yourself comfortable by creating a soothing ambiance: get a warm drink, put on some music, or light a candle. Take a few deep breaths, relax, and when you are ready, answer the following questions honestly and thoroughly.

1. Summarize the past two weeks in a sentence.

2. Looking back, what are you most proud of?

3. What are some inner blocks and fears you noticed?

4. What important lessons did you learn?

5. What brought you the most joy?

6. What surprised you the most?

7. How are you doing in terms of loving yourself?

8. How has your relationship with yourself evolved?

9. How has your relationship with others evolved?

10. How has your attitude toward life evolved?

11. What tools, practices, or teachers have helped you the most?

13. What were your favorite and least favorite exercises? Explain.

14. What are you most grateful for at the moment?

15. What are things you would like to improve on in the upcoming two weeks?

Would you like to add anything else?

Today, as the daily exercise, either repeat your favorite exercise of the past two weeks or do an activity that feels good to your soul.

What did you do?

Day 76

Today, I...

> ***"Love your skin, give oil a go."***
> ***- Shu Uemura***

EXERCISE 76: Warm Oil Self-Massage

In Ayurveda medicine (a Hindu alternative form of medicine), there is a practice involving warm oil self-massage called "Abhyanga," which is extolled for its many benefits. It improves the skin's softness and suppleness, tones the muscles, flushes toxins, relaxes and calms the nerves, stimulates the mind, helps with sleep patterns, promotes hair growth, etc.

It is generally performed with different oils and herbs depending on your particular dosha (Vata, Pitta, or Kapha), which is one of three energies that are believed to circulate within the body and govern a person's disposition, emotional tendencies, physical attributes, and so forth. If you have never heard of Ayurveda and its principles, I invite you to further research the concepts of this ancient form of healthcare.

Today, find a moment before your morning or evening shower to give yourself an intuitive warm oil self-massage by following the steps below. This is an opportunity to connect with your body in a gentle and loving way.

Before you begin, make sure the room temperature is at a comfortable setting, and create a soothing ambiance. Be as conscious and present as possible during the massage – feel your body as you touch it and watch it respond. Allow your mind to relax and enjoy this well-deserved moment of luxurious self-care.

Postpone giving yourself a massage if you are going through your menstrual cycle, have a skin condition (breakouts, irritation, rash, hives, eczema, etc.), are recovering from surgery, are going through an illness, or have a wound or cut on your body. Also make sure to test oil and herbs on a small area of your body 24 hours ahead of time to prevent any allergic reaction.

Self-massage steps:

1. Gently warm your oil by either putting the container under hot water or placing a small bowl of oil in a bath of hot water.
2. Undress.
3. Optional: Take a small amount of oil in the palm of your hand and begin by gently massaging your scalp in a circular motion with the tip of your fingers.
4. Work down your face, ears, and neck.
5. Continue down your body using your palms, fingers, and thumbs. Alternate between circular motions (on your joints and areas such as your chest and your buttocks) and long strokes (on the elongated parts of your body such as your back, arms, and legs), always moving toward your heart. Massage your abdomen in a circular motion moving up on the right side of the abdomen, then across, then down on the left side. The back can be a difficult area to reach so just do your best.
6. Keep the pressure light on your face and heart area, but apply varying pressure where it feels good. Make sure to follow your intuitive guidance and stay present to what feels good to your body.
7. Give extra attention to your hands and feet; it will be very relaxing.
8. If you have time, allow your body to absorb and benefit from the oil for 10 to 15 minutes.
9. When you feel ready, take a warm shower or bath. Soap your sensitive areas as you normally would, but be gentler on the rest of your body. Finish by softly patting your body dry.

Helpful Tips:

- To avoid slipping or making an oily mess, sit (or stand) on a towel during your massage. Wipe off excess oil from the soles of your feet, and be very careful going in the shower or bathtub.
- Some people choose to dry brush their skin before massaging their body with the warm oil. If you choose to start with this step, make sure to brush your skin with a dry brush or loofah beginning at your extremities and brushing toward your heart in order to drain the lymphatic system.
- Use oils that you have around the house, such as olive oil, argan oil, coconut oil, jojoba oil, or almond oil.
- You can choose to use oils and herbs according to your dosha. You can choose to purchase premade herbal oils, or you can use common oils, such as sesame for Vata, coconut oil for Pitta, and olive oil for Kapha.
- If you are curious about your dosha, follow the links below, and take one of the following online quizzes.
- VPK by Maharishi Ayurveda (Dosha Test) http://www.mapi.com/doshas/dosha-test/index.html
- Banyan Botanicals (Dosha Quiz) https://www.banyanbotanicals.com/info/prakriti-quiz/
- The Doctor Oz Show (Dosha Quiz) https://www.doctoroz.com/quiz/ayurvedic-body-type-find-your-dosha

Things that made me feel good today:

Things I noticed about myself:

Things I am grateful for:

Thoughts on the daily exercise:

Would you like to add anything else?

Today, I...

> *"Today I will do something just for the fun of it. I will find something to do that's just for me and I won't worry about what I should be doing. I will learn how to make myself feel good and enjoy life to the fullest."*
>
> **- Melody Beattie**

EXERCISE 77: A Fun List

By now, I hope that you understand how essential it is to balance your responsibilities and obligations with activities that bring you joy. To feel balanced, harmonious, and happy, you must tend to your heart's needs and desires – your joy and well-being must be your priority. Unfortunately, people are so often consumed by their to-do lists and their distractions that they feel disoriented as soon as they have a bit of free time on their hands. They have no idea what to do with themselves and cannot seem to recall what activities they truly enjoy. As an alternative, they will "kill" time by diving back into unfulfilling distractions or occupations (e.g. watching television, burying themselves in social media, etc.), which will tilt their inner balance unfavorably, leaving them feeling weary, fatigued, bored, or stressed.

Today, sit down and begin a "Fun List" of all the activities you really delight in. They must be activities, hobbies, or pastimes that you can easily do whenever you have some leisure time. Anytime you discover a new enjoyable or amusing activity, add it to your ongoing list. Make sure to carve out some time to check off some of the items on your list every day, including today.

Examples

- Fly your drone or a kite.
- Listen to or play music.
- Read or write a book.
- Make miniatures or build a model kit.
- Watch documentaries or bake desserts.
- Make 3D puzzles or play solitaire.
- Go on long walks or go ice skating.
- Do some paper crafts or paint.
- Take pictures or create vlogs.
- Blow bubbles or take up knitting.
- Write in your journal or write a blog.
- Meditate or make Ikebana flower arrangements.

My Fun List

Things that made me feel good today:

Things I noticed about myself:

Things I am grateful for:

Thoughts on the daily exercise:

Would you like to add anything else?

Day 78

Today, I...

> *"Choose your exercise using the same criteria you'd apply to choosing a date - that is, attractive to you and able to hold your interest for an hour."*
>
> **- Victoria Moran**

EXERCISE 78: A Physical Activity That You Enjoy

Everybody knows that regular physical activity is good for a person's health and well-being. The list of benefits is endless and includes, but is not limited to, warding off certain deadly diseases such as cancer or coronary heart disease, helping with certain conditions such as depression or insomnia, improving your muscle strength, slowing down the aging process, losing weight, lowering your blood pressure, improving your overall mood and outlook on life, etc. With such promises, you would think people would be more engaged in moving their bodies but, in reality, an alarming majority of people unfortunately choose to remain sedentary.

When asked why they refuse to partake in physical activities, people will commonly give the same responses: "I don't have time," "I'm too tired," "It's boring," "I don't know where to start," "I feel awkward going to the gym alone," or "the gym is too expensive." Regrettably, physical activity has a negative reputation – it's generally viewed as grueling work you must toil through in exchange for slow gains or progress. In addition, to be fair, it can be a little overwhelming and make anyone feel a tad insecure to walk into a gym as a beginner among the more experienced and ripped individuals. The solution? Stop seeing physical activity as something painful that you have to endure. Stop thinking of the gym as the only place you can exercise. And, before joining a gym, do several walkthroughs and make sure to ask questions about their coaching and training services and their policies to be positive you are comfortable and satisfied with their facility and personnel.

You must transcend the way you perceive physical activity, start seeing it as an opportunity to care for your body and health. Then, find exercises, practices, or sports that feel fun and exciting to you; you must find something that you really love and would not mind doing regularly. This will ensure that you stick to a healthy exercise routine while having a good time.

Today, take some time to do a physical activity that you enjoy. Choose something that does not feel like a chore but instead feels like an exhilarating and self-loving pastime. It can be something you already love doing or something completely new and different. If you already have a consistent fitness routine, this will be an easy exercise for you and you will have a blast. However, if you are new to exercise, do not pressure yourself, be gentle with your body, and enjoy moving in a fun and loving way.

Your body is the medium that helps you experience this reality, and it is much easier to preserve a healthy body than to heal an unhealthy and neglected body, so do your body a favor and care for it lovingly.

Remember to consult your healthcare provider prior to exercising if you are experiencing certain health issues or if you have not exercised in a long time. Also, remember to stay hydrated and do some warm-up and cool-down stretches and exercises.

Examples

- Turn on some music and dance.
- Do some indoor rock climbing.
- Go for a jog or on a walk with your best friend.
- Play tennis or badminton.
- Go rollerblading or Freeline skating.
- Go bowling or golfing.
- Go paddle boarding or kayaking.
- Take a Capoeira class or a Zumba class.
- Run around and play with your kids.
- Go ice skating or skiing
- Put in your favorite Wii FIT game.
- Follow an exercise channel like TiffanyRotheWorkouts, Blogilates or FitnessBlender on YouTube.

What activity(ies) did you partake in?

Things that made me feel good today:

Things I noticed about myself:

Things I am grateful for:

Thoughts on the daily exercise:

Would you like to add anything else?

Today, I...

> *"Remember, wisdom comes from everywhere, I am always searching for ideas that can inspire me or others to reach another level."*
>
> **- Les Brown**

EXERCISE 79: Compile Some Wisdom

In our wonderful world, we can learn a lot of helpful information and gain valuable guidance thanks to people and other mediums such as books, documentaries, articles, blogs, videos, podcasts, and classes. The more you gather information, the more you grow, and the more you can make educated decisions. Too often, individuals rely solely on their personal experiences to help them through life, or they look for knowledge and wisdom after it is long overdue. People around this planet have precious experiences, know-how, and insight that could be advantageous to you – leap at the opportunity!

Today, compile some wisdom from others. Either ask people you admire to share with you the best piece of advice they have ever received, or look for advice from role models that inspire you. If you want to have a bit of fun, you can ask your friends and followers on social media. Allow your intuition to assist you during the entire process. At the end of the day, choose the five recommendations that you find the most useful or valuable, and record them below.

Helpful Tip:You could begin a "Wisdom Journal" where you compile all the best advice you receive, and use it as a reference anytime you need motivation, inspiration, or creative ideas.

My Favorite Recommendations

Things that made me feel good today:

Things I noticed about myself:

Things I am grateful for:

Thoughts on the daily exercise:

Would you like to add anything else?

Today, I...

> *"Effective listening is more than simply avoiding the bad habit of interrupting others while they are speaking or finishing their sentences. It's being content to listen to the entire thought of someone rather than waiting impatiently for your chance to respond."*
>
> **- Richard Carlson**

EXERCISE 80: Do Not Interrupt

Do you appreciate being interrupted by people who jump in, mid-conversation, to finish your sentences or who eagerly want to share their thoughts and feelings? The rude interjections frustrate everyone, but most individuals are as guilty as the ones they blame. In most cases, people are too preoccupied with what they want to say to listen to what you are saying, and unless you have practiced developing your listening skills, you are probably as guilty as they are.

Today, make a conscious effort not to interrupt anyone who speaks to you as long as they are not aggressively communicating with or insulting you in any way. This will not be an easy task, and you will probably find yourself automatically falling back into your habitual patterns. As soon as you catch yourself, deliberately refocus your attention on the speaker's conversation. Be patient with yourself, and celebrate yourself for putting effort into listening as best as you can. The more you practice listening attentively, the easier it will become. To be attentive, you must be willing to be present, and abstain as much as you can from thinking about replies or from having judgments of any kind. Allow the person in front of you to share, completely, what they want to say at their own speed and from their own point of view. Be open to learning something new and pay attention to what is being said. Only ask questions or give feedback when the person is finished talking, or if they request your opinion. This is a valuable life skill that I recommend you implement in your daily life as it will undoubtedly open new doors for you in terms of relationships, knowledge, patience, and mindfulness.

Be aware that people around you may respond to your attentiveness with awkwardness and even a tad of uneasiness, nervousness, or frustration. It's a natural reaction; they are not in the habit of being able to formulate a complete thought without interruption. If they question your new behavior, just kindly reassure them that you are trying to get better at listening and being mindful.

Things that made me feel good today:

Things I noticed about myself:

Things I am grateful for:

Thoughts on the daily exercise:

Would you like to add anything else?

Today, I...

> *"The more you believe it, the more it starts to become real for you. This is why it is so very important to believe in positive things, rather than negative things. Whatever you believe, you will find that you are correct. The universe has a way of presenting to you exactly what you believe. If you think life is great, you are correct. If you think life is tough, you will be proved correct too."*
>
> ***- Anita Moorjani***

EXERCISE 81: Dispose of Negativity

From the time of your birth, you have gathered many different fears and negative beliefs that hold you back from being the best version of yourself and from experiencing life to its fullest potential. In order to change these negative patterns, you must reprogram your subconscious mind. However, before you can start reprogramming your mind, you will need to unearth the inconspicuous negativity playing in the background.

Today, find a moment when you will be uninterrupted for a least an hour. Get something to drink, make yourself comfortable, take a few conscious breaths, and relax. When you are ready, write down on a blank piece of paper all the fears and negative beliefs you think hold you back from being your best self. Try to be as honest as you can with yourself, and do not worry about figuring it all out – this is something you will be working on for the rest of your life. As one aspect of your life improves, other things that need your attention will surface and will give you the opportunity to grow further. For now, you will notice what needs your attention today, and that's plenty. Once you are done writing everything down, on the following page, for each negative belief and fear fill in an "I used to believe... But now..." statement, affirming something more in line with what you want to believe. Make sure that your statements reframe your perspective in a way that you agree with and that is believable for you. For instance, do not say "I used to believe I was ugly, but now I know I'm beautiful," if you do not truly believe that – instead, say something like "I used to believe I was ugly, but now I am learning to see the beauty in myself."

It can be helpful to question your beliefs by asking questions such as "What evidence do I have that this is the truth?" "Is this serving me or keeping me in my misery?" "What value is there in keeping this fear or belief?" "Is there a more positive way to see this?" or "What do I need to believe to be my best self?" Once you are done doing that for each negative fear and belief, dispose of the page that is covered in negativity as you see fit. You can cut it in a hundred little pieces and throw it away. You can burn it, just be mindful not to burn yourself or start a fire. Or, you can rip it to shreds and flush it down the toilet. Just make sure to get it out of your living space.

This symbolic gesture communicates to your subconscious mind that you are severing the relationship and attachment with an old way of thinking. As you discard and clean up, you can say a silent prayer, affirm positive declarations, or simply feel gratitude for the experience. Do what feels good. Moving forward, try as best as you can to reframe your negative thoughts and beliefs as soon as they surface.

Examples

- I used to believe no one would like me if I was my authentic self, but now I know that by being myself I will be happier and attract like-minded people.
- I used to believe I was doomed to live in my boring routine, but now I realize that I have the power to create change in my life.
- I used to believe I wasn't as intelligent as my peers, but now I see it was all because of my own insecurities and choose to appreciate what I bring to the table.
- I used to believe the world was a scary place, but now I understand that watching too much news is the cause; the world is as friendly as I make my mind about it.
- I used to believe that everyone's life was better than mine, but now I choose not to compare myself with others and realize that everyone goes through difficulties.
- I used to believe I was unlucky, but now I recognize that I make my own luck.

I used to believe

but now

I used to believe

but now

I used to believe

but now

I used to believe

but now

I used to believe

but now

I used to believe

but now

I used to believe

but now

I used to believe

but now

I used to believe

but now

I used to believe

but now

I used to believe

but now

I used to believe

but now

I used to believe

but now

I used to believe

but now

I used to believe

but now

I used to believe

but now

I used to believe

but now

I used to believe

but now

I used to believe

but now

I used to believe

but now

I used to believe

but now

I used to believe

but now

I used to believe

but now

Things that made me feel good today:

Things I noticed about myself:

Things I am grateful for:

Thoughts on the daily exercise:

Would you like to add anything else?

Day 82

Today, I...

> ***"The eye is the jewel of the body."***
> ***- Henry David Thoreau***

EXERCISE 82: Revitalize Your Eyes

Do you ever take the time to consider how amazing your eyes are? Take your eyes off the page for a moment, look around you and notice all the wonderful things you are able to see. Appreciate the incredible gift that is your eyesight for a few minutes.

Your eyes have some of the most overworked muscles in your body, and now more than ever they are subjected to conditions that provoke unfavorable consequences such as eye fatigue or eye strain. Most people can relate to experiencing one of the following symptoms daily: burning or itchy eyes, watery or dry eyes, some redness, some inflammation, heaviness of the eyelids, occasional visual blurriness, and even eye pain. These common eye problems can be caused by excessive use of digital devices, prolonged staring at a computer screen or television, considerable amounts of reading, weather conditions, exposure to fans or interior cooling and heating systems, overly bright lights or poor lighting, pollution, and dietary deficiencies. There are many ways to help your eyes (see tips below), and the following process is one of the fastest ways to alleviate any discomfort you are consciously or unconsciously experiencing.

Today, experience relief and revitalize your eyes by placing a nice cool compress on them for 10 to 30 minutes. Before you begin, choose and prepare the medium you will use, lay down comfortably in a darkened room, place a cooling agent on your eyes, and relax completely. You can choose to turn on some relaxing music, play some nature sounds, or lay in silence. Be present and conscious, enjoy the relief your eyes feel during the process and appreciate how refreshed your eyes feel afterward.

Please take good care of your eyes, as neglect and overstrain could eventually lead to more serious issues, such as cataracts and loss of vision.

Examples

- Soak cotton pads in cucumber juice, unsweetened chilled black coffee, or cool water, squeeze out excess liquid and place over eyes for 15 to 20 minutes. Keep a few tissues in hand to wipe excess liquid running down your face. When you are done rinse your eyes with fresh water.
- Place two organic green tea or chamomile tea bags in hot water for one to two minutes, take out of water, cool, and place bags over eyes for 15 to 20 minutes. Keep a few tissues in hand to wipe excess liquid running down your face. When you are done rinse your eyes with fresh water.
- Wet two cotton balls with chilled rose water or cornflower water, and gently dab your eyelids for 3 to 5 minutes.
- Use a cooling gel eye mask.
- Use some gel eye packs.
- Use some refreshing cucumber eye pads.

Helpful Tips: Here are other ways to help your eyes.

- Wear sunglasses when you are outside.
- Wear computer or gaming glasses.
- Wear photophobia glasses for light sensitivity.
- Wear a hat when spending long periods of time outside.
- Avoid harsh lighting and invest in better lighting such as incandescent bulbs or energy-saving warm white compact fluorescent lights (CFLs).
- Eat a diet rich in fruits and vegetables.
- Look away from your computer or television every 15-20 minutes and close your eyes for a few seconds.
- Follow the 20-20-20 rule: Look up from your work every 20 minutes and look at an object 20 feet away for 20 seconds.
- Do some eye-yoga exercises.
- Make sure your prescribed glasses and contact lenses are up to date.
- Make sure to care for your contact lenses as prescribed by your doctor.
- Avoid the glare from windows.
- Minimize driving at night.
- Get enough sleep.
- Blink more often.
- Use preservative-free artificial tears eye drops.

Things that made me feel good today:

Things I noticed about myself:

Things I am grateful for:

Thoughts on the daily exercise:

Would you like to add anything else?

Today, I...

> ***"Touch comes before sight, before speech. It is the first language and the last, and it always tells the truth."***
> ***- Margaret Atwood***

EXERCISE 83: *Touch and Feel*

The sense of touch is the first sense to develop as an embryo grows and it is crucial for the healthy development of an infant. As we mature, the sense of touch continues to play an important role in our lives. It contributes to our physical and mental health, helps us navigate the world, facilitates or deepens our connection with others, and allows us to experience life fully.

The sense of touch is not found in a particular location and is experienced throughout the body; it is always active (for most of us), and unlike our other senses, we are incapable of pausing it (e.g. the ability to pinch our nose to cease smelling or close our eyes to interrupt our sight). The process of touching and feeling is complex and amazing – hot, cold, smooth, rough, soft, hard, pleasure, pain, wet, and dry are all tactile experiences that allow you to experience the world and bond with this reality internally (emotional and mental) and externally (physical). Knowing all this, it is mind-blowing to think that it's one of the most underappreciated senses.

Today, celebrate your ability to touch and feel. Be as present as possible throughout your day, and allow your body to awaken to as many sensations as possible. Begin now, feel the contact between your body and the chair you are sitting on, feel the clothes against your skin, the contact of your tongue against the roof of your mouth, and so forth. Explore and tune in to your sense of touch as much as possible and attentively observe how you react physically, mentally, and emotionally to all the different stimuli. Note your observations below.

Examples

- Hug and touch a loved one.
- Pay attention to the texture of the food you are eating.
- Feel the air brush against your skin.
- Be present to water running down your body.
- Feel the keys of your keyboard under your fingertips.
- Run your fingers through your pet's fur and enjoy the texture.
- Be aware of how the current temperature affects your body.
- Give or receive a massage.
- Feel the contact as you hold your child's hand.
- Be present to the sensation of putting lotion on your skin.
- Feel your heartbeat.
- Notice how the ground feels under your feet.

Things that made me feel good today:

Things I noticed about myself:

Things I am grateful for:

Thoughts on the daily exercise:

Would you like to add anything else?

Day 84

Today, I...

> ***"If you can dream it, you can make it so."***
> ***- Belva Davis***

EXERCISE 84: *Desktop Wallpaper Slideshow*

Keeping an ideal or a dream alive when things are going great is much easier than keeping your mind on the right stuff when things are not easy or when things are outright challenging. However, it is undeniable that keeping a clear vision of your intentions and goals is vital if you want to experience constant positive improvements. To do that, you must surround yourself with subliminal messages that continually communicate your desired outcomes to your subconscious mind. In other words, to reprogram your subconscious mind you must feed it new and better-quality information, repeatedly, until it rejects the old patterns and embraces the upgraded programs. One of the best ways to do that is to surround yourself with things and images that trigger within you strong emotions that are aligned with your intended results – it's not enough to place a fruit basket on your kitchen table or look at images of someone meditating if those things do not make you truly feel healthy. You must choose to surround yourself with things that resonate with you at an emotional level. Things that make you feel like you have already achieved your goals, or at least give you the feeling that it's possible for you. Doing this will help keep you focused and committed, by providing a constant stream of inspiration and motivation.

Today, create a "Desktop Wallpaper Slideshow" showcasing your dreams, your desires, and your objectives. You will need a couple of hours to do this activity. Put on some pleasant music, get yourself a snack and something to drink, and make yourself comfortable. Think about your dreams and desires. What images, quotes, or words reflect your intentions? Your goals? Your aspirations?

When you are ready, open a new folder on your computer, name it, and save it. Next, save images from the internet that resonate and align with your objectives into that folder. Remember to incorporate pictures of people, things, places, and quotes that generate positive feelings, thoughts, and emotions. Lastly, create the slideshow.

Use the following instructions if need be:
- Windows: https://www.windowscentral.com/enable-windows10-slideshow-and-battery
- Mac: https://support.apple.com/en-us/HT2478

Watch this slideshow often, taking the time to visualize, and fill yourself with uplifting energy and emotions – watching it first thing in the morning and last thing before retiring at night are great options. I highly recommend including motivational messages and reminders of your greatness, your potential, and your worthiness – you know what you need help with, so make sure you choose accordingly. Moving forward, anytime you find images that positively resonate with you, add them to your folder.

Your slideshow should include images that encourage feelings of self-love and appreciation.

Things that made me feel good today:

Things I noticed about myself:

Things I am grateful for:

Thoughts on the daily exercise:

Would you like to add anything else?

Day 85

Today, I...

> ***"Any time I get to blow bubbles pretty much lights me up."***
> ***- David Helvarg***

EXERCISE 85: Blow Bubbles

Who doesn't love blowing bubbles? Blowing bubbles has to be one of the most fun and uplifting activities that anyone can truly delight in, regardless of age.

It's unbelievable that simply making bubbles with a bit of soapy solution can relieve stress, deepen your bond with loved ones (especially the young ones), improve your sleep, create positive emotions, help you breathe more mindfully and become more present.

Today, have some fun and blow bubbles. You can choose to do this activity alone, with loved ones, or include it in an event you are hosting. Let your inner child come out and play and allow yourself to be silly. Blow small bubbles and big bubbles, run after them, pop them, and have a blast. Be as present as possible and let yourself bubble up with positive emotions.

Remember, blowing bubbles inside can result in a slippery and sticky mess, so make sure to blow them outside. Consider purchasing or finding a recipe for an eco-friendly and non-toxic bubble solution.

Examples

- Get a generic bottle of bubbles.
- Have fun with a bubble-blowing gun.
- Go all out with a bubble machine.
- Make huge bubbles with bubble wands.
- Be creative and use a fly swatter.
- If it's cold outside, make "frozen" bubbles.

Helpful Tips: Here are two ways to take your bubble-blowing experience a step further:

- To relieve stress and anxiety, every time you blow a bubble, imagine you are blowing the negative feelings and energies out, and feel relief and gratitude as you watch your "worry bubbles" blow away and pop.
- Think of something you dream of manifesting and blow your "dream bubbles"

Things that made me feel good today:

Things I noticed about myself:

Things I am grateful for:

Thoughts on the daily exercise:

Would you like to add anything else?

Today, I...

> *"People always say 'Motivation is great but it doesn't last.' I just tell them, bathing does not last either, that is why I recommend it daily."*
>
> *- Zig Ziglar*

EXERCISE 86: Listen to a Motivational Speaker

Certain teachers and mentors preach that we must be self-motivated to accomplish anything in life. Unquestionably, acquiring this skill is important because no one other than you knows exactly what you need, what triggers your mind, and what speaks to your heart and soul. However, regardless of whether you can self-motivate or not, a little outside motivation can assist you in many different ways. Motivational speakers can help you discover what is holding you back, they can stimulate you to go beyond your current challenges and blockages, and they can motivate you to achieve your dreams and goals. They can help you design a roadmap, they can widen your perspective, they can teach you useful techniques, they can boost your morale, and they can invigorate you with uplifting messages and truths. A lot can be gained from learning and listening to such inspiring mentors.

Today, you can either listen to your favorite motivational speaker, listen to someone different (for a fresh perspective), or go on a platform like YouTube to watch a compilation video of various speakers. You can attend an event, watch an online video, or listen to an audio recording. You can choose to listen to motivational messages first thing in the morning, before going to bed at night, or during naptime (to reprogram your subconscious mind). You can also have fun and listen to them while exercising, taking a shower, driving to work, doing chores, doing something more creative, or any time you need a pep talk.

Be attentive and let the message(s) speak to you – hold on to what resonates with you and let go of the rest. Below write a short summary about who you listened to, what impacted you the most, and what you will take away from this experience.

Examples

- Les Brown
- Eric Thomas
- Jim Rohn
- Gary Vaynerchuk
- Lisa Nichols
- Tony Robbins
- Mel Robbins
- Steve Harvey
- Sean Stephenson
- Iyanla Vanzant
- Robin Sharma
- Zig Ziglar
- Alexandra Villarroel Abrego
- Chris Gardner
- Brian Tracy
- Joyce Meyer
- T.D Jakes
- Nick Vujicic
- Joel Osteen
- Bob Proctor

Things that made me feel good today:

Things I noticed about myself:

Things I am grateful for:

Thoughts on the daily exercise:

Would you like to add anything else?

Today, I...

> ***"I love the smell of the universe in the morning."***
> ***- Neil deGrasse Tyson***

EXERCISE 87: Smell the Universe

When was the last time you stopped and smelled the roses? In general, unless someone is detecting a delightful fragrance or a disagreeable odor, they tend to ignore their sense of smell. You may want to use your nose more mindfully when you realize that your olfactory sense influences you more than you probably imagine. Among other things, it affects your sense of taste, triggers certain emotions and memories, and even helps you unknowingly smell out a potential mate or someone's fear. Case in point, without your sense of smell all your food would be flavorless, your sense of taste alone would only allow you to notice if something was sweet, sour, salty, bitter and umami*. Just think of how food tastes when you are eating with a head cold and a stuffy nose.

Different smells have the potential to affect you in various ways – while some fragrances will calm and relax you, uplift and energize you, or put you in a sexy mood, others will turn your stomach, repulse you, and turn you off. Additionally, they can transport you back to your childhood, the arms of a past lover, a bad hangover, your favorite season, or worse, a traumatic experience.

The olfactory sense has such an impact on your body, mind, and spirit that it is worthwhile to surround yourself with pleasant all-natural scents and fragrances, or even explore aromatherapy – an alternative form of healing that uses aromatic essential oils extracted from herbs, plants, and fruits to support physical, psychological, and spiritual well-being.

Today, be mindful and smell the world around you. Smell your morning coffee or tea, your soap, your food, flowers, herbs, spices, essential oils, perfumes or colognes, your environment, etc. Have fun smelling as many things as you can (this can be a wonderful opportunity to invite friends or family members to participate in a "What's that Smell?" guessing game). Observe how your body reacts to certain scents – what feelings, emotions, or recollections surface. At the end of the day, reflect on your experience, and write down your favorite and least favorite smells. From this moment forward, always make sure to nurture your sense of smell by smelling beautiful natural aromas that are healing and make you feel good.

Consult your healthcare provider before using essential oils, especially if you are pregnant, have small children, or are dealing with certain health conditions. Always read guidelines carefully.

Helpful Tips: Try reaping the benefits of the following essential oils by inhaling them with the help of an aromatherapy inhaler, by putting a few drops on a cotton ball, by wearing aromatherapy/aromatic jewelry, or by using an aromatherapy essential oil diffuser:

- Lavender helps with sleep and relaxation.
- Lemon uplifts and helps boost your energy.
- Frankincense helps calm the body and mind.
- Orange helps with self-image and confidence.
- Ylang Ylang helps with anger management and depression.
- Jasmine helps with fear and insecurity.
- Palo Santo helps with feelings of loneliness and restores peacefulness.
- Patchouli helps with fatigue and stress.

In the table below, write down the smells you have enjoyed the most and the least today:

Favorite Smells	**Least Favorite Smells**

**Umami: a taste sensation that is meaty or savory and is produced by several amino acids and nucleotides (such as glutamate and aspartate) (ref. Merriam-Webster)*

Things that made me feel good today:

Things I noticed about myself:

Things I am grateful for:

Thoughts on the daily exercise:

Would you like to add anything else?

Today, I...

> **"Heroes give hope."**
> ***- Amit Kalantri***

EXERCISE 88: Showcase a Hero

In a world where people are bombarded with negative media, it is crucial to gather and share as much positive and inspiring information as possible. Constantly watching, listening, and hearing such negative messages overwhelms people and misleads them into believing that the world is a scary place full of horrible people. In truth, yes, there are some pretty horrible things happening in the world, and yes, there are some disturbed human beings, but on the flip side there are also amazing things going on, and there are beautiful people.

At our primal state, as a self-preservation mechanism, we are programmed to look for all the negatives around us, and that is why "bad news" sells. However, as an evolved conscious being, you can choose what you will feed your mind. Ask yourself this question: "If worldwide there was more evil than good, why would the media need to play the same stories over and over?" Loving yourself means to be conscious and picky about where you put your attention.

Here, I am not asking you to ignore facts, but I am suggesting that you choose to see all the facts – if you take the time to look around, you will notice there is a lot more positivity in the world than there is negativity.

For the most part, people are benevolent, sympathetic, and willing to go above and beyond to help others – just look at what happens during an accident or a crisis. Moreover, according to Giving USA's 2018 report (https://givingusa.org), charitable donations increased, totaling $410.02 billion in 2017 – this number is even more astonishing when you realize that it only reflects donations made to American charities.

Heroes come in all shapes and sizes; they are human beings, like you and me, committed to giving of themselves and doing their very best daily, regardless of hardships and circumstances. Heroes understand their choices make an impact; they believe they can make a difference and create a better tomorrow. Heroes give us hope, courage, and inspire us to be better versions of ourselves.

A hero is someone who will hand a warm blanket to a homeless, donate to a charity, organize a food drive, adopt an abandoned animal, stand up to terrorists for the right to girl education, or smile at you when you need it most.

Today, showcase a hero – a person that you admire and value for the impact they have had on your life or in the world. You can choose to make a social media post thanking them or simply acknowledging them and their contributions. Additionally, if applicable, you can always encourage your followers to donate to their charity or to join their movement (remember to post links people can follow). You could also encourage others to showcase their favorite hero present or past.

Remember, it is important to feature the positive souls making a positive difference – to encourage and support them is to encourage and support a better world for us all.

Whom did you showcase today? How did you do it?

Things that made me feel good today:

Things I noticed about myself:

Things I am grateful for:

Thoughts on the daily exercise:

Would you like to add anything else?

Today, I...

> ***"It's not selfish to love yourself, take care of yourself, and to make your happiness a priority. It's necessary."***
> ***- Mandy Hale***

EXERCISE 89: *Go Ahead and Pamper Yourself*

It's astounding to think that most people prioritize things such as work, school, obligations, schedules, and other people, over caring for themselves. Giving of yourself and of your time is noble, even necessary, but unless you create time to care for your own wellness and well-being, you will inevitably experience fatigue, stress, resentment, and anger.

As we grow up, we are often taught to believe that we should think of ourselves last, that thinking of ourselves first is selfish and conceited; nothing could be further from the truth. You cannot give anything from an empty vessel, and if you do not take time for yourself to recharge and refill, you will begin experiencing physical, mental, emotional, and spiritual imbalances. However busy your schedule might be, however much your children and partner "need" you, however long your to-do list is – before scheduling anything, begin your days scheduling time for yourself. If all you can manage is ten minutes, do that, but if you can pen in one hour or more, do not hesitate. You must stop believing the false ideologies that you have been forced-fed – nothing is more important than you are: not your children, parents, lover, friends, or pet, and, definitely not your work, school, commitments, or obligations. Bar none, you are the most significant person in your world. Yes, you. This does not mean that you cannot love someone deeply or attend to the stuff of life; it just means that by acknowledging that you are the most important person in your reality and by loving yourself and caring for yourself accordingly, you will be able to love others more completely and accomplish tasks more successfully. I understand this might be a difficult concept to accept, but please contemplate this notion, and try to see it from your soul's perspective. Caring for yourself is an act of self-love and it helps you connect with yourself in an intimate and loving way. It lifts your spirit and revitalizes you. It promotes positive self-image and confidence.

Finally, it gives you time and space to enjoy your own company. The more you connect with your whole self (body, mind, and spirit) by doing loving things for yourself, the better apt you will be to care for anyone or anything else. Always remember that a positive state of being facilitates things, while a negative state blocks everything.

Today, go ahead and pamper yourself. Schedule some time to do something that relaxes you, reenergizes you, and makes you feel amazing. Be as conscious as possible and enjoy your own company. Pay attention to how you feel during and after your self-care session, and afterwards, also notice how differently you interact with others or carry out tasks.

Be mindful to take time for yourself every day – you deserve the best.

Examples

- Spend some time in a hot tub or a mud bath.
- Go get a foot massage or a facial.
- Get your hair done.
- Have a pajama day.
- Indulge in a face mask.
- Meditate.
- Light some candles and listen to some music.
- Enjoy some acupuncture or acupressure.
- Take a nice nap.
- Have a spa day.
- Get a room at a nice hotel and get room service.
- Have a Netflix marathon.
- Color in your favorite coloring book.
- Take your time getting ready.
- Dance to some uplifting tunes.
- Write affirmations, or journal.

What did you do to pamper yourself?

Things that made me feel good today:

Things I noticed about myself:

Things I am grateful for:

Thoughts on the daily exercise:

Would you like to add anything else?

Pause. Breathe. Take a moment to realize how far you have come!

It is important to look back to the very first day you began this program and contemplate how much you have learned, how much you have grown, and how much things have changed within yourself and in your life.

In this moment, wherever your self-love gauge is, feel gratitude toward yourself for giving yourself the opportunity to grow this love to the best of your abilities. As you get ready to embark on the next part of this journey, open your heart to miracles and possibilities.

Always remember that you deserve the best.

> ***"Whatever you do, don't do it halfway."***
> ***- Bob Beamon***

Since Day One, you have probably experienced ups and downs. You may have felt excited, hopeful, and motivated at times, while at other times you may have felt fatigued, distressed, or annoyed. At some point, you may have even felt the daily exercises were taking too much of your time. These feelings, thoughts, and emotions will continue to surface, but please, do not give up and instead persevere. This program is long, and a long time is what it will take for you to learn how to authentically love yourself. However long and arduous this journey may seem, this is just the beginning of your walk with self-love. It will all become easier – trust the process.

This program was created to assist you in finding your own compass, until self-love and self-care become natural and automatic responses. I encourage you to continue this journey with me until you are ready to walk it alone. You have nothing to lose and everything to win. Love yourself enough to give yourself the gift of self-love.

Today, I...

> *"Everything you want to be, you already are. You're simply on the path to discovering it."*
> *- Alicia Keys*

EXERCISE 90: Bi-Weekly Report

It is time to pause and reflect on the past two weeks. Complete this exercise when you can have at least one hour of undisturbed time. Make yourself comfortable by creating a soothing ambiance: get a warm drink, put on some music, or light a candle. Take a few deep breaths, relax, and when you are ready, answer the following questions honestly and thoroughly.

1. Summarize the past two weeks in a sentence.

2. Looking back, what are you most proud of?

3. What are some inner blocks and fears you noticed?

4. What important lessons did you learn?

5. What brought you the most joy?

6. What surprised you the most?

7. How are you doing in terms of loving yourself?

8. How has your relationship with yourself evolved?

9. How has your relationship with others evolved?

10. How has your attitude toward life evolved?

11. What tools, practices, or teachers have helped you the most?

13. What were your favorite and least favorite exercises? Explain.

14. What are you most grateful for at the moment?

15. What are things you would like to improve on in the upcoming two weeks?

Would you like to add anything else?

Today, as the daily exercise, either repeat your favorite exercise of the past two weeks or do an activity that feels good to your soul.

What did you do?

Today, I...

> ***"Food is not rational. Food is culture, habit, craving and identity."***
> ***- Jonathan Safran Foer***

EXERCISE 91: Be Thy Food

The history of humanity and food are understandably intertwined, as food is essential to our survival – it sustains us, enables us to grow, and provides us with the energy to thrive and remain alive. Delving deeper into the history of food is captivating as it helps us discover how it has influenced civilizations, cultures, traditions, economies, and politics. As for the actual chemistry of food, most of us are aware that to be healthy, a balanced diet including carbohydrates, proteins, fats, vitamins, and minerals, is necessary – yet, the complexity and depth of the composition of any given foodstuff escapes us.

Still, for those of us lucky enough to eat to our heart's content, the subject of food is usually far from exciting and often results in thoughts such as "I feel like eating this or that," "What should I eat?" or "I don't know what to eat." Furthermore, all too often food choices are not outcomes of conscious healthy dietary selections, but instead, sadly depend on factors such as time, cost, habits, moods, and ease of preparation.

Today, step out of your unhealthy and/or unconscious relationship with food, and be thy food. Ask yourself: "If I were a prepared food, what type of food would I be?" Would you be a salad? A dessert? A sandwich? A soup? Think about color, flavor, texture, simplicity or complexity, raw or cooked, and any other details that can help inspire your choice. Have fun coming up with a dish that personifies you; when you've made your decision, choose to prepare it or buy it, and finally, if at all possible, share it with others. You can even decide to take it a step further and organize a meal where each member of your family elects to be a certain course and a certain dish – as you all enjoy the meal together, ask everyone to explain why they chose that specific course and/or foodstuff. Another option is to invite a few friends over for a potluck asking them to bring a dish that personifies either themselves or the host (you). It will be amusing to see what people come up with – only do this if you have a good sense of humor, this is meant to be an enjoyable and goofy activity, not a reason for feelings to be hurt. Have your guests take turns explaining why they chose their dish. Whichever way you choose to explore this exercise, remember to be creative, have fun, play, be silly, laugh, and allow your inner child to have a great time.

What food did you choose and why?

Things that made me feel good today:

Things I noticed about myself:

Things I am grateful for:

Thoughts on the daily exercise:

Would you like to add anything else?

Day 92

Today, I...

> ***"It's a great day for a ball game; let's play two!"***
> ***- Ernie Banks***

EXERCISE 92: Play with a Ball

A ball – such a simple concept, but such an amazing object. Regardless of gender or culture, most children around the world have played with a ball at some point or another. It is fascinating to realize that this ancient invention still holds our attention today and continues to have an important place in most societies – some of the most popular sports watched and played worldwide, such as soccer, basketball, or baseball all include the use of a ball.

Beyond the childlike fun, the numerous health benefits, and the bonding opportunities that can result from participating in ball games or sports, there are also other interesting advantages that are worth mentioning: improved balance and coordination, increased sharpness of the mind, development of focus and concentration, cultivation of patience, and enhancement of predictability skills.

Today, have a good time and play with a ball. You can choose to take part in any game or sport involving the use of a ball. Do something that you love or try something different and exciting. You can choose to play alone or invite friends, colleagues, or family members to join in on the fun. Enjoy yourself and allow your inner child to come out and play.

Examples

- Enjoy a few games of foosball.
- Partake in a game of beach ball relay.
- Join a bowling tournament.
- Have fun playing bubble soccer.
- Learn how to dribble a basketball.
- Dive into a game of water polo.
- Play a double match of tennis.
- Try your hand at juggling.
- Go shoot some pool.
- Challenge yourself with a paddle ball.
- Hit the green and play some golf.
- Toss any kind of ball back and forth.

What did you play?

Things that made me feel good today:

Things I noticed about myself:

Things I am grateful for:

Thoughts on the daily exercise:

Would you like to add anything else?

Day 93

Today, I...

> ***"Habits are where our lives and careers and bodies are made."***
> ***- Seth Godin***

EXERCISE 93: Notice Your Habits

A habit is the result of a choice that has been made repetitively. Your habitual patterns, what you continually think about, and how you repeatedly behave are predominantly responsible for the personality you have become and the life you are experiencing today.

All your habits are born following this three-step process: a trigger, a habitual thought or action, and a reward. In other words, it's the unconscious anticipation and craving of a certain reward that perpetuates all your positive and negative habits. For instance, the difference between someone who procrastinates and someone who is proactive can be that one has associated laziness with comfort and relaxation, while the other has associated action with peace of mind and a feeling of accomplishment.

To live life on your terms, you must observe your mental and behavioral habits, and understand what keeps them alive, especially if your current habits are not giving you the results that you desire. Once you become conscious of your patterns and the "why" behind each one of them, you will then be more capable of changing the habits that sabotage you.

Today, notice your habits, their triggers, and the apparent rewards you reap from them. Take notes throughout the day on your phone or a notepad. At the end of the day, for each mental or behavioral habit you have discovered, ask yourself the following question: "Is this habit serving me or hurting me?" For every negative habit that you find, think about a habit that is better aligned with your dreams and desires. Once you have identified your new objectives and the new habits you want to adopt, think of the actions you need to take. Create new triggers and come up with alluring rewards that are in line with your goals and intentions. Make sure your rewards are truly enticing, as they will help focus your attention and produce the positive emotions you need to succeed. Complete the table on the following page. This activity will probably take more than one day to complete, but begin today and make sure to finish it during the week.

Remember, rewiring your brain takes time, and while some of your habits will only take about a month to change, others can take up to six months or more. Commit, persevere, be consistent, and most of all be patient with yourself.

Helpful Tips:

- Do not try to change more than one or two habits at a time. Attempting too many changes at once may result in failure.
- If you are not sure about what new routines to adopt, investigate the habits of successful people or people you admire who have achieved the objectives you aspire to accomplish.
- Always choose habits that intuitively feel good and positively resonate with you.
- Always choose rewards that are more appealing than the previous.
- Visualize yourself embodying your new habits, especially when you notice old patterns creeping in.
- Create a daily log and keep track of your progress.
- Eliminate as many negative triggers as possible from your surroundings (ex: throw away the junk food if you want to lose weight, or throw away your ex's photos if you want to begin dating again).
- Create and repeat positive affirmations relating to your goals and intentions.
- Keep yourself motivated and inspired by reading and listening to positive messages.
- Take better decisions by remaining as conscious and present as possible.

Examples

Current Habits	Current Triggers	Current (Perceived) Rewards	New Objective	Required Action	New Habits	New Triggers	New Rewards
Watching too much TV.	Boredom, silence, eating, insomnia.	Excitement, entertainment, escape from real life.	Be more active.	Cancel cable subscription, move TV, or just unplug.	Go for daily walks	Have tennis shoes, bottle of water and hat ready next to front door. Go right after dinner.	A nice evevning bath.
Endless hours on social media.	Apps on my phone.	Sense of belonging, entertainment, connecting with others.	Learn a new language: Spanish.	Move social media apps into a folder in phone's secondary screen.	Practice Spanish 30 minutes every day.	Download a language app such as Duolingo and place it on home screen.	Being able to talk with the locals during my vacation in Spain. Feeling victorious.

Current Habits	Current Triggers	Current (Perceived) Rewards	New Objective	Required Action	New Habits	New Triggers	New Rewards

Current Habits	Current Triggers	Current (Perceived) Rewards	New Objective	Required Action	New Habits	New Triggers	New Rewards

Things that made me feel good today:

Things I noticed about myself:

Things I am grateful for:

Thoughts on the daily exercise:

Would you like to add anything else?

Day 94

Today, I...

> ***"If I don't laugh at least 20 times a day - it hasn't been a good day."***
> ***- Jordin Sparks***

EXERCISE 94: Find the Funnies

Take a moment and contemplate how often you laugh in a typical day. If you are like the average human being, chances are you spend little time on feeling joyful and lighthearted, and a lot more time feeling bored, stressed, frustrated, angry, and worried.

Focusing on negativity and continually looking for reasons to be upset will never make you feel good, and it will prevent you from experiencing a healthy level of happiness. On the other hand, looking at the bright side of things and enjoying good hearty laughs feels amazing and offers some outstanding benefits. It will lower your stress levels, help you cope with difficult situations, relieve depression and anxiety, reduce aggressiveness, help oxygenate your body, exercise different muscle groups, and even make you more attractive. So, out with the gloomy and in with the happy – it's time to experience some joie de vivre!

Today, make the effort to step out of your humdrum, adopt a carefree (not careless) attitude, and find the funnies. Wherever you go, whatever you do, look for the humor in everything, including your own goofy ways. Actively look for reasons to have fun and laugh as much as you can. At the end of the day, record the five things that made you laugh the most.

Remember, be kind enough not to laugh at the expense of others and sweet enough to share a good laugh with family and friends.

Examples

- Observe the funny things your pets or wild critters do.
- Look for funny billboards or signs.
- Laugh at the silly things you do or the funny things that happen to you.
- Listen for funny slips of the tongue.
- Read funny quotes or jokes.
- Watch funny videos or a comedy.
- Delight in the humor of a child.
- Giggle at some hilarious memes.
- Watch the Instagram or Snapchat Stories of some favorite comedians.
- Practice laughter yoga.

Top 5 Funnies

Things that made me feel good today:

Things I noticed about myself:

Things I am grateful for:

Thoughts on the daily exercise:

Would you like to add anything else?

Day 95

Today, I...

> *"Several times a day, stop and just listen. Open your hearing 360 degrees, as if your ears were giant radar dishes. Listen to the obvious sounds, and the subtle sounds - in your body, in the room, in the building, and outside. Listen as if you had just landed from a foreign planet and didn't know what was making these sounds. See if you can hear all sounds as music being played just for you. Even in what is called silence there is sound. To hear such subtle sound, the mind must be very quiet."*
>
> **- Jan Chozen Bays**

EXERCISE 95: Stop and Listen

Sounds are all around us, from the humming of cars in the streets to the clicking of a computer's keyboard; from the inhale and exhale of your breath to the snoring of your dog – even silence is not silent. We don't necessarily hear every sound thanks to adaptation; the brain does an amazing job of tuning out any background noises that have a persistent and repetitive sound pattern. Left to its own devices, the brain only brings our attention to sounds it deems of the utmost importance for our well-being or survival. For example, on a busy street you may tune out the sounds of traffic but hear everything your friend is saying. While driving you probably block out the sound of your car's engine unless something starts rattling. Finally, chances are, you will not hear the conversation of a group of people standing at a distance from you unless you hear someone mention your name.

The gift of hearing is beneficial for our health and well-being, it is also a wonderful ability that allows us to enjoy the most beautiful sounds: the cooing of a baby, the splashing of the ocean's waves, the crackling of a warm fire, notes played on a favorite instrument, etc. That said, there are also those dreaded sounds that will make you climb up the walls, such as a loud siren, a piercing scream, or nails on a chalkboard. It's interesting to note that different sounds have profound effects on us; some will soothe, comfort, and inspire, while others will disrupt a person's concentration, increase their blood pressure, and even cause stress and trauma.

Today, stop and listen to the sounds around you, deeply and mindfully. Pay close attention to all the different sounds without judgments and labels. Be present to the way they make you feel. At the end of the day, think about the sounds you enjoyed, the sounds you usually would not have noticed, and the sounds that irritated you. Complete the graphics below.

If you live with a serious hearing impairment and are not able to complete this activity take time to feel and enjoy the vibration of objects and the environment around you (e.g. the vibration transmission from a road's surface, using an electric toothbrush, drumming on a hollow surface or a drum, holding up a balloon in a noisy area or concert, rattling some maracas, using a power tool, etc.). At the end of the day report your favorite and your least favorite vibrations in the graphics below.

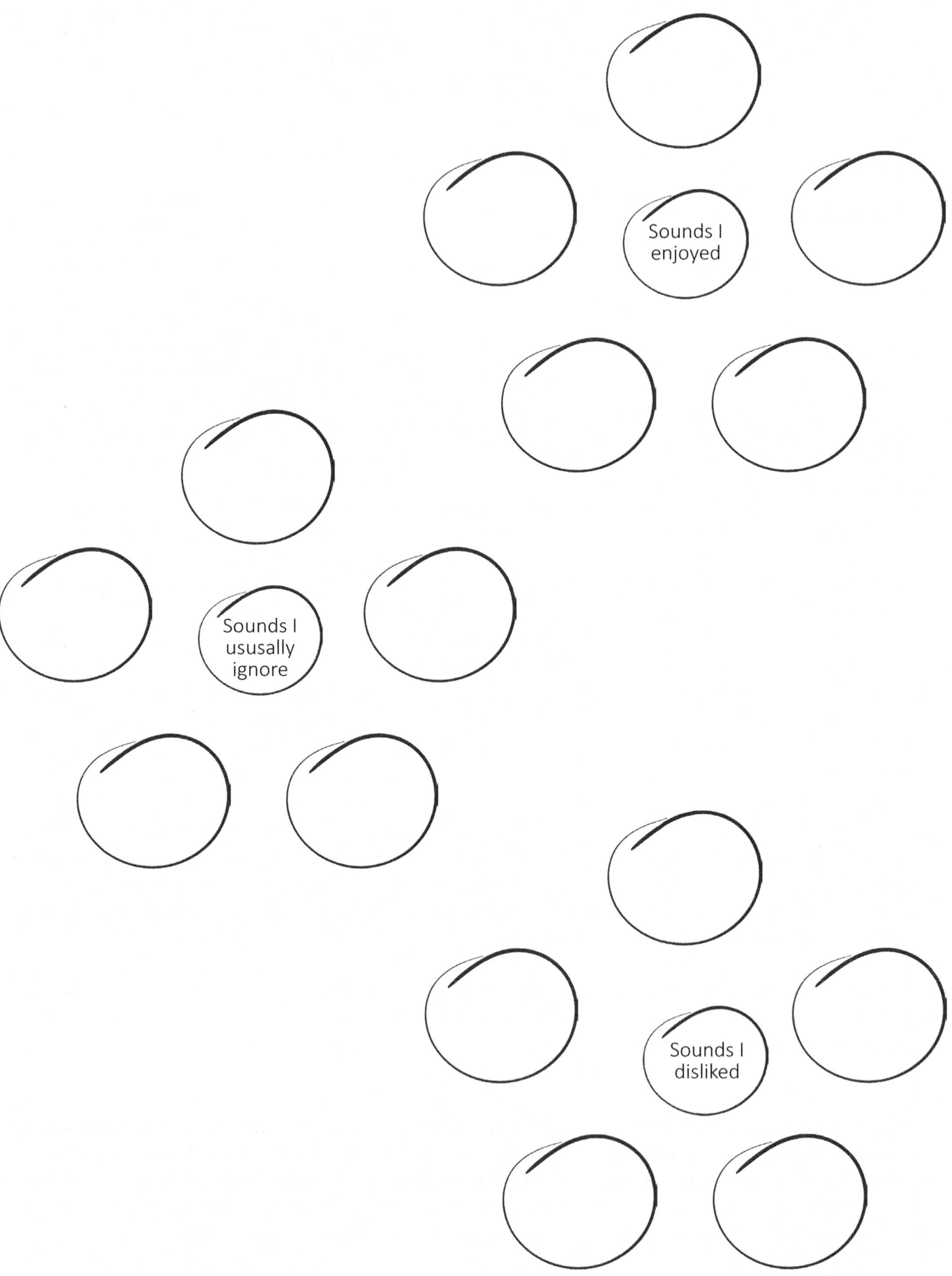
Sounds I enjoyed
Sounds I ususally ignore
Sounds I disliked

Things that made me feel good today:

Things I noticed about myself:

Things I am grateful for:

Thoughts on the daily exercise:

Would you like to add anything else?

Today, I...

> *"Your best champion and cheerleader is yourself. Always be proud of your accomplishments, big or small."*
> *- Ayanna Howard*

EXERCISE 96: All Accomplishments Matter

Regardless of someone's level of self-confidence, their personal circumstances, and where they stand in relation to their aspirations and objectives, it is common for people to glorify others' accomplishments and devalue their own. Of course, it is important to praise and support people who are doing well, but it is just as important (if not more) to recognize your own accomplishments, however big or small they may seem to you. For some of you, getting out of bed today was a great victory, while for others eating carrots instead of chips is a personal triumph, and still for others signing a great business deal will be the peak of your day.

Being human, in and of itself, is such a feat! There are so many things that you accomplish daily without realizing it. Loving yourself is all about celebrating and appreciating your own efforts, not minimizing them or being self-critical about what you haven't done (yet). The more you pay attention and acknowledge all the things that you do, the more you will value yourself, the more self-worth you will develop, the more confident you will become, and the more you will want to take on new things.

Today, remember that all your accomplishments matter; nothing is too small or too big. Write down the list of everything you achieve during the day no matter how silly or insignificant you think it may be. At the end of your day, look back at your list, and take the time to feel a real sense of satisfaction and gratitude for everything you have done today.

I highly recommend adopting this practice as part of your daily routine; you can choose to note everything in a planner, a calendar, or your phone. As an alternative, you can even record each personal achievement on a voice recorder or your phone throughout the day and listen to your recording in the evening. Doing this will considerably improve your self-worth and confidence, and it will be a great motivator to accomplish greater objectives.

Examples

- Brushing your teeth.
- Doing the daily exercise.
- Typing an email.
- Showering.
- Opening the door for someone.
- Making the bed.
- Listening to someone without interrupting.
- Brushing your hair.
- Playing with your pet.
- Emptying the dishwasher.
- Reminding someone of something.
- Making coffee or tea.
- Submitting a term paper on time.
- Helping the kids with homework.
- Driving to work.
- Working on a new project.
- Jogging 30 minutes on the treadmill.
- Buying a sandwich for a homeless person.
- Going to your therapist.
- Being on time.

My Accomplishments

Things that made me feel good today:

Things I noticed about myself:

Things I am grateful for:

Thoughts on the daily exercise:

Would you like to add anything else?

Today, I...

> *"You cannot get through a single day without having an impact on the world around you. What you do makes a difference and you have to decide what kind of a difference you want to make."*
> **- Jane Goodall**

EXERCISE 97: Think Green

It used to be that whenever individuals would mention "going green" or being "environmentally friendly," they would immediately be stereotyped as a hippie. Nowadays, most people have evolved and understand that caring for Mother Earth is of the utmost importance if we want all species to thrive, and if we care about handing over a healthy planet to future generations – our children, our grandchildren, their children and so forth.

Being environmentally friendly is a lifestyle choice centered on mindfulness and conscious living. Many choose to ignore the green trend because it can be inconvenient and a bit overwhelming. However, this is an issue that concerns all of us, and for things to improve, we each must take some measure of responsibility for the state of our home. We must cultivate compassion and gratitude for the Earth, and lovingly care for our environment – doing this helps the planet, our brothers and sisters around the globe, future generations, and ourselves.

Today, think green and do a benevolent act for Gaia (ancient Greek name meaning Earth). Be conscious and take time to evaluate your impact on the planet. When you are finished, think of all the different ways you can be more environmentally friendly.

Remember, this is an issue that will not disappear; if ignored, it will only worsen. We are all called to play our part – may your footprints leave a positive, meaningful, and inspiring legacy.

Examples

- Become a vegan.
- Stop using disposable plastic.
- Recycle your old cell phones.
- Walk or bike to work.
- Plant a tree.
- Reduce your amount of waste.
- Carpool with coworkers.
- Support green businesses.
- Invest in solar panels.
- Take shorter showers.
- Watch a documentary with friends on the subject.
- Reuse your cardboard boxes.
- Turn off the lights when you get out of a room.
- Eat organic foods.
- Donate to an eco-friendly charity.
- Use reusable shopping bags.

Helpful Tips: Educate yourself by watching documentaries that delve into topics regarding our environment, and get inspired by watching documentaries that show you the beauty of our planet and its inhabitants:

- Tomorrow (https://www.tomorrow-documentary.com)
- COWSPIRACY: the sustainability secret (http://www.cowspiracy.com)
- Before the Flood (https://www.beforetheflood.com)
- Time to Choose (http://www.timetochoose.com)
- Bag It (http://www.bagitmovie.com)
- BBC's Planet Earth, Planet Earth II, Life Story, The Blue Planet, etc. (https://www.bbcearth.com)

**Most of these documentaries are available on Netflix, Amazon, YouTube, or Vudu.*

What green action(s) did you take today?

Things that made me feel good today:

Things I noticed about myself:

Things I am grateful for:

Thoughts on the daily exercise:

Would you like to add anything else?

Today, I...

> *"Don't take your health for granted. Don't take your body for granted. Do something today that communicates to your body that you desire to care for it. Tomorrow is not promised."*
> ***- Jada Pinkett Smith***

EXERCISE 98: *Look After That Body*

Once upon a time, you came into this world with a body – your very own body and all its unique attributes. At some point, you decided to categorize what you liked and did not like about that body. When did it happen and who was to blame? Was it your parents' expressions and words? The collective (mixed) messages and intimidating looks? Did the culture you grew up in demand certain traits and expect certain shapes? Or, was an accident or a disease responsible?

In reality, it isn't what your body looks like that is to blame; it's the way you perceive your body in contrast to the world around you, and the way you feel the world perceives you, which shape your opinions. Your missing limb, your weight, your skin type, the texture of your hair, your birthmark, your pigmentation, your wrinkles, your ears, and all the things that you choose to love or loathe about yourself have nothing to do with your body but everything to do with the way you choose to see your body. The way you see yourself affects your entire being (mind, body, and spirit) and it determines the way you care for yourself, the way you value yourself, and the way you present yourself to the world. It is important to realize and recognize that there is no such thing as an ugly body – including yours. All bodies are beautiful. To love yourself, to awaken to your unique beauty, and to walk the world with authentic confidence, you must first put some distance between you and all the ideas you have about your body. Stop taking this amazing organism so personally and begin seeing it as it truly is – astonishing, extraordinary, fascinating, intelligent, resilient, strong, and unique – a phenomenal creation.

Now, for a bit of fun, imagine that a loved one could ask you to watch over their body for an entire day. How would you care for it?

Today, look after your body the same way you would if it were the body of someone dear to you. Care for it, dress it, feed it, hydrate it, exercise it, and nurture it with great love and care. Be as conscious as possible throughout the day; listen to your body's needs and desires and do your best to see your body without judgments and labels. This exercise may feel uncomfortable and a bit foolish, but please, do it anyway. This process will begin to open your eyes to your body's magnificence. Make sure to record your impressions at the end of the day.

Did you do anything differently? Were you more attentive or nicer toward your body? How do you feel about your body now?

Things that made me feel good today:

Things I noticed about myself:

Things I am grateful for:

Thoughts on the daily exercise:

Would you like to add anything else?

Day 99

Today, I...

> *"When you recover or discover something that nourishes your soul and brings joy, care enough about yourself to make room for it in your life."*
> ***- Jean Shinoda Bolen***

EXERCISE 99: Connect with Your Inner Wisdom

Every day, a significant amount of time is spent on activities that deplete your energy and stifle your soul. This leads to mental obstructions, such as negative and obsessive thinking, or emotional blocks, such as anguish, anger, and stress. Altogether these circumstances prevent you from hearing the guidance of your ultimate self – an intelligence uncorrupted by ego that is innate to you alone. Going through life without the assistance of this inner wisdom can lead to unnecessary challenges and crises which themselves provoke emotional and physical issues, such as stress, depression, anxiety, high blood pressure, migraines, ulcers, etc.

Being able to connect with this guidance is essential because your higher self knows the road toward your best life, can help you through challenges, and has the answers to your questions. The first step toward developing this connection is to be open to receiving the information. From there, there are several ways to facilitate the "line of communication" between your personality and your soul: deep relaxation, meditation or a meditative practice (e.g. jogging, coloring, listening to instrumental music, etc.), and taking part in pleasurable and exhilarating activities.

Today, connect with your inner wisdom. When you wake up, take a moment to think about three to five things you can do that will relax you, help you get in a meditative state, or make you blissful and cheerful. Deliberately choose to complete those things during the day, even if it means reorganizing your agenda. Enjoy yourself, be present, and be open to receive guidance without feeling needy – needing things to be a certain way, being impatient, or giving in to (the energy of) desperation will close the connection. Feel free to ask a question or seek assistance from your higher self and see if any information comes through. Conversely, at this stage, I would suggest keeping things light; simply be attentive to your intuition, while delighting in activities that enable the connection between your earthly self and your higher self. At the end of the day, journal any insights you have gathered. Depending on the amount of negative emotions you are dealing with presently, you may or may not be able to connect right away. Do not lose hope; be gentle with yourself, and continue to enjoy daily routines that support that spiritual connection. We should all strive to listen and follow our intuition daily, as it is a sure way to step into our dreams and the life we all deserve.

Remember, the voice of your mind tries to reason while your intuition offers information without explanation. Your inner wisdom will never compulsively repeat anything, be forceful, or analytical.

Helpful Tips: Here are a few activities that can help you connect with your intuition:

- Take time for some yoga or tai chi.
- Try your hand at handmade pottery or glass blowing.
- Practice breathing or candle gazing meditation.
- Do some cooking or vacuum the floors.
- Delight in a massage or spa treatment.
- Enjoy a good swim or nature walk.
- Watch clouds during the day or the stars at night.
- Draw some doodles or do some finger painting.
- Be still in the shower or relax in a bath.
- Go rowing or cycling.
- Do some gardening or just watch nature's critters.
- Go find some seashells or special pebbles.
- Watch the sunrise or the sunset.
- Do some automatic writing or journaling as soon as you wake up.

Things that made me feel good today:

Things I noticed about myself:

Things I am grateful for:

Thoughts on the daily exercise:

Would you like to add anything else?

Day 100

Today, I...

> ***"Either you run the day or the day runs you."***
> ***- Jim Rohn***

EXERCISE 100: Organize Your Time

For centuries, time has been a debated subject among great philosophers, and still is today. Despite our opinions on the matter, we can all agree that time is the most important currency that humanity is given.

Nowadays only a minority of individuals continue to live, as did our ancestors, a life free from the constraints of time choosing instead to follow their inner impulses and serendipity; while most of us have had to adapt to a world regimented by clocks, calendars, and timetables. Consequently, most humans today answer to a 24-hours-a-day schedule. Although it may seem like a reasonable amount of time, most people report having trouble managing their time – they are either overwhelmed by their long to-do lists, unable to accomplish all their daily tasks, or struggle to find enough time to balance what they must do versus what they want to do. On the other hand, for some individuals, time seems interminable, and they have no idea what to do with the time they have. It goes without saying that in either case, managing your time is quite necessary, as neglecting to do so can result in high levels of frustration, stress, and distress.

Today, organize you time in a way that will benefit you. This exercise will span an entire week, since attempting a shorter time period would not give you scalable results, or a means to truly estimate whether this strategy works for you. You will initially need about one hour to complete this activity and 10 to 15 minutes for every other day.

Brainstorm and write down a list of everything you have to do and want to do in the next seven days in the correct areas on the next pages. To have complete balance and harmony, no area should be neglected.

In the event that you have little to do during the day and find that time goes by slowly, make the effort to step out of your comfort zone, and try to find new activities that can entertain you, help you connect to others, or even make a difference.

Spiritual (e.g. pray, meditate, contemplate, journal, go on a silent retreat, burn sage, etc.):

Self-Love/Self-Care (e.g. create a self-love altar or space, dry brush, dress nice, see a therapist, etc.):

Personal Development (e.g. read, take an online course, hire a mentor, improve skill, etc.):

Health/Sports (e.g. drink 48 oz. H2O, exercise, stretch daily, eat more veggies, run a marathon, etc.):

Work/School & Related Activities (e.g. finish project, call client, hire new staff, attend meeting, etc.):

Household & Related activities (e.g. mow the lawn, do the laundry, prep meals, pay bills, etc.):

Fun/Hobbies (e.g. bingo night, make doll clothes, play the cello, tend edible garden, Aikido class, etc.):

Family time (e.g. board game night, play with kids, call grandma, send gift to nephew, etc.):

Significant other (e.g. date night, quality time, text sweet words, slide a kind post-it note in lunch, etc.):

Social (e.g. friends night out, meet a new person, go kayaking with coworkers, sing in a choir, etc.):

Contribution (e.g. donate blood, sponsor a child, sign a petition at https://www.change.org/, etc.):

Miscellaneous:

Now, think of seven ways you could reward yourself if you accomplished your daily goals and jot them down below. Then, think of a reward you would love to give yourself if you accomplished all your weekly goals and write it down. Make sure to choose rewards that really satisfy you. Please, do not skip this step – it is an important part of the process.

Examples

- Buy yourself something nice.
- Spend some time alone.
- Watch a movie.
- Indulge in a sweet.
- Order in.
- Take a nap.
- Go somewhere special.
- Play a game.
- Read a book.
- Take a day off.
- Go to the beach.
- Attend a play.
- Go to an art gallery.
- Go for a swim.
- Hang out with friends.

From there, prioritize your list by writing down your three main goals for each day; make sure to arrange goals in a balanced way. Then, add two "bonus" goals per day – choose two additional objectives that are not requirements but that you would enjoy accomplishing. Finally, assign a reward for each day and the master reward at the end.

Days	Main Goal #1	Main Goal #2	Main Goal #3	Bonus #1	Bonus #2	Reward
Day 1: ________						
Day 2: ________						
Day 3: ________						
Day 4: ________						
Day 5: ________						
Day 6: ________						
Day 7: ________						
Master Reward:						

Once you are done, make sure to assign each goal to a block of time in your planner, journal, or calendar. If at all possible, for that block of time, avoid distractions and stay focused on the task at hand. Do your best to accomplish all your goals, and make sure to reward yourself for every successful day. At the end of the week, if you have effectively achieved all your goals, treat yourself to your master reward.

Remember, if this approach does not work for you, do not be discouraged. Simply research and test other techniques until you find one that works better for you.

Things that made me feel good today:

Things I noticed about myself:

Things I am grateful for:

Thoughts on the daily exercise:

Would you like to add anything else?

Today, I...

> ***"Everyone eats and drinks, but few appreciate taste."***
> ***- Confucius***

EXERCISE 101: Taste and Appreciate

Answer this, when was the last time you took time to savor anything? If you are like most, you are too busy talking to someone, watching television, fixated on your phone, or just occupied with another activity to really notice the flavors of the foods and drinks that you are consuming.

When most individuals think about the way something tastes, they usually think in terms of something tasting "good" or "bad." That said, really tasting and savoring something is a lot more involved. The gustatory sense is complex and goes far beyond your taste buds registering sweetness, saltiness, bitterness, sourness, and umami. It influences what foods we are attracted to, it affects our appetite, and combined with our sense of smell, it gives us the possibility to experience a multitude of flavors.

Nature offers a cornucopia of delicious fruits, vegetables, nuts, and grains. Throughout time, different societies have found remarkable methods to fuse these foods with herbs and spices in flavorful and unique ways; opening doors to new delicious culinary creations.

Neglecting or ignoring your sense of taste robs you from experiencing these delightful adventures.

Today, stop multitasking, and instead take a moment to taste and appreciate the foods and beverages you consume. During the day, each time you are about to eat or drink something, try to do it alone and in silence without any distractions. Take a bite or a sip at a time, go slowly, and savor all the flavors. Be conscious of the tastes, the smells, and observe the way you respond physically. Discern how different tastes and flavors make you feel. This activity may be a bit challenging at first but be patient and persevere. To make things easier, eat before you are famished and drink before you're parched. It is also a good idea to play around with different tastes. At the end of the day, note your observations in the table below.

Here is a cool little factoid for those of you trying to eat smaller portions – taking the time to mindfully taste the flavors of the foods you eat will automatically cut down on the quantity of food you consume.

Helpful Tips: Here are a few ideas to help you explore your sense of taste:

- Try to savor foods with the five basic tastes: sweet, salty, sour, bitter, and umami.
- Be adventurous and taste new foods and drinks.
- Have a fun evening with your family and organize a blind taste test. For example, you could buy several brands of orange juice, salsa, potato chips, or hummus. Place a sample of each brand in small paper cups and assign a number to each cup. Place the containers with the name brands in plain sight and place your samples in front of each participant. Ask everyone to guess the correct brand. The winner will be the person with the most correct answers.
- Invite a few close friends over and have everyone play a "Guess What It Is" taste testing game. Place five to ten samples of different things, such as juices, jellies, dips, spreads, nut butters, or condiments in small paper sample cups, and assign numbers to each cup. Blindfold your guests, have each one taste the sample, take cups away and have each participant write down their guesses on a piece of paper. The participant with the most correct answers wins the game.

Remember, always take everyone's food allergies, sensitivities, and ethical choices in consideration.

Favorite Tastes	**Least Favorite Tastes**

Things that made me feel good today:

Things I noticed about myself:

Things I am grateful for:

Thoughts on the daily exercise:

Would you like to add anything else?

Day 102

Today, I...

> ***"Treat people the way you want to be treated. Talk to people the way you want to be talked to."***
> ***- Hussein Nishah***

EXERCISE 102: Speak Kindly

Communication plays an essential role in all aspects of life. The manner in which we express ourselves and communicate with others – including our exchanges over the phone, email, text, and social networking websites – matters and can be the catalyst of either great opportunities or terrible setbacks. It's also important to realize that the way in which we choose to communicate affects our own well-being and can leave us feeling emotionally satisfied or miserable. Therefore, honestly observing and assessing how you communicate with different people, such as relatives, friends, coworkers, or even strangers, is significant. (Ironically, you will notice that those closest to you are frequently the ones with whom you make the least amount of efforts in terms of communication. However, the guilt, the stress, and the frustration that follow these unpleasant interactions affects you the most.)

Communicating in a mindful way and continually improving on the way you interact with others, whether they are close to you or not, is vital for healthy relationships, your personal growth, and your well-being. An easy but powerful way to improve the way you interact with others is to be kind.

Being kind here means to take into consideration both your feelings and the feelings of the person you are communicating with; to strive for both parties to get the most out of the interaction, even if occasionally it means saying "no" or simply walking away.

Today, be mindful and speak kindly whenever possible. Throughout the day, take time to pause before your interactions, whether written, in person, or through a device. Think of ways you can make the most of the experience for all parties. Be attentive, be present, and do your best not to subconsciously or mechanically express yourself (i.e. mindless or reactive chatter).

Remember, being kind never means that you should allow others to bully or abuse you. Before being kind to anyone, you must first be kind toward yourself. Sometimes that means saying "no" to things you do not want to do; sometimes it means clearly expressing the way you feel; sometimes it means hanging up the phone or walking away, and sometimes it means freeing yourself from the toxic people who are in your life.

Helpful Tips: Here are some suggestions to facilitate kinder exchanges:

- Do not ignore people that speak to you in a friendly way. Do not ignore your loved ones' phone calls. Do not ignore emails from people expecting answers. Do not ignore text messages.
- Smile and say hello to people.
- Try not to use negative words or statements when you speak to people, as it predisposes them to undesirable feelings and reactions. For instance, instead of saying "I can't talk to you right now!" maybe say, "I would love to speak with you, but I am in the middle of something at the moment. I'll make sure to call you as soon as I'm finished."
- The kindest thing you can do when someone is speaking to you is to attentively listen without interrupting them.
- Pay attention to the tone of your voice (children included). You never need to raise your voice unless you are involved in a crisis, such as needing help or trying to save someone.
- Look at people when they speak to you (i.e. not your phone, not other people walking by, not the television, etc.).
- Say "Please," "Thank You," "You're Welcome," and "Bless you." (Use "thank you" and not "thanks," as "thank you" speaks directly to the person).
- Watch your body language and your facial expressions, as sometimes they communicate a lot louder than your words.
- Be generous with your compliments. A compliment has the capacity to change someone's life.
- Put yourself in other people's shoes and treat them with all the care, kindness, and respect you would like to be treated with yourself, regardless of age, gender, status, job position, nationality, etc.

Things that made me feel good today:

Things I noticed about myself:

Things I am grateful for:

Thoughts on the daily exercise:

Would you like to add anything else?

Day 103

Today, I...

> ***"Intuitive eating is about having a healthy relationship with food and your body. It's about enjoying food and honoring your body's signals of hunger and fullness. Intuitive eating means letting go of all the guilt that surrounds food."***
> ***- Michelle P. Gallant***

EXERCISE 103: Eat Intuitively

If you do a quick search on intuitive eating, you will find a lot of information about weight loss and dieting. Here, intuitive eating is approached from a more holistic perspective – a process that will essentially help you reconnect with your body in a more loving way, while simultaneously developing a more harmonious relationship with food.

Unfortunately, many have given up their right to choose what is best for their bodies. They willingly and mindlessly implement dogmas that decree what and when they should eat. They allow fads and diets to dictate what (or how much) they should or should not consume. Meanwhile there's always a new study professing the benefits of certain foods or disproving other studies – this week nutmeg may be the new miraculous thing to include in all meals; next week it may be bashed by some study and replaced with cinnamon.

Intuitive eating is based on a simple principle: your body knows what it needs, how much it needs, and when it needs it – trust its wisdom.

Today, do not look at the clock, do not stick to your usual diet, and allow yourself to eat intuitively – it goes without saying that you should not indulge in any foods to which you are allergic or sensitive. Throughout the day, tune in to your body and feed it what it wants when it wants. This means that if you wake up and your body craves baked Japanese sweet potatoes with hot sauce or a warm bowl of cinnamon baked apples with a big scoop of banana nice cream, go right ahead and enjoy guilt-free. On the other hand, if you do not feel hunger pangs until late morning then do not eat anything (unless you suffer from a disorder, condition, or illness that requires you to eat three to six meals a day). Let go of all the self-judgments or "rules," and have fun with this activity. Allow your body to be in charge for once, not your mind, not your emotions, not other people, and not technology. Be as conscious as possible of your body's needs and wants during the entire day, and keep yourself from activities or circumstances that trigger mindless or compulsive eating.

If you would like to continue eating intuitively, I suggest that you first begin by gradually lowering your consumption of processed foods as they confuse your body and trick your mind. Increase your consumption of fruits, veggies, and other whole foods (e.g. nuts, seeds, grains, legumes, beans, etc.) that are minimally processed or non-chemically processed. By doing this, your body will slowly relearn to self-regulate, and it will only consume the specific foods and the quantity it absolutely needs in order to heal itself and perform at its fullest potential.

Please understand that individuals dealing with an eating disorder, an illness, or a medical condition may not be good candidates for intuitive eating. If you are facing such a challenge, the most loving thing you can do for yourself is to either contact your healthcare provider or an experienced professional that can provide help, assistance, and guidance.

What did you eat today? How did it feel?

Things that made me feel good today:

Things I noticed about myself:

Things I am grateful for:

Thoughts on the daily exercise:

Would you like to add anything else?

Day 104

Today, I...

> ***"We're all just memories of our future selves."***
> ***- Reggie Watts***

EXERCISE 104: Message the Future You

When we look back on our life, it's easy to contemplate all the things we would say to our younger self, given the opportunity – the guidance, the advice, the support, and all the reassurance. Well, going back in time isn't possible, but what you can do is communicate and share a message, including your thoughts, your dreams, your intentions and goals, or your gratitude, with a future version of yourself.

As you learn to love yourself, life will undoubtedly change, and you will certainly evolve – seeing an older version of yourself deliver a heartfelt message will be endearing, but most importantly it will help remind you of your journey, and that will be incredibly rewarding.

Today, send a message to the future you by recording a video of yourself on your phone, a camera, or a camcorder. Say whatever you feel like saying to that forthcoming self. You may choose to give certain details concerning the status of things in your life today; you can share your dreams and goals, you can share some inspiration, or anything you believe your future self will appreciate. When you are done recording the video, save it in a folder on your phone or computer with the title "Watch me _ _ / _ _ / _ _" (dated one year from now.) If you want, you can also put a reminder on your calendar or planner. Do not watch this video for an entire year, regardless of temptation.

Doing this video can also serve as a catalyst to get you motivated to do certain things you have been putting off, or to accomplish certain goals you want to have achieved by the time you view the recording. Make sure to enjoy this process and be authentic; you do not have to look perfect or say the perfect thing – simply speak from the heart – your future self will thank you for it.

Things that made me feel good today:

Things I noticed about myself:

Things I am grateful for:

Thoughts on the daily exercise:

Would you like to add anything else?

Today, I...

> ***"Make it thy business to know thyself, which is the most difficult lesson in the world"***
> ***- Miguel de Cervantes***

EXERCISE 105: Bi-Weekly Report

It is time to pause and reflect on the past two weeks. Complete this exercise when you can have at least one hour of undisturbed time. Make yourself comfortable by creating a soothing ambiance: get a warm drink, put on some music, or light a candle. Take a few deep breaths, relax, and when you are ready, answer the following questions honestly and thoroughly.

1. Summarize the past two weeks in a sentence.

2. Looking back, what are you most proud of?

3. What are some inner blocks and fears you noticed?

4. What important lessons did you learn?

5. What brought you the most joy?

6. What surprised you the most?

7. How are you doing in terms of loving yourself?

8. How has your relationship with yourself evolved?

9. How has your relationship with others evolved?

10. How has your attitude toward life evolved?

11. What tools, practices, or teachers have helped you the most?

13. What were your favorite and least favorite exercises? Explain.

14. What are you most grateful for at the moment?

15. What are things you would like to improve on in the upcoming two weeks?

Would you like to add anything else?

Today, as the daily exercise, either repeat your favorite exercise of the past two weeks or do an activity that feels good to your soul.

What did you do?

Day 106

Today, I...

> ***"Helping people and putting smiles on their faces is a great, great thing. God only knows why more people don't do it more often."***
> ***- Wayne Gerard Trotman***

EXERCISE 106: Give Something of Value

There are countless ways to help people by donating time, money, services or goods, and volunteering. However, people often associate giving with extreme cases or situations, and forget that from time to time everyday people also need some assistance.

At some point in your life, you have probably confronted some challenge that annoyed, troubled, or distressed you, and for which you thankfully found an answer.

Take a moment to think back to a time where you gained valuable assistance, and reflect on the one thing that helped ease your hurdle and benefited you.

Today, decide to give something that is of value to you to someone around you or to a stranger who could benefit from it. Depending on the particular item, it may be a bit hard to let go, but true giving is not measured by what is easy, but by what is good. Look around your home and identify things that could help others, and choose the one thing that you feel will produce the greatest joy. Of course, feel free to donate more than one valuable thing. If you can, explain to the receiver why you are presenting them with that gift and explain how it benefited you. In the event that you cannot explain, maybe attach a note. Either way, celebrate the opportunity to make a positive difference in another person's life.

I firmly believe that our legacies reside in how we serve others and the gifts of kindness we offer along the way.

Examples

- Give a book that has helped you.
- Offer a DVD that has changed your life.
- Donate a painting that has inspired you.
- Donate the nice suit that got you the job.
- Give a poem that gave you strength.
- Bless someone with a prayer that healed you.
- Give the number of a great therapist who can assist.
- Offer a cookbook that has helped you transition to veganism.

What did you give? Why?

Things that made me feel good today:

Things I noticed about myself:

Things I am grateful for:

Thoughts on the daily exercise:

Would you like to add anything else?

Day 107

Today, I...

> ***"It's hard to stay flexible if you don't stretch. I think if you train the right way you'll be flexible. There are people that don't appreciate the value of stretching. I think it's very important."***
> **- Darren Shahlavi**

EXERCISE 107: Do Some Stretching Exercises

Stretching exercises are often recommended pre- and post-workout as measures to prevent muscle, tendon, and ligament injuries. However, stretching exercises are not solely part of a fitness routine; they are also excellent to relax your muscles, reduce stress, improve sleep, gain flexibility and range of motion, improve posture and balance, and alleviate muscular stiffness and soreness. Whether you are physically active, follow a regular exercise program, or lead more of a sedentary lifestyle, you can benefit from adding a few flexibility exercises into your daily routine.

Today, do some stretching exercises and, if possible, make sure to target all the major muscle groups. You can choose to simply carry out some light stretches, select something soothing to the mind like Yoga, or step it up a notch and undertake something a little more dynamic and physically stimulating like Pilates – just pick a process that includes a lot of stretching exercises. Enjoy each stretch and be as present as possible with each of your movements, remaining mindful of how your body feels. Take your time; delight in bending, pulling, and elongating your muscles. Be careful not to lock your joints into place and not to force a painful movement beyond the slight pulling feeling that is common with such exercises. Lastly, take care not to hold your breath and make sure to continue breathing evenly and regularly during all the different exercises.

Before beginning any exercise regimen or taking on a new physical activity, remember to evaluate the best options for you; it is always a good idea to first contact and talk to your physician.

Examples

- Follow a stretching routine on YouTube.
- Join a Pilates or dance class.
- Follow a flexibility workout on DVD.
- Begin a Tai Chi or Yoga practice.

Things that made me feel good today:

Things I noticed about myself:

Things I am grateful for:

Thoughts on the daily exercise:

Would you like to add anything else?

Day 108

Today, I...

> *"I think the reason that I like so many different games is because I like the way my brain works when I'm playing games. It's more fun."*
> **- John Romero**

EXERCISE 108: Puzzle and Tease Your Brain

When it comes to mind games, researchers do not always agree on whether they are useful or not. Some suggest that these brain training games help improve memory, concentration, decision-making abilities, multitasking, and the added benefit of reducing the risks of developing Alzheimer's disease or dementia. Others refute those claims, stressing that the evidence only demonstrates that such games have helped individuals get better at a specific game but failed to prevent cognitive decline, and furthermore, failed at showing any improvement in the participants' lifestyles.

Pushing aside scientific claims, it's easy to see that brain games offer some advantages that can be easily verified. Getting involved in any activity that perplexes the mind will logically develop certain skills and abilities, such as patience, focus, and recollection. It will also improve brain plasticity and, depending on the games, it will develop specific skill sets, such as strategizing, problem-solving, or mathematical and linguistic performance – most importantly it will be stimulating and fun.

Today, puzzle and tease your brain by playing a mind game. You can choose a logic puzzle, a brainteaser, a strategy game, or brain training exercises. Choose an activity that you particularly like or try your hand at something new – just make sure to give free rein to your inner child and enjoy an unrestricted, guilt-free, playtime session.

Examples

- Crossword or Word Search puzzles
- Memory or Trivial Pursuit
- Poker or Bridge
- PEAK or LUMOSITY apps
- Chess or Checkers
- Sudoku or Kakuro
- Tetris or Pacman
- Dominoes or Mahjong
- Rubik's Cube or Bop it
- Mancala or Backgammon
- Wheel of Fortune or Jeopardy
- Bingo or Yahtzee

How did you puzzle and tease your brain?

Things that made me feel good today:

Things I noticed about myself:

Things I am grateful for:

Thoughts on the daily exercise:

Would you like to add anything else?

Today, I...

> *"Color provokes a psychic vibration. Color hides a power still unknown but real, which acts on every part of the human body."*
>
> *- Wassily Kandinsky*

EXERCISE 109: Color Your World

Marketing and branding professionals have long understood the psychological effect of color on human behavior, and they strategically use different hues to influence consumers. While cultural background and personal experience can sway people's perspective, in general people tend to react in similar ways to certain colors, such as yellow, blue, or green.

Color is all around us and continually influences the way we feel and behave whether we know it or not – to the extent that therapists use color therapy (also known as chromotherapy), to heal and relieve people suffering from different physical, emotional, and psychological ailments. Needless to say, color plays an important role in your daily life, and you should take advantage of this knowledge to assist you with whatever you are creating, but most importantly to care for yourself in a healthier way.

Today, look at the tips below, or research information on color psychology, and color your world to fit your needs and intentions. Whether you feel a bit down and need a mood booster, suffer from anxiety and want some peace of mind, or simply want to feel more confident – colors can help. Keep in mind that you may react differently based on your culture, your life experiences, your belief system, and your preferences. Throughout the day, try to notice how your three bodies (body, mind, spirit) react to various colors. Moving forward, play with different colors until you figure out what colors you need to surround yourself with, dress with, and use to get the best possible results – your very own color palette.

Too much of any color can create an imbalance in the long term; for instance, painting the walls of a room black can lead a person to depression and suicidal thoughts. Different hues or color combinations can also influence you in various ways.

Helpful Tips: Here are a few basic color associations to help you begin:

BLACK
Positive: Sophistication, elegance, power, confidence, mysteriousness, security, protective, grounding.
Negative: Emptiness, depression, coldness, unfriendliness, aggressive, intimidating, overwhelming.

WHITE
Positive: Cleanliness, freshness, innocence, simplicity, clarity, purity, openness, hope, organization.
Negative: Coldness, distant, unfriendliness, superiority, isolation, emptiness.

GRAY
Positive: Emotional balance, stability, quiet, calm, wisdom, methodical, neutrality, practicality, modern.
Negative: Timidity, depression, hibernation, lethargy, indecisiveness, dullness.

RED
Positive: Passion, love, action, confidence, courage, metabolic stimulation, energizing, enthusiasm.
Negative: Aggressiveness, antagonistic, demanding, impulsive, anxiety, danger, warning, pain, increases blood pressure and heart rate.

PINK
Positive: Femininity, sweetness, nurture, warmth, love, softness, compassion, youthfulness, playfulness, plumps up the skin.
Negative: Immaturity, neediness, shallowness, emasculating.

ORANGE
Positive: Friendliness, warmth, energizing, optimism, strength, creativity, fun, joy, stimulates appetite.
Negative: Laziness, childishness, intense, anxiety.

YELLOW
Positive: Happy, cheerful, self-esteem, creativity, spontaneity, friendliness, activates memory.
Negative: Instability, irrationality, irresponsibility, overstimulation, exhaustion.

PURPLE
Positive: Luxury, royalty, spirituality, intuitive, contemplative, uplifting, calming, creativity.
Negative: Cold, aloofness, overthinking, apathy, impatience.

BLUE
Positive: Calm, soothing, trustworthiness, faithfulness, loyalty, dependability, intelligence, concentration.
Negative: Coldness, melancholic, detached, withdrawn, depression

GREEN
Positive: Freshness, harmony, balance, serenity, safety, healing, mental and physical relaxation.
Negative: Guilt, jealousy, cautious, inexperience.

BROWN
Positive: Reliability, stability, strength, warmth, comfort, simplicity, friendliness, earthiness, grounding.
Negative: Inflexible, gloominess, stingy, predictability

How did you color your world today? How did it feel?

Things that made me feel good today:

Things I noticed about myself:

Things I am grateful for:

Thoughts on the daily exercise:

Would you like to add anything else?

Day 110

Today, I...

> *"Smile and smile often. Smile regularly. Smile when you don't feel like it and you will feel like it when you smile."*
> **- B. J. Palmer**

EXERCISE 110: Turn That Frown into a Great Big Smile

Whatever a person is thinking or feeling is usually reflected on their face. At the office, in the school halls, on the subway, or even in the safety of their homes, people are often preoccupied with the things that worry or upset them.

We are intrinsically wired to look for the negatives – our survival mechanism causes our mind to anticipate and prevent any potential threat, essentially protecting us from perceived or real dangers. However, each time we make a negative facial expression, a negatively charged message is sent to the brain, reinforcing the negative thought-patterns, which ultimately influences our moods.

In other words, unhappy facial expressions translate into unhappy emotions, and happy expressions translate into happy emotions. Furthermore, the power of your facial expressions does not stop there. They also influence how people with whom you come into contact perceive you, respond to you, and feel themselves. You can test this theory for yourself, by looking at people around you and seeing how their different facial expressions make you feel.

Interestingly enough, because of the interconnectedness between our mind, our body, and our emotions, we can make ourselves (and others) feel better by simply faking the happiest of expressions – a big smile. You do not need to be in a happy mood or have any particular reason to smile; if you smile on purpose long enough, you will trick your brain into thinking it has a reason to feel good. Smiling often will bring about other positive advantages, such as feeling more relaxed, being more approachable, improving communication with others, looking more attractive, and feeling more cheerful.

Today, turn that frown into a great big smile as often as possible; spread some joy by sharing your beaming smile with as many people as you can, including the people closest to you. Try to remain present whenever you smile; take note of the way you feel and observe how people react to you.

Remember to use common sense and your intuition. Some people sometimes can regrettably misinterpret your smile, so please smile plentifully but mindfully.

Things that made me feel good today:

Things I noticed about myself:

Things I am grateful for:

Thoughts on the daily exercise:

Would you like to add anything else?

Today, I...

> ***"Of all the senses, sight must be the most delightful."***
> ***- Helen Keller***

EXERCISE 111: *Explore Your Sense of Sight*

People are repeatedly told that they are amazing and unique beings, but they never really take the time to appreciate how true that is. This uniqueness comes through in your personality, your thought-patterns, your behaviors, and your anatomy. In this activity we will focus on one of these exceptional features, your eyes.

Did you know that your iris has 256 unique characteristics? Or, that your eye is the second most complex organ in your body after the brain? This extraordinary organ helps you learn 80% of what you know, can distinguish millions of colors, heals rapidly, and most importantly allows you to view the world around you.

Most of us are incredibly blessed to have the ability to observe this vibrant and beautiful life. There are so many things to look at, enjoy, and appreciate – it's mind-blowing to think that most people rarely take the time to see the world around them.

As individuals, we habitually are so wrapped up in thinking, labeling, and interpreting the world around us, we tend to neglect seeing things as they are.

Today, explore your sense of sight without labeling or judging. Simply observe your environment and the people around you as objectively as you can. This means that instead of looking at a tree thinking, "That's a pretty tree! I wonder how old it is?" mindfully observe the shape, colors, textures, and details of the tree without labels. Or instead of seeing a person and thinking, "Such big eyes and such a nice smile. What a lovely outfit!" attentively notice the person's traits, their pigmentation, shape, and all the details, without labels or the internal dialogue. Begin by looking at things around you, small things, or your own hands; take a few conscious breaths, relax, and view all the details as if you were seeing this object for the first time without the vocabulary, judgments, opinions, or beliefs that you would ordinarily have. Throughout the day, do this activity with different things or beings; be conscious to avoid automatically defaulting to words, associations, and thoughts.

Deliberately choose to step back and see things neutrally. Appreciate the things or beings you observe for their specific and unique details. Look at all their features, their intrinsic beauty, and watch how everything begins to appear differently. At the end of the day, write down your observations.

What surprised you about seeing things with fresh eyes?

Things that made me feel good today:

Things I noticed about myself:

Things I am grateful for:

Thoughts on the daily exercise:

Would you like to add anything else?

Day 112

Today, I...

> *"I like doing arts and crafts, so I would probably go to one of those fun little ceramic places and go paint some plates and do something fun like that."*
> ***- Christina Milian***

EXERCISE 112: Create an Arts and Craft Project

As young children, girls and boys love being creative and continually play with colors, textures, and different mediums. As the years go by, most adults, regardless of gender, lose touch with that creative spark. Fear of looking silly or immature, worries of being judged, taking things too seriously, self-imposed rules, and skewed beliefs (i.e. being an adult means you must act seriously, or part of being a grown-up is replacing fun with work) are all responsible for this reluctance to enjoy creative and artistic activities. However, allowing your inner artist to surface, and creating things with your hands, offers amazing benefits. It is a way to relieve your daily stresses, a means to express yourself without restrictions, a way to meditate and reflect, a door to innovative and inspired ideas, and a way to avoid boredom. Furthermore, it is important to mention that many who suffer from PTSD, addictions, emotional distress or trauma, grief, chronic pain, illnesses, and disorders have also demonstrated positive results through creative outlets or art therapy.

Today, let your guard down, your inner child out, and create an arts and craft project. This activity is supposed to help you step out of your comfort zone, but it is also meant to be fun and enjoyable. The goal here is for you to create more space for hands-on creativity in your life; therefore, it is important that you enjoy this exercise. If you are reluctant to create anything, start with something easy, but if you are an avid crafter try your hand at something new. You can choose to create something on your own, but if you are open to turning this into a group activity, you are welcome to join a class or host a craft party. Allow yourself to be child-like and have a good time.

Examples

- Paint a white shirt or a pair of canvas sneakers.
- Take a class at an art supply store.
- Pick an exciting project from Pinterest or Instructables.
- Turn an old wheelbarrow or used tire into a planter.
- Purchase a DIY craft kit from Etsy or Michaels.
- Make baskets out of plastic bags.
- Host a jewelry or wreath making party.
- Make papier-mâché masks or bowls.
- Refurbish a dresser or an old chair.
- Make a succulent or cacti planter.
- Do some face or body painting.
- Go to a craft studio and paint a mandala, or do some pottery painting.

What did you create?

Things that made me feel good today:

Things I noticed about myself:

Things I am grateful for:

Thoughts on the daily exercise:

Would you like to add anything else?

Today, I...

> ***"The human foot is a masterpiece of engineering and a work of art."***
> ***- Leonardo da Vinci***

EXERCISE 113: Get Off Your Feet

Feet, the foundation that support your body, are complex structures that house a quarter of your body's bones (26 bones in each foot to be exact). Yet it is interesting to note that they are prone to injuries, ailments, and infections. Unaware, most people walk all over them, neglect them, and never give them the proper care they deserve.

The first step to caring for your feet is to have a good foot hygiene. The foot has 250,000 sweat glands that excrete more than half a cup of sweat a day, therefore adopting a good hygiene routine is vital for the health of your feet. Washing them every day, scrubbing them, drying them completely, trimming and brushing your toenails, alternating the shoes you wear, wearing clean socks, and changing them at least twice a day should all become a part of your daily habits.

Beyond cleanliness, your feet deserve to be pampered and cared for. Creating day-to-day rituals to care for your feet will help in keeping the skin, the bones, and the muscles healthy and functioning properly.

Today, get off your feet and give them some tender loving care. This activity can be done at any time, but afternoon and evening hours are best as they are the periods during which the feet are the most swollen and uncomfortable. Create a serene ambiance, if possible, and care for your feet; find ways to rejuvenate them and relieve tension. Relax and be conscious of how your feet feel during the entire process and afterward.

Health issues can show up on your feet long before they become a problem, so examine your feet regularly (use a mirror if you have a hard time bending). Contact a healthcare professional if you notice any of the following symptoms: bumps, bruises, hairless toes, tingling, numbness, change of color or irregularities on toenails, dry flaky skin, sores that won't heal, change of temperature in feet (cold or hot), heel pain, swollen ankle(s), or any unusual changes and discomforts.

Examples

- Give yourself a foot massage or get one.
- Soak your feet in a foot bath.
- Roll a tennis ball under each foot.
- Use an acupressure foot mat.
- Indulge in a foot mask.
- Dip your feet in a bucket filled with ice and water.
- Moisturize your feet and put socks.
- Get an appointment with a reflexologist.
- Do some foot stretches.
- Exfoliate your feet.

Helpful Tips: Here are other ways to prevent foot problems:

- Do not share footwear with anyone.
- Wear flip-flops, sandals or slippers in gyms, locker rooms, showers, and public bathing areas.
- Let your toes breathe.
- Wear shoes that fit well.
- Avoid foods that are high in salt.
- Avoid wearing high heels too often.
- Let nails breathe between nail-polish applications.
- See a podiatrist for your ingrown nails.
- Do not share your yoga mat.
- Bring your own pedicure utensils to the salon and make sure the foot baths are clean.

How did you care for your feet?

Things that made me feel good today:

Things I noticed about myself:

Things I am grateful for:

Thoughts on the daily exercise:

Would you like to add anything else?

Today, I...

> *"I want to write, but more than that, I want to bring out all kinds of things that lie buried deep in my heart."*
> *- Anne Frank*

EXERCISE 114: Free Write

Day in and day out people go through life holding on to thousands of thoughts, feelings, and emotions concerning their experiences, their to-do lists, things seen on television or social media, complaints and resentments, repressed emotions, fears and joys, goals and dreams, appointments and obligations, hidden secrets, etc. Layers upon layers of information and emotional tension that can negatively impact the three bodies (body, mind, and spirit). Having an outlet to release all this "stuff" can be incredibly therapeutic and liberating. Free writing is one of those fantastic ways of letting everything out – to free write is to write everything that comes to mind, regardless of what it is without censoring, judging, or holding back. It's putting down on paper your random thoughts, memories, painful experiences, opinions, hopes, and anything that surfaces on the moment. It allows you to free yourself, feel relief, and gain a better perspective. It helps you get acquainted with the voices of your inner child, your conscious and subconscious minds, your spirit, and all the different parts of you.

Today, first thing in the morning, sit in silence and free write. You will need about an hour of undisturbed time to complete this activity. Before you begin, take a few conscious breaths and completely relax. When you are ready, just write anything that you are thinking of – do not think about what to write, forget about things looking neat, ignore grammatical and spelling rules, and just give freedom to whatever chooses to surface. Write as much as you can for 10 to 15 minutes until you feel that you are done. You can choose to write on the following pages, you can opt to type it all out on your computer, or if you prefer, you can express your thoughts on loose leaf paper. Withholding any thought from being written defies the purpose of this exercise, so please make sure to write down every thought that you notice without restraint (if privacy is a concern, you can choose to dispose of your writings afterward). When you are done writing, go back and read everything you have written – cross out anything that is not relevant but highlight and contemplate the information that is inspiring, interesting, comforting, or revealing. Doing this regularly will allow you to develop a better relationship with yourself, heal from certain past or present hurts, find solutions to questions, and lighten your load.

Remember, there is no "right way" or "wrong way" to do this. At first, this exercise will feel awkward because your brain will want to answer questions such as "What am I supposed to write about?" And, that's perfectly fine, just write whatever comes up.

(In order for you to better understand the gist of this example, I have written it with proper spelling, style, and punctuation.)

"I'm tired. I didn't feel like getting up. Now I'm going to be tired all day! This cup of tea is so good! Okay, let's start. What am I supposed to write about? This is ridiculous. I have nothing to say. Maybe I should go back to bed.

This is a tricky exercise, but I think I might discover new things about myself. I might even make sense of things that are not making any sense right now.

Today is Tuesday, remember you have an appointment at 3:00 pm. Should I wear the black slacks or the gray slacks? It really doesn't matter as long as you walk in there, head high, and confident. You got this! I've never liked having all the attention on me. Maybe it all began in 2nd grade when Marc made fun of me. It's funny how something that happened so long ago can still affect me today. How can I fix that? Stretch yourself and step out of your comfort zone until it feels comfortable.

Wait, what was that sound? Are the kids up already? There it goes. No more me time. Oh! It was the dog. I shouldn't feel this way about the kids though. I love them so much, they are my life. There's nothing to feel bad about, you deserve time for yourself. A lot has been going on lately; maybe I should ask mom if they can spend the weekend with her, so that I can enjoy some me time. I like that, good idea.

It looks like it's going to be a beautiful day! It's so sunny already and the birds sound so happy. I love spring, everything being reborn. I think I'll have a smoothie for breakfast. Maybe banana, papaya and mango. Yum! That sounds so delish! ..."

Free Writing

Things that made me feel good today:

Things I noticed about myself:

Things I am grateful for:

Thoughts on the daily exercise:

Would you like to add anything else?

Day 115

Today, I...

> *"Try everything that can be done. Be deliberate. Be spontaneous. Be thoughtful and painstaking. Be abandoned and impulsive. Learn your own possibilities."*
> **- George Bellows**

EXERCISE 115: Be Spontaneous

One of the biggest complaints that people have is about how stuck they feel in their daily routines and how unhappy and bored it makes them. While a routine can at times be helpful and comforting, it doesn't really teach your brain anything new and, unfortunately, repetition over time can create a dull humdrum. Get up, brush teeth, drink coffee, make bed, shower, eat breakfast, go to work, eat lunch, talk to the same people, have the same conversations, finish work, get home, shower, prepare dinner, eat dinner, watch television, go to bed. Almost everyone can relate to a similar pattern in their daily lives. This can be crushing to a person's spirit, as it wants nothing more than to explore, experience, learn, and discover.

Having a routine and making plans are necessary and have their place; however, making space in your days for spontaneity will ensure that you invite some joy, some fun, and a whole lot of excitement back into your life.

Today, be spontaneous and be open to new possibilities. First thing in the morning, make an intention stating your desire to be spontaneous throughout the day, and let your inner compass take the lead. You do not need to reschedule or cancel your plans; just say yes to things you would usually turn down, make conversation with people who cross your path, go watch a play or visit a comedy club, eat on a roof top, buy a meal for a homeless person, have your business meeting at a coffee shop, take the kids to the park – simply allow your intuition to guide you, and have an exciting time infusing your day with unplanned experiences. Be as conscious as you can throughout the day, and listen to your inner voice as it presents delightful opportunities – you will need to let go of your inhibitions, dismiss your mind's chatter, and the opinions of others. At the end of the day, write down a list of all the things you did, and explain how this experience made you feel. Moving forward, consider including more spontaneity in your daily life, as it will open many doors and expand your reality.

Remember, being spontaneous does not mean to be reckless or impulsive. It means paying attention to your inner voice and having a good time. Therefore, safety and common sense must still prevail.

What spontaneous actions did you take? How did you feel about it?

Things that made me feel good today:

Things I noticed about myself:

Things I am grateful for:

Thoughts on the daily exercise:

Would you like to add anything else?

Today, I...

> *"Heaven and Earth give themselves. Air, water, plants, animals, and humans give themselves to each other. It is in this giving-themselves-to-each-other that we actually live. Whether you appreciate it or not, it is true."*
>
> *- Kodo Sawaki*

EXERCISE 116: Lend a Helping Hand

Would you agree that when you intentionally help someone, especially if you assist them without expecting anything in return, you come out of it feeling really good?

An overwhelming majority of people are inherently benevolent and willing to help and support others. However, this willingness to lend a hand often correlates to some kind of crisis – hunger, poverty, disease, catastrophe, accident, loss, and many other unfortunate circumstances. While this is commendable, it is also important to remember that kindness does not need negative circumstances to manifest.

Every day, we are given opportunities to extend kindness and positively impact people – this includes the people we work with, the people we see regularly, and the people who are closest to us. Sometimes making someone's day can simply mean taking a load off their shoulders, assisting them with a certain task, or teaching them something valuable. Think of times when people around you have done nice things for you. Maybe your neighbor offered to relieve you from a mundane chore like mowing the lawn, or perhaps a coworker volunteered to take on your workload so that you could attend your child's recital, or yet again, your grandma may have taught you how to make a cherished family recipe.

Today, lend a helping hand and assist someone by either taking on a task, doing a chore, or by teaching something valuable. You can choose to help any number of people, but first and foremost, make sure to show kindness to someone in your circle. Whatever you choose to take on, you must do willingly and without any expectations whatsoever. This exercise is not about what you can get, but what you can give – the impact that you, as a human being, can have on this planet. Put your heart into this activity and be conscious of the feelings that surface. It is normal to have some expectations at first, so do not judge yourself for feeling any particular way; just be mindful not to have an attitude if you do not get the reaction you silently would have liked to receive. The more you practice giving freely, the more freely you will give.

Remember, this is not an exercise that encourages you to discount your well-being for the welfare of others. This is not about accepting to take on all of other people's workload or responsibilities. Be mindful of your feelings and always make sure to do things that resonate with you.

Examples

- Make or buy coffee for your secretary.
- Help a senior cross the street.
- Help someone carry their groceries.
- Bring a dish to a new mom and dad.
- Take the trash out for your parents.
- Teach your teenager how to budget.
- Help someone who is moving.
- Offer to cover the shift of someone who has a doctor's appointment.
- Allow people to merge-in during traffic.
- Offer to do some pro bono work for deserving person.

How did you lend a helping hand?

Things that made me feel good today:

Things I noticed about myself:

Things I am grateful for:

Thoughts on the daily exercise:

Would you like to add anything else?

Day 117

Today, I...

> *"I don't have any particular thing I do ritualistically. I do the same thing every day. I get up. Drink a lot of water. Have a wheatgrass shot. Drink some green juice. Eat as healthy as I can."*
>
> ***- Erykah Badu***

EXERCISE 117: Hydrate Positively

Being largely composed of water it's clear that drinking water is essential for the health of our bodies. A common recommendation for the average adult is to drink at least half their body weight in ounces. Still, most fall short of that number, and a great many prefer ingesting unhealthy substitutes that are packed full of sugar and other chemical additives; these substances cause havoc in the body and often result in weight gain, tooth decay, dehydration, and even certain diseases.

Today, skip the sodas, the store-bought juices, or the energy drinks, and hydrate positively. Drink plenty of water, and for added nutrition and goodness, include delicious, all natural, freshly made drinks. Do not add sugar or sweeteners, as they are unhealthy choices. This activity will be easier for some than for others, but take into account that it's the best decision for your body. Take pleasure in giving your body what it needs and deserves. Be aware of the way you feel mentally, emotionally, and physically throughout the day. As always, keep in mind that loving yourself is about making positive choices for your mind, body, and spirit.

Remember, if you are accustomed to consuming many sugared and highly caffeinated drinks, you may get jittery and a bit uncomfortable. You may even develop a headache. This is your body detoxing and just doing its best to adjust. Should you decide to continue this activity, these symptoms will pass after a few days.

Examples

- Have a cup of sugar-free Moroccan mint tea.
- Detox with some lemon water.
- Delight in a fresh green juice.
- Have some cucumber and mint infused water.
- Indulge in a nice smoothie.
- Enjoy some fresh coconut water.
- Sip on some sugar-free green iced tea with a slice of lemon.
- Enjoy a fresh watermelon or passion fruit juice.

Things that made me feel good today:

Things I noticed about myself:

Things I am grateful for:

Thoughts on the daily exercise:

Would you like to add anything else?

Day 118

Today, I...

> *"It's a choice if you want to change your life for the better. Life is cause and effect, it's all about choices. And what you do today can deter the next 30 years of your life."*
>
> **- Cory Hardrict**

EXERCISE 118: Cause and Effect

The universal law of cause and effect dictates that your choices, actions, and thoughts are all responsible for the life you currently live and the results you will produce in the future. This can seem a bit harsh to those who would argue that people are not always 100% responsible for their fate. However, we can all agree that having the power to decide, the ultimate power to choose, we are in fact mostly responsible for the majority of what manifests in our reality. If you welcome people with a big smile when they walk in your store, you will probably increase your chances of making a sale and having repeat customers. If you exercise regularly and eat whole foods, chances are you will be healthier and feel more energized. If you repeatedly drive fast, you are likely to get a ticket or get into an accident.

Finally, if you always think everyone is out to get you, in due time you may very well end up lonely, with no friends. These are all examples of how everyday choices can have impacting consequences.

Today, take some time to contemplate what role cause and effect play in your life. What choices have led you to the life that you live today? What results can you expect if you continue making the same choices, taking the same actions, and thinking the same thoughts? Make sure to think about how you are applying the law of cause and effect in every area of your life. When you are done contemplating on the matter, evaluate whether your current patterns match your intentions, your goals, and your grandest vision for yourself. If they do not, think about what different choices and changes would be more aligned to your objectives, and fill in the table on the following pages.

Helpful Tips: Here are a few tips to help you make better decisions for yourself:

- Always take at least one to two conscious breaths before saying anything, reacting to anything, or doing anything.
- Remain aware of your power to choose in every moment and always consider the possible consequences that could ensue.
- Always ask yourself questions such as "How is this choice going to impact my life?" "What results can I expect?" "Does this choice reflect my intentions and goals?" "Will this decision benefit me and others in the long run?" and "What are the positive and negative consequences that I can expect if I continue making this choice?"

Past choices, thoughts, and actions	**Current results**	**Anticipated outcomes if I keep making the same choices**

New choices, thoughts, and actions	How I plan to stick to these choices	Anticipated outcomes if I stick to my plan

Things that made me feel good today:

Things I noticed about myself:

Things I am grateful for:

Thoughts on the daily exercise:

Would you like to add anything else?

Today, I...

> ***"Things don't spiral out of control when we surrender them; they spiral out of control when we try to control them!"***
> ***- Marianne Williamson***

EXERCISE 119: Surrender

Most human beings subconsciously or consciously feel the need to control everything in their lives; this includes circumstances, events, and even other people and creatures. Needing people to act a certain way, needing to look a certain way, needing the kids to behave a certain way, needing to work a certain job, needing to feel happy, needing to find true love, needing answers – just a constant longing for life to play out on their terms. Yet the more a person needs control, the more stress, anguish, and misery they will experience.

Being intentional and having goals or expectations is wonderful, but being inflexible and needing things to be a certain way will cause you to suffer.

Life is made in such a manner that you are bound to experience contrast – however, life will also present you with opportunities to grow and learn. Therefore, you will certainly deal with things beyond your control; pushing or fighting against those things, and always trying to have your way will only give you more grief, sorrow, and unhappiness. On the other hand, when you surrender to a power or process greater than yourself – when you accept that you do not have all the answers and choose to release control – magic and miracles often abound. Fascinating studies concerning the power of surrender and the power of "thy will be done" have shown astounding results. Here, surrender does not mean to give up; it means to release the need for control and accept that help, guidance, and wisdom come from a power bigger than yourself. Whether you believe that power to be God, Universal Intelligence, Life, Love, your Higher Self, or your Subconscious Mind does not matter; the true power resides in the letting go and the trusting.

Today, surrender a problem, worry, or situation beyond your control to a power greater than yourself, and trust that an answer or miracle is on its way to you. You will need about an hour of undisturbed time to complete this activity. When you are ready, create a soothing atmosphere, take a few conscious breaths, and relax. Take a moment to think about one thing you feel you would like assistance with and write a detailed letter to the source of your faith or conviction. Share, release, and hand over the issue to that greater power, and before you finish, remember to express gratitude for the answer that is forthcoming.

When you are done, take a few deep breaths, relax, feel gratitude, and let go. Throughout the day, stay alert, open, and mindful; look for signs and opportunities, and pursue any insight you receive. Here, action is implied; if you ask for assistance, it is important that you act on the insights you receive. This can be a tricky exercise for some of you, especially for those who feel safe being in control. Take this opportunity to assess your resistance and your relationship with both control and surrender. Furthermore, some of you may worry that you will not get the things you want or that something terrible might happen if you just let go and surrender. Whenever that happens, step into the present moment, and realize that those fears are all attempts from your mind to keep control. Respond to those thought patterns with a question such as "what if something magical and incredible happens?" a declaration such as "I am safe and protected!" or an affirmation such as "I am open to receive the very best of everything."

Remember, whether you are a "control freak" or not, things not going according to plan may be a blessing in disguise, an opportunity, or a gift – so just, be open to possibilities, and surrender more and more every day until it becomes natural and comfortable.

Dear ,

Things that made me feel good today:

Things I noticed about myself:

Things I am grateful for:

Thoughts on the daily exercise:

Would you like to add anything else?

Today, I...

> *"We are here to change. We are here to grow, develop and unfold. We are progressive beings that have infinite capacity."*
> **- Michael Beckwith**

EXERCISE 120: End-of-Phase Report

Congratulations! You have successfully completed PHASE I and will now begin PHASE II. As you end one phase and get ready to enter another, it is time to pause and reflect on the past 60 days. Complete this exercise when you can have at least one hour of undisturbed time. Make yourself comfortable by creating a soothing ambiance: get a warm drink, put on some music, or light a candle. Take a few deep breaths, relax, and when you are ready, answer these questions honestly and thoroughly.

1. What were your greatest successes and/or achievements during this phase?

2. What brought you the most joy during this phase?

3. What are fears and challenges you are still facing?

4. What are the biggest changes you have noticed about yourself?

5. What are the biggest changes you have noticed in your relationships?

6. What are the biggest changes you have noticed in your life?

7. What has become easier for you since beginning this journey?

8. What are you the most grateful for at the moment?

9. What are the things you still must work on or improve?

10. What teacher(s) or tools (practices, documentaries, exercises, etc.) have helped you the most during this phase?

11. What are the greatest lessons you have learned during this phase?

12. On a scale of 1 to 10, with 10 being the most positive, how satisfied are you with your progress so far? Explain.

Completely dissatisfied				Neutral					Completely satisfied
1	2	3	4	5	6	7	8	9	10

13. On a scale of 1 to 10, with 10 being the most positive, how comfortable are you with trying new things? Explain.

Very uncomfortable				Neutral					Very comfortable
1	2	3	4	5	6	7	8	9	10

14. On a scale of 1 to 10, with 10 being the most positive, are you satisfied with the amount of commitment you have put into Phase I? How can you improve?

Completely dissatisfied				Neutral					Completely satisfied
1	2	3	4	5	6	7	8	9	10

15. On a scale of 1 to 10, with 10 being the most positive, how much do you love yourself now? Explain.

I loathe myself				Neutral					I love myself completely
1	2	3	4	5	6	7	8	9	10

Would you like to add anything else?

You did it! Now, it's time to celebrate by doing something special or giving yourself a gift. Please do not skip this step, as it is significant for your present and future progress. Positive reinforcement will assure future success in changing certain behaviors, certain patterns, and achieving your dreams and goals.

Today, I celebrated completing ***PHASE II*** by

Phase 3: Let Love Blossom

Reminder: This final phase will give birth to the first blossoms of true self-love. You will be asked to make additional efforts in the daily exercises.

At this stage, you will be more appreciative and loving toward your three bodies (body, mind, and spirit), and it will be easier for you to find a good balance between the three. Theories and philosophies become internalized – you will go beyond simply intellectually understanding certain concepts; you will embody them, or at least understand them in a more intrinsic and profound way.

You will know that, while at times some unexpected or unfortunate events may happen, you always have control over your perspective and choices. You will enjoy your own company and understand the value of being your number one priority. You will gain a newfound gratitude for your life. You will find joy in experiencing new things and stepping out of your comfort zone.

Day 121

Today, I...

> ***"You must love and care for yourself, because that's when the best comes out."***
> ***- Tina Turner***

EXERCISE 121: Self-Care Practices

Oftentimes self-care falls under the umbrella of Band-Aid activities aimed at relieving stress, fatigue, or distress. While self-care can be used as a treatment, it really should be utilized as a proactive measure. Loving yourself entails caring for yourself, and it should be an integral part of your daily routine. It is a philosophy that goes beyond popular or mainstream self-care rituals (e.g. bubble baths, meditation, mani-pedi, etc.) – it is about honoring yourself. Caring for the self should be a holistic practice that encompasses caring for the mind, the body, and the spirit, in a balanced and harmonious way. Neglecting your needs and giving priority to things outside yourself will deplete your energy and cause you emotional and mental distress.

To be your best self and create the life that you desire, you must learn to maintain your inner equilibrium by using and recycling your energy in ways that serve you. The easiest and fastest way to do that is by doing activities that nurture, nourish, and uplift your three bodies (body, mind, and spirit).

Today, be attentive to your needs and desires by making a list of six simple self-care practices you can incorporate in your day. Before you begin, look at the different categories on the graphic. Close your eyes, take a few conscious breaths, and relax. Think of different activities that could improve each area today. Pick one for each category and an additional bonus one that's special to you. Enjoy checking off all the different activities you have planned for this day.

Remember, you are the most important being in your life, and you deserve to take time to honor yourself and treat yourself lovingly and respectfully.

Examples

PHYSICAL	Have green juice
MENTAL	Read before bed
EMOTIONAL	Mindful breathing
SPIRITUAL	Gratitude list
SOCIAL	Have lunch with best friend at favorite restaurant
BONUS	Go to bed early

PHYSICAL	
MENTAL	
EMOTIONAL	
SPIRITUAL	
SOCIAL	
BONUS	

Things that made me feel good today:

Things I noticed about myself:

Things I am grateful for:

Thoughts on the daily exercise:

Would you like to add anything else?

Day 122

Today, I...

> *"You must feed your mind even as you feed your body, and to make your mind healthy, you must feed it nourishing, wholesome thoughts."*
> **- Norman Vincent Peale**

EXERCISE 122: Inspirational Message

No one can ever really predict when the Muses of inspiration will visit and expand a person's perceptions, hopes, and dreams. Inspiration can be found in many unusual places – watching a movie, during meditation, listening to a speech, reading a poem, overlooking a nice scenery, going through a life-changing event, or for no apparent reason. While inspiration does not affect everyone in the same way, on some degree or another, it cuts through perceived limitations, gives people wings, and transports them to lands of potential and possibilities. Being inspired helps you peek beyond the realm of your ordinary routine; it renews your enthusiasm, sparks your creativity, helps you find purpose, and makes you feel joyful. Making time every day to nourish and nurture your spirit will expand your inner vision and help you reach new heights in all the areas of your life.

Today, make time, preferably in the morning, to listen to an inspirational message. You can choose to listen to your favorite speaker or feel free to enjoy a new point of view. You can go to an event, a place of worship, watch an online video, or listen to a podcast. Enjoy the message and open yourself to be inspired. Afterward, write a short summary explaining what inspired you or moved you the most and your take-away from the message.

Examples

- Dalai Lama
- Malala Yousafzai
- Desmond Tutu
- Deepak Chopra
- Oprah Winfrey
- Wayne Dyer
- Prince Ea
- Brené Brown
- Matthieu Ricard
- Immaculée Ilibagiza
- Turia Pitt
- Jay Shetty
- Lizzie Velásquez
- Marie Forleo
- Eckhart Tolle
- King Nahh (Kids)
- Dr. Michael Bernard Beckwith
- Esther Hicks
- Sadhguru Jaggi Vasudev
- Neil Donald Walsch

Things that made me feel good today:

Things I noticed about myself:

Things I am grateful for:

Thoughts on the daily exercise:

Would you like to add anything else?

Day 123

Today, I...

> ***"People think that you have to do something huge, like go to Africa and build a school, but you can make a small change in a day. If you change Wednesday, then you change Thursday. Pretty soon it's a week, then a month, then a year. It's bite-size, as opposed to feeling like you have to turn your life inside out to make changes."***
> ***- Hoda Kotb***

EXERCISE 123: Change the World

What will be your legacy? This question will be more or less important to you, depending on your age and the stage of life you find yourself in presently. However, it's a pertinent question, one you should ponder regardless of your age or circumstances.

Most people think of their legacy as the culmination of successes, measurable and remarkable projects, and a progeny – all "things" that will ultimately bolster their name or their family's reputation. Here, the word legacy is seen from a unique perspective; it is seen as the culmination of selfless contributions an individual (in this case, you) will have made during their lifetime – acts of kindness that will have had a notable impact, not just on one individual or family, but on the entire world.

People often think that leading a meaningful, purposeful, and significant life must involve something huge, impressive, or out of reach. Nothing could be further from the truth. Yes, the world is changed by inventing new technologies, finding cures for untreatable illnesses, creating exceptional products, building schools, donating food and medicine, or championing social causes. However, the world is also changed by telling a child she is worthy, planting a tree, signing a petition, sharing a warm meal, rescuing an animal, and smiling at a passerby. Think back on events that have had a positive impact in your life; chances are, the most important ones come from what many would consider insignificant moments. Be a gift to the world; begin where you are, do one small act of kindness after another, and witness how everything improves around you.

Today, change the world! Take a few deep breaths, relax, and create a list of five things you can do to be impactful and helpful during the day. Think of the ripples you want to create as a giver, through your actions. Do not mindlessly accomplish the different tasks on your list; make sure to remain conscious of the effect you are having on the planet and the beings around you. Take joy in the process, give without expectations, and take time to appreciate your capacity to change the world positively.

Remember, we each have our part to play; we are the ones who make this world a better place. What other people do, or do not do, is none of your business. You can only be responsible for who you are and what you bring to the whole. Therefore, brighten the world, shine your light wherever you go, and leave a lasting legacy.

Examples

- Leave a nice review.
- Host a pantry donation party.
- Compliment your boss.
- Buy a toy for your neighbor's pet.
- Leave extra coins at the Laundromat.
- Buy someone lunch.
- Hold the elevator for someone.
- Say "I love you" to someone you love.
- Organize a neighborhood cleanup.
- Donate some clothes.
- Buy a case of water for a construction crew.
- Be patient.
- Buy a hot drink for a homeless person.
- Be kind to a customer.
- Listen without interrupting.
- Put seeds out for critters.
- Play with your kids.
- Send a sweet text to a friend.

How did you change the world today?

Things that made me feel good today:

Things I noticed about myself:

Things I am grateful for:

Thoughts on the daily exercise:

Would you like to add anything else?

Day 124

Today, I...

> ***"Thought is the labor of the intellect, reverie is its pleasure."***
> ***- Victor Hugo***

EXERCISE 124: Time to Unplug

Since childhood, people have been repeatedly snapped out of their reveries, asked to pay attention and to focus. Daydreaming has a bad reputation and is often synonymous with "escapism," "waste of time," "laziness," "avoidance," or "distraction" – but, as it so happens, there are many benefits to letting your mind travel and wander. Daydreaming can be a positive and healthy habit that allows you to pull back from the outside world, connect to your inner world, and dive into a world of possibilities.

Giving way to your wandering mind can assist with problem solving, increasing creativity, improving memory, helping plan the future, organizing thoughts, relieving boredom, giving your brain a break, and making you feel good. Far from being a futile pastime, daydreaming is a natural process that greatly contributes to our overall well-being.

Today, take some time to unplug and allow your mind to wander. You can choose to take several mind-breaks during the day, or you can choose to create a time slot to enjoy your mini mental vacation. You do not need to do anything in particular; just turn off all your electronic devices (to not be disturbed), make yourself comfortable, and let your mind do the rest. Let your imagination take the lead, and enjoy this leisurely time, guilt-free.

Helpful Tips: Here are some ideas to help with your daydreaming experience:

- If you tend to daydream negatively, instead of allowing your mind to pick your fantasies randomly, plant a seed by asking a positive question such as "What is my ideal scenario?" or "What is the best thing that could happen to me right now?"
- Your daydreams can help you observe how you see yourself in the world or help you pinpoint certain issues. Pay attention to recurring patterns that place you in the role of a martyr, a victim, or a transgressor. Watch for the hidden messages of repetitive daydreams.
- If you have a hard time daydreaming, try to look up at the sky or your ceiling, go for a walk, read a book (fiction is preferred here), or close your eyes and sit in silence.

Things that made me feel good today:

Things I noticed about myself:

Things I am grateful for:

Thoughts on the daily exercise:

Would you like to add anything else?

Day 125

Today, I...

> ***"The only thing better than singing is more singing."***
> ***- Ella Fitzgerald***

EXERCISE 125: *Sing Out Loud*

Singing has played a significant role in the evolution of people for thousands of years and remains a practice of communities worldwide, regardless of location, tradition, and spiritual beliefs. Whether you sing in your shower or on a stage, are in tune or think you are tone deaf, are an introvert or a boisterous extrovert (originally coined extravert by Carl Jung), singing is incredibly therapeutic and liberating.

The positive effects of singing are countless and include strengthening of the immune system, increased lung capacity, improved breathing, toning of facial muscles, stress reduction, social bonding, added confidence, and emotional well-being.

Today, let go of your preconceived notions regarding your voice or singing abilities (if you have any), and sing out loud any chance you get. Release your inhibitions and enjoy yourself. Take notice of how good you feel while you are singing your favorite tunes, and be conscious of how you feel mentally, emotionally, and physically afterwards.

Remember, this activity is supposed to make you happy, so no sad or depressing songs allowed.

Examples

- Join a choir.
- Take some singing lessons.
- Make a playlist of your favorite songs and sing along.
- Go to a concert and join in the singing.
- Do some vocal exercises.
- Go to a karaoke bar.
- Sing a cappella with some friends.
- Make up songs about anything.

What's your favorite song(s) to sing?

Things that made me feel good today:

Things I noticed about myself:

Things I am grateful for:

Thoughts on the daily exercise:

Would you like to add anything else?

Day 126

Today, I...

> ***"Hiking is the best workout!... You can hike for three hours and not even realize you're working out. And, hiking alone lets me have some time to myself."***
>
> ***- Jamie Luner***

EXERCISE 126: Urban Hiking

People often dream of traveling to faraway lands and jump on every opportunity to get out of the city they live in; meanwhile, it's not uncommon for the same people to live somewhere for years without ever taking the time to explore or visit the area. That said, even when a person has taken the time to visit and discover their city or town, there are still undiscovered locations and opportunities for great sightseeing.

A fun activity to rattle your routine is to go urban hiking. The premise behind this concept is to hike in the scenic and green areas of your city or smack dab in the midst of the concrete jungle. You can choose to plan your hike ahead of time and locate particular terrains, staircases, parks, or zones you want to undertake, or you can be daring and let the flow of your intuition lead you. Regardless of how you decide to proceed, this is a great way to appreciate your area in a completely different way.

Today, put on your tennis shoes, grab a bottle of water, and go urban hiking. You can choose to go alone or organize an expedition with friends. You can also decide to hike for a few hours or make it a day's adventure. The point here is to have fun, not exert yourself, so remain mindful of your body. Be curious, look at the environment with fresh eyes, and appreciate the beauty of your region. Remember to breathe and be conscious during this escapade.

Staying conscious of your surroundings is an important part of this activity for entertainment purposes, but it can also be valuable for your safety.

Helpful Tips: Here are a few safety measures to keep in mind:

- Be mindful of weather conditions and take necessary precautions.
- Stay hydrated.
- Avoid unsafe areas.
- Pay attention to traffic lights. Look left, right, and left again before crossing a street, and always use crosswalks when crossing.
- Take a small first-aid kit along with you.
- Avoid listening to music with earphones or headphones at a high volume in order to hear what's going on around you.

Where did you go? What did you discover?

Things that made me feel good today:

Things I noticed about myself:

Things I am grateful for:

Thoughts on the daily exercise:

Would you like to add anything else?

Day 127

Today, I...

> *"For me, it's the unexpected and surprising combinations of produce that are the most exciting and lure me into the kitchen for a little bit of experimenting. Apples and sweet potatoes together? Who knew? Carrots with grapes? Okay. I may not be Julia Child, but I can do pretty well with a simple recipe and a lot of enthusiasm."*
>
> ***- Marlo Thomas***

EXERCISE 127: Try a New Recipe

It is safe to say that in most households, when it comes to food choices, people tend to be creatures of habit. We all have a tendency to stick to a routine diet, generally throwing together the same dishes week after week or purchasing the same take-out foods. Often, there's good cause, between hectic schedules and obligations, there's not much time or energy left at the end of the day to come up with new meal plans or attempt new recipes. This is nothing that can't be fixed with a little prior planning and organization.

A lot of information can be found online regarding make-ahead meals and meal planning for any budget, any experience level, and any time constraint; it is worth investigating and researching. It is also worthwhile to consider the health advantages of eating home-cooked meals, as they usually are healthier than catered or readymade foods – the latter often being high in fats, sugars, and additives. Furthermore, expanding your gastronomic portfolio and eating new foods can significantly improve your health by enabling the absorption of new nutrients into your body. Finally, cooking can help you de-stress from your daily worries, increase your creativity, create amazing memories, and virtually open up a completely new world of tastes and flavors for you. So, contemplate adjusting or changing your perspective concerning what cooking means for you and what it means for your body.

Today, be adventurous and try a new recipe. Pull out a recipe you've been wanting to try, test a recipe saved in a Pinterest folder, or reach for a cookbook. Make sure to read the recipe all the way to the end, purchase and gather all the ingredients, prepare your mise en place[1], put on some music, and have a fantastic time. You can enjoy this activity alone or decide to involve family and friends. It's also a fantastic opportunity to include children in a fun and educational activity – most of all they will delight in spending quality time with you.

[1] *Mise en place (MEEZ ahn plahs) is a French term for having all your ingredients measured, cut, peeled, sliced, grated, etc. before you start cooking. Pans are prepared. Mixing bowls, tools and equipment set out. It is a technique chefs use to assemble meals quickly and effortlessly. http://food.unl.edu/use-mise-en-place-make-meal-preparation-easier*

Remember to create a plan B in case your recipe does not come out as expected. If it works out, great; if it does not work out, great! Whether your recipe is a success or not, just enjoy your culinary adventure! Bon appétit!

Helpful Tips: Here are a few ideas to motivate you in case you do not enjoy cooking or think of it as a chore:

- Choose a fun dish like DIY pizza, and have the entire family get involved.
- Make a dish for a loved one (e.g. your college kids or your grandparents).
- Make a dish, like a stew or soup, and distribute it in to-go cups with lids to homeless individuals.
- Have a cooking party, invite friends over, and have fun cooking together.
- Take a cooking class, and go learn a recipe or two – have fun and make it a date night.
- Do something easy like a smoothie, a sandwich, or a salad.

What recipe did you try? Did you enjoy it?

Things that made me feel good today:

Things I noticed about myself:

Things I am grateful for:

Thoughts on the daily exercise:

Would you like to add anything else?

Day 128

Today, I...

> *"You have been criticizing yourself for years, and it hasn't worked. Try approving of yourself and see what happens."*
> **- Louise L. Hay**

EXERCISE 128: Negative Self-Talk

What if I told you negative self-talk is just a bad habit that you can change? It feels like such a natural and innate occurrence that it can be hard to believe all inner criticism and judgments are actually just the outcome of a thinking disposition. A pattern of thinking you have practiced so many times and for so long that it has in fact become part of your programming – who you are.

The good news is that like any bad habit or negative programming, you can change it! To begin, you must observe your default settings – what you automatically or repeatedly say to yourself and say to others about yourself. If you doubt how powerful your self-talk can be, just pay attention to those inner and outer conversations, and notice how they affect you – you will be flabbergasted.

If you are in the habit of repeating to yourself and others that things are "hard," chances are, you confront a lot of hardships; if you talk to yourself and others about how "overweight" you are, chances are you are dealing with weight issues, unhealthy eating habits, or an eating disorder; if you talk about the news and how everything is "scary," you probably suffer from stress or anxiety. Stop filling your dialogues with "I can't," "I/they should," "I/they need to," "I/they never," 'I don't have," "If only," "I'll never," "I'm too... stupid/ugly/old/young/fat/skinny/poor/unlucky," etc. This kind of talk impacts you, the people around you, and your reality. Feeding your mind heaps of negativity never makes you feel good and never results in positive outcomes.

Today, catch your inner and outer negative self-talk and reverse it. Refuse to give in to self-sabotage, self-hatred, and self-destruction. Being loving toward yourself is all about celebrating yourself and being your own best friend. Jot down some of the patterns you notice in the tables (see following pages), and replace them with more positive suggestions that are empowering and believable for you – be mindful, creating statements that are too far outside your belief system will create adverse reactions. From this day forward, begin to include more positive self-talk into your days. Be more conscious of your (inner and outer) dialogues, and choose words that are aligned with your hopes, desires, and the dreams you have for yourself. Whether you believe this works or not does not matter; your mind is (always) listening, and your subconscious mind is (always) recording regardless of what you think. So, be kind, loving, and compassionate toward yourself because you deserve the best of everything.

Remember: your current programming took years of repetition – be patient with yourself. Instead of being unkind toward yourself with judgments and criticism, celebrate yourself for taking positive steps toward changing and upgrading your inner and outer dialogues. Also keep in mind that contrary to popular belief, putting yourself down in front of people is not funny, attractive or pleasing, nor does it make you humble or empathetic. You help no one and certainly not yourself by belittling yourself. So, stand up within yourself, and change your talk.

Helpful Tips: Here are a few ways you can choose to practice positive self-talk:

- Silently repeat positive and empowering statements, mantras, or affirmations.
- Write affirmations and positive statements.
- Write affirmations on post-it notes and tape them on your bathroom mirror – read them any chance you get.
- Repeat positive declarations or incantations (in your shower, while doing chores, at the top of a mountain, in front of a mirror, etc.).
- Share positive, uplifting, fun, and inspiring conversations with others.
- Record positive statements and listen to them several times a day.

I suggest completely eradicating negative words that are emotionally charged from your vocabulary such as "hate," "terrible," "worthless," etc.

Instead of...	**Try this...**
I have a bad memory.	My memory is so much better lately.
I can't change. It's just the way I am.	I am changing for the better! This is fun!
Nothing good ever happens to me.	The more I look for good, the easier things get.
All the good ones are taken. I'll end up alone.	I deserve the best. I deserve to be loved. I now attract the perfect one for me – someone funny, kind, and who loves me as much as I love them.
There are a lot of bad people in the world.	Wherever I go, I meet sweet and kind people.
I always get sick! I have a weak immune system.	Every day, in every way, I get better and better. I get stronger and stronger. My body is healthy. My cells are healthy, my bones are healthy, and my organs are healthy. My heart is healthy, my blood is healthy, and my whole being is healthy. I am grateful for the intelligence of my body, and I trust its power to heal itself.
I'm never going to amount to much.	Many started at the bottom and found a way up! I deserve the same! I am capable, I am committed, and I am now working toward my success.

Instead of...	Try this...

Instead of...	Try this...

Things that made me feel good today:

Things I noticed about myself:

Things I am grateful for:

Thoughts on the daily exercise:

Would you like to add anything else?

Day 129

Today, I...

> ***"Kindness in words creates confidence. Kindness in thinking creates profoundness. Kindness in giving creates love."***
> ***- Lao Tzu***

EXERCISE 129: Surprise a Stranger

It is always heartwarming to read stories or see videos of good Samaritans giving away gifts to strangers. Witnessing human goodness gives hope and generates positive feelings within each of us. Everyone is capable of carrying out acts of random kindness – you have most certainly done it a few times yourself around the holidays or during selfless moments.

Oftentimes, gift giving is primarily reserved for people whom we know or care about, and while it's fun and exciting to give gifts to those around us, there is an incredibly refreshing and uplifting feeling that comes with freely offering something to a complete stranger. Giving a gift to someone we do not know takes a degree of creativity, courage, generosity, and enthusiasm – it is exciting and a little scary because it asks us to step out of our conventional gift giving "traditions," but the rewards are all the more meaningful. Not only do you gain from putting effort and thought into making someone's day, but in turn you also get to surprise someone in the most delightful and unexpected way. Imagine the ripple effect that can result from taking such actions, from making someone feel special, from giving someone hope and joy. By being kind and generous, not only do you prove to yourself that goodness can change the world, but you also spark those same thoughts and feelings in others.

Today, surprise a stranger by giving them a gift. You can choose to offer your gift openly, or you can choose to remain anonymous and be discrete. Put heart in the giving and remember that your intention matters more than any reaction you may or may not receive. Having any expectations defeats the purpose, so focus on giving and nothing else. Be conscious and present during the process, and let your inner child and spirit rejoice in this caring act. Allow yourself to feel good and feel gratitude for the ability to make a difference. Write about your experience on the next page.

Please remember that some people might be wary of receiving gifts from strangers, therefore do not be pushy or insistent if someone refuses your gift. Be understanding, polite, and kind. Maybe try offering it to someone else. If you decide to give a gift to a child or pet, first make sure to discreetly ask their guardian(s) so as not to upset the potential receiver.

Examples

- Offer goodie bags or origami animals to passersby.
- Leave a pretty plant in front of an unacquainted neighbor's door.
- Pay for the order of the person behind you at a drive-through.
- Hand a gift card to a crossing guard or a nurse.
- Leave a book with a note on a seat at a train station.
- Leave some new toothbrushes and toothpaste in a public restroom.
- Leave a free bag of chips in a vending machine.
- Buy a few balls or some sidewalk chalk and leave them at a kid's park.
- Give a scarf, a hat, or your spare change jar to a homeless person.
- Give an umbrella to someone at a bus stop.
- Bake cookies and bring them to a fire station near you.
- Leave a nice "Thank you" card on the seat of your LYFT or UBER driver's car.

What did you do? What happened? How did you feel?

Things that made me feel good today:

Things I noticed about myself:

Things I am grateful for:

Thoughts on the daily exercise:

Would you like to add anything else?

Day 130

Today, I...

> *"Your problem is you're... too busy holding onto your unworthiness."*
> *- Ram Dass*

EXERCISE 130: List Your Qualities

Unless you enjoy a healthy degree of self-esteem, you may engage in self-condemnation and self-degradation. This can seem like an overstatement until you begin paying attention to the way you put yourself down – the amount of times in a day where you focus on your perceived flaws, where you speak about your shortcomings, rehash your so-called weaknesses, and replay past mistakes. You may even go as far as having the worst expectations for yourself – you expect to fail, to be rejected, to get hurt, to act foolishly, to be ridiculed, etc.

Unfortunately, this kind of mindset begins developing early on and is later reinforced through other people such as parents, teachers, authority figures, partners, bullies, etc. That said, presently, you are the one keeping it alive.

Continually programming your subconscious mind with negative messages results in beliefs and behaviors that match the negative messages. Negative programming will lead you to accept certain conditions and relationships that a positive and healthy mind would not find acceptable. What you feed your mind influences how you see yourself and has a direct impact on your personal standards. If you don't think much of yourself, you won't get much; if you are abusive with yourself, you might attract controlling and abusive relationships; if you have little faith in yourself and your potential, it will be impossible for you to succeed.

Cease thinking or saying things like "I'm clumsy," "I'm gross," "I'm a loser," "I'm too old," "I'm not as smart as my friends," or "I'm not funny like my brother." Be compassionate, gentle, forgiving, and loving toward yourself. By doing so, you will progressively change and upgrade your programming, which in turn will reshape your personal value system and your self-worth. The final outcome will be a complete transformation of yourself, your relationships, and your life.

Today, remind yourself of your worthiness and focus on positive traits by writing a list of qualities you have on the next pages. For this activity, you cannot ask anyone for help. You can choose to name positive character traits, strengths, skills, good habits, and physical attributes. It is important that you go into this exercise with a positive frame of mind, not a defeatist, skeptical, or exasperated attitude.

This task may be somewhat challenging depending on your level of self-esteem; be conscious of any resistance you feel, and simply remind yourself that feeling this way does not have to be a permanent situation. Be gentle, loving, and patient with yourself. If you cannot complete the entire list in one sitting, just walk around with a small notepad, and list some of your best qualities as they come to you. The more you acknowledge your strengths and abilities, the more you will see yourself in a loving and empowered way, and the kinder you are when communicating with yourself, the more you will blossom. Let go of your unworthiness and embrace your greatness!

My Qualities

Things that made me feel good today:

Things I noticed about myself:

Things I am grateful for:

Thoughts on the daily exercise:

Would you like to add anything else?

Day 131

Today, I...

> ***"Planning is bringing the future into the present so that you can do something about it now."***
> ***- Alan Lakein***

EXERCISE 131: Plan ahead

There are two schools of thought when it comes to planning: there are the dedicated planners who believe that success can only be obtained by creating judicious plans, and there are the more laid-back individuals who advocate letting things naturally unfold, by living in the moment and going with the flow of life. Both have merit. Whether you agree with one philosophy versus another or feel that maintaining a balance between both makes more sense to you, planning for some things can be helpful. It can be the difference between enjoying peace of mind or feeling emotionally distressed.

We all have demanding tasks or obligations we must take on, things we feel we ought to do, and unexpected situations we must deal with. Avoidance, not getting organized, or waiting last minute – often causes undue stress and anguish that can easily be averted by making certain arrangements. Planning can give you back some control, help you organize your time, and relieve you from pressure, worry, and anticipation.

Today, take the time to plan ahead. Think about something in your life that you do not usually plan for, or that you have avoided doing. Use the graphic on the next page to create a brief strategy for the next three to seven days. This can seem a bit tedious if you are new to this, so remember to be easy with yourself; it does not have to be perfect and it does not need to be complicated – a simple plan can work wonders. Finally, implement your plan as best as you can; remain open regarding possible changes, and keep track of how this system makes you feel. Does it help you relax? Is it helpful? Do you feel better? When you are done, come back and share your experience.

Examples

- Create a meal plan.
- Plan out your outfits.
- Create a workout plan.
- Plan a payment schedule for upcoming expenses.
- Plan out your study and homework schedule.
- Organize your to-do list.
- Pencil in your appointments.
- Plan your blog or social media posts.
- Plan your self-care activities.
- Plan your child's weekly homeschool schedule.
- Plan the steps you will need to take to de-clutter your house or office.
- Plan the steps you need to take in order to accomplish a project.

Day 1

Day 2

Day 3

Day 4

Day 5

Day 6

Day 7

What did you gain from planning ahead?

Things that made me feel good today:

Things I noticed about myself:

Things I am grateful for:

Thoughts on the daily exercise:

Would you like to add anything else?

Day 132

Today, I...

> ***"You can't be happy when you are complaining: Complaining amplifies problems, it doesn't diminish them. Complaining only increases being upset; it doesn't lessen it. If complaining made people feel better, then the biggest complainers would be the happiest people."***
>
> ***- Will Bowen***

EXERCISE 132: No Complaining

Does this sound familiar? There's toothpaste in the sink: complain. All the seats are taken on the subway: complain. Your boss gave you a last-minute assignment: complain. You are not losing weight as fast as you would like to: complain. Taxes are going to increase again this year: complain. The cashier gave you a look: complain. Your best friend cannot make it to your birthday: complain. And so on, and so forth. It seems like a long list, doesn't it? Complaining is remarkably prevalent and mainstream – an accepted behavior, a default response, a beloved distraction, and the focus of most conversations. The problem with complaining, is that while it may seem to help (e.g. ranting and venting may appear to relieve tension and stress), it does not solve your problems. Actually, it agitates you and negatively affects the people around you. Here are some (internal or external) drawbacks you can expect from repetitively complaining: adverse programming of your subconscious mind, feelings of powerlessness and frustration, depression or anxiety, lower self-esteem, less trust from people around you, and increasing isolation. On the other hand, cutting back on this bad habit or altogether eliminating it will help you in many ways. It will improve your outlook and your perspective, help resolve problems and concerns, and attract better relationships; you will gain trust from people around you, feel better about yourself, and feel more relaxed and peaceful.

Today, no complaining. Resist the urge to dwell on inner complaints or to voice mean, negative, offensive, and irritating comments and/or discussions. This will not be an easy process, and you will likely revert to your default behavior quite a bit. Do not be upset or self-critical; understand that growing out of your current patterns will take time. Try to remain conscious of your urges without giving in to them.

Please remember that there is a big difference between complaining, whining, and nagging versus stating facts or addressing issues in an effective and constructive way. Rambling on and spewing negativity serves no purpose, whereas being proactive, voicing certain concerns, or speaking sensibly about certain matters can help you resolve issues and find solutions.

Helpful Tips: Here are a few ideas to help you resist complaining:

- Whenever you have a complaint, write it down. Go over your list at the end of the day and evaluate whether they were useful or not.
- Instead of focusing on what bothers you, think of possible solutions to your problem, or take action to remedy the situation.
- Reframe your complaint to a more positive outlook (e.g. Instead of "I'm so tired of this traffic!" go with "Now I have time to listen to my audiobook!").
- Refocus – think a better thought, get involved in a mind consuming activity, move your body, do some breathing exercises, or become present.
- Look for things to be grateful for.
- Instead of talking or thinking about your complaints, put them on paper and dispose of it.
- Remind yourself of the consequences of complaining.
- Question your reasons for complaining (e.g. "Why am I complaining?" or "What triggered this complaint?"), the value of your complaint (e.g. "Will complaining help the current situation?" or "What am I trying to accomplish by complaining?"), look for the real cause of your complaints (e.g. "What is really bothering me?" or "What do I want that I am not getting?"), or ask yourself how you can improve the situation you are complaining about (e.g. "What can I do at this moment to improve the situation?" or "What would be a better use of my time?").
- Repeat a mantra or affirmation.
- Pray – the short version of the serenity prayer can be helpful. ("God grant me the serenity to accept the things I cannot change; courage to change the things I can, and wisdom to know the difference.").
- Stay away from chronic complainers and surround yourself with positive people.
- Redirect conversations in a more productive way. Talk about your latest project, the last good movie you saw or book you read, the success of a common friend, etc.

Things that made me feel good today:

Things I noticed about myself:

Things I am grateful for:

Thoughts on the daily exercise:

Would you like to add anything else?

Day 133

Today, I...

> ***"The Earth would die***
> ***If the sun stopped***
> ***kissing her."***
> ***- Hafiz***

EXERCISE 133: Step into the Sunshine

We all have been forewarned of the damaging effects of sun overexposure – from mild concerns, such as premature skin aging, to more serious ones, such as sunburns, skin rashes, or skin cancer. However, you may have also heard or been told by your physician that spending some time in the sun is a great way to absorb vitamin D (essential for the absorption of calcium and phosphorus). In fact, it is worth noting that there are many benefits to enjoying some sunlight. Sensible sun exposure can help prevent certain cancers, multiple sclerosis, depression symptoms, or SAD (Seasonal Affective Disorder). It can also heal some skin disorders, such as psoriasis, acne, and eczema. Moreover, it can increase your energy and stamina, lift your mood, and boost your immune system. In conclusion, it is important to be mindful and not carelessly spend too much time under the sun's rays, but it is just as vital to not completely avoid the sun. The sun is essential for our well-being; without it, all things and all beings on our planet would perish.

Today, step into the sunshine. For this exercise, choose the early morning rays as they are gentler – depending on where you live that could range anywhere from 7:00 AM to 10:00 AM. Enjoy a sunbath for 10 to 20 minutes; just keep in mind your habitual level of exposure and remember to be mindful of your skin's sensitivity. For instance, people who have fair skin and spend little time in the sun should probably begin with 5 to 8 minutes the first day and maybe progressively work their way up to 13 to 15 minutes. Be present and enjoy the warmth of the sun on your skin, but step away as soon as it becomes unpleasant or uncomfortable. For those of you who are having a cloudy, rainy, or snowy day, still do your best to step outside, or at least open a window for a few minutes; you will still gain a lot from getting a bit of fresh air.

People have mixed feelings about using sunblock or sunscreen, and as always you should conduct your own research and draw your own conclusions. However, for the purpose of this activity, consider not putting anything on your epidermis and allowing the sun to embrace your bare skin. In the event that you are unable to bypass wearing sunblock or sunscreen, or are unable to go in the sun because of a certain skin condition, allergy, or medication, please follow the guidelines of your healthcare provider and consider repeating a previous activity that you have enjoyed.

Helpful Tips: Here are a few ideas to enjoy your time in the sun:

- Practice sun salutation or yoga.
- Meditate or contemplate.
- Go for a jog or a walk.
- Lay down on the dirt or sand and soak up the rays.
- Visit your local farmers market or flea market.
- Do some gardening or yard work.
- Go skateboarding or rollerblading.
- Enjoy a breakfast picnic or have breakfast on the terrace of a café.
- Play with your children or furry babies.
- Wash your car or pressure wash your driveway.
- Go swimming or sailing.
- Practice tai chi or qigong.

How did you enjoy your time in the sun?

Things that made me feel good today:

Things I noticed about myself:

Things I am grateful for:

Thoughts on the daily exercise:

Would you like to add anything else?

Today, I...

> ***"Spending time with the ones who are dear to you is like being in a dream, is it not?"***
> ***- Sakura Tsukuba***

EXERCISE 134: Quality Time

With the busyness of life, it can be difficult to create time for the people you love or care about. Finding that extra time slot or mustering enough energy to spend quality time with loved ones, can be challenging, but it's essential for you and for them.

Here, quality time is defined as moments of time you come together with your loved one(s), to enjoy their company, strengthen your relationship, and give them your complete attention. Sometimes people get confused and think that quantity equals quality; however, seeing your loved ones or being in the same room without taking the time to communicate, share, get involved, and bond is not conducive to a real connection. For instance, this can be the case between parents and their children or long-married couples – they live together and spend a lot of time together, but sometimes know very little about one another, or are barely engaged in each other's worlds.

Having deep connections with your family, your friends, and even your pets is valuable for you and for them. It will diminish loneliness, lift your mood, improve your health, and prevent or ease symptoms of depression and anxiety. Best of all, it will help you deepen your relationships, create amazing memories, and enjoy feelings of gratitude, happiness, and fulfillment.

Today, spend some quality time with your loved one(s). This activity does not have to take long; nevertheless, it must be a meaningful and memorable moment. Choose to spend this time in a manner that is pleasing to everyone. Be present and mindful during this get-together, and make sure to connect emotionally with your favorite being(s).

Please remember to exclude reprimands, criticism, and unsolicited advice from your quality time. It is okay to encourage, share wisdom, and motivate, but do it mindfully and compassionately, so that quality time does not become an unpleasant and dreaded time. If things need to be addressed, do it during a more appropriate moment.

Examples

- Have family dinners and talk about your day.
- Enjoy a family reunion.
- Go to the restaurant with your friends and catch up.
- Play with your children or your pets.
- Read your kids a bedtime story.
- Do some volunteering with your teens.
- Make crafts or bake with loved ones.
- Visit your parents (or grandparents), or instead take them to the movies.
- Skype or Facetime with friends or family members who are far away.
- Make a snack for your kids when they come home from school and talk about their day.
- Go on a hike or a walk with loved ones.
- Go on an exciting scavenger hunt with family and friends.

Who did you spend quality time with and how did you enjoy each other?

Things that made me feel good today:

Things I noticed about myself:

Things I am grateful for:

Thoughts on the daily exercise:

Would you like to add anything else?

Today, I...

> ***"Until you make the unconscious conscious, it will direct your life and you will call it fate."***
> ***- Carl G. Jung***

EXERCISE 135: Bi-Weekly Report

It is time to pause and reflect on the past two weeks. Complete this exercise when you can have at least one hour of undisturbed time. Make yourself comfortable by creating a soothing ambiance: get a warm drink, put on some music, or light a candle. Take a few deep breaths, relax, and when you are ready, answer the following questions honestly and thoroughly.

1. Summarize the past two weeks in a sentence.

2. Looking back, what are you most proud of?

3. What are some inner blocks and fears you noticed?

4. What important lessons did you learn?

5. What brought you the most joy?

6. What surprised you the most?

7. How are you doing in terms of loving yourself?

8. How has your relationship with yourself evolved?

9. How has your relationship with others evolved?

10. How has your attitude toward life evolved?

11. What tools, practices, or teachers have helped you the most?

13. What were your favorite and least favorite exercises? Explain.

14. What are you most grateful for at the moment?

15. What are things you would like to improve on in the upcoming two weeks?

Would you like to add anything else?

Today, as the daily exercise, either repeat your favorite exercise of the past two weeks or do an activity that feels good to your soul.

What did you do?

Day 136

Today, I...

> ***"If you're good to your body, your body's good to you."***
> ***- Jermain Defoe***

EXERCISE 136: Legs Up

It's not uncommon for people to complain about achy legs at the end of the day. While some individuals feel slightly uncomfortable and tired, others are more seriously affected and experience symptoms such as pain, heaviness, and inflammation. Setting aside certain diseases and conditions, this can be the consequence of overexerting the muscles, sitting or standing for long periods of time, dehydration, heat, or wearing high heels all day.

A wonderful way to quickly relieve your lower limbs is to elevate them. Elevating your legs will alleviate muscle tension, relieve venous pressure, help blood flow more easily to the heart, drain build-up fluids, calm your nervous system, and help you relax.

There are different ways to practice elevating your legs. Depending on your comfort level, you can prop them with pillows so that they rest just above your hips, you can lift them above your heart with the help of a leg rest cushion, or you can choose to put them straight up a wall.

Today, find a moment at the end of the day to relax and put your legs up. To fully enjoy this activity, create a soothing ambiance, and if possible, do it when you will not be disturbed. Assume a position that is relaxing and pleasant – make sure to pay attention to how your body feels and be mindful to respond kindly to its needs. Relax and breathe consciously throughout the exercise. Keep your legs up for ten to 15 minutes, or until you no longer feel comfortable. When you are done, slowly and gently come out of your position.

Remember, if you are experiencing severe symptoms, such as acute leg pain, abnormal swelling or discoloration, do not dismiss them, and consult with a healthcare professional immediately as they may be the sign of a serious medical condition. If you have heart or blood pressure problems, please contact your physician before elevating your legs.

Helpful Tips: Here are other ways to care for your legs:

- Stay hydrated.
- Wear comfortable shoes.
- Do not walk or stand for extended periods on high heels.
- Eat a healthy diet with lots of fruits and veggies.
- Wear compression socks.
- Avoid wearing tight clothing.
- Self-massage with a foam roller.
- Get a professional massage.
- Exercise (water exercises are excellent).
- Limit your salt intake.

Things that made me feel good today:

Things I noticed about myself:

Things I am grateful for:

Thoughts on the daily exercise:

Would you like to add anything else?

Today, I...

> *"In every single thing you do, you are choosing a direction. Your life is a product of choices."*
> **- Dr. Kathleen Hall**

EXERCISE 137: Better Choices

Every day individuals make thousands of choices that shape their lives. To understand the power of choice is to understand that every choice you make creates your reality. If you spend any amount of time contemplating how your choices – from the seemingly insignificant to the more important – affect your life, you will be fascinated by the various possibilities each choice offers. Saying yes or no, turning left or right, deciding to eat a salad or a cheeseburger, screaming at your children or talking with them, speaking up or staying silent, expecting the best or expecting the worst, praising or criticizing – countless choices that continually write your story and impact the reality of others. Thus, it's astonishing to think that you incessantly allow your subconscious mind to make these choices for you.

Your choices must be made consciously and mindfully in order for you to grow into a greater version of yourself and live a life that is in accord with your dreams and desires.

Today, make better choices for yourself. This activity does not need to be complicated; all you have to do is make choices that are just a little bit better than the choices you would usually make. Envision, to the best of your ability, the different possibilities and eventualities each choice offers, and choose the alternative that promises results that are more positive. Of course, it will be challenging to notice every decision you make because there are thousands in a day; just do your best. The objective here is to remind you that your choices affect you and others. It's a way of empowering you to take control of your choice-making capabilities, and to assist you in becoming mindful of your ability to choose consciously. If you made choices daily that were just a little better than the day prior, you would reap incredible results – a new you, a new life, and a whole new reality.

Please remember, this is not an exercise designed for you to focus on how "bad" or "good" your choices are. It is an opportunity to become lucid of your choices and their impact; a process to grow into a deliberate decision-maker.

Examples

- Dress a little nicer than usual.
- Instead of eating cereal for breakfast, eat some oatmeal.
- Apply to more than one job.
- Don't text while talking with someone, instead give them your complete attention.
- Do one more set or one more rep at the gym.
- Ride your bike instead of driving your car.
- Instead of watching two hours of television, limit your screen time to one hour.
- Drink one more glass of water.
- Don't hit the snooze button, and get up as soon as your alarm rings.
- Instead of being reactive, take a couple of breaths before interacting with others.

Things that made me feel good today:

Things I noticed about myself:

Things I am grateful for:

Thoughts on the daily exercise:

Would you like to add anything else?

Day 138

Today, I...

> ***"Social media demands a lot of us on top of our already demanding lives. So, let's disconnect as we need to and renew our interest and ourselves."***
>
> ***- Simon Mainwaring***

EXERCISE 138: Social Media Break

Reading the title of this activity probably ignited different reactions in people. Some of you may welcome the idea, others may feel annoyed, and finally some almost certainly feel twinges of anxiety. Worldwide, people have become increasingly reliant on social media, and daily many spend hours upon hours jumping from one platform to another.

Social media is brilliant and offers wonderful advantages in terms of connections, partnerships, business, and job opportunities. It can also help people keep in touch, discover the world, learn new things, and expand their horizons. However, social media can also be the cause of some undesirable consequences. Like a drug, it can be addictive; it can become a time waster, incite stalking tendencies, provoke accidents, be a self-esteem crusher, a bully's playground, a trigger for violence or jealousy, and give birth to conditions such as anxiety and depression. For these reasons, it's important to distance yourself from social media every once in a while.

Taking a time-out from social media can shift your perspective, relieve stress, improve self-worth, deepen connections with family and friends, increase productivity, reduce exposure to negativity, and help you be present.

Today, take a social media break. As always, the activities in this book are all about making you feel good, so there are no time limits you need to respect. Ideally, you will choose to challenge yourself and stay away the entire day (or the entire week), but if all you can tolerate are a couple of hours, then do that. This will not be an easy process for some of you; you can counteract any withdrawals or negative side effects by planning activities to occupy your time during this short break. For instance, you could decide to wake up and read a book instead of jumping on your phone; you could choose to practice mindfulness throughout the day, spend time with a friend, focus on work, or do something fun and creative. As always, try to do things that make you feel good. Notice the way you feel during the entire day (with compassion, not judgment), and remain as conscious as possible. At the end of the day, journal your observations on the following page.

Social media getting the best of you? Feeling drained or envious of others? Worried of how you look, and of how many likes you will get on your next post? Be daring and take a mini vacation; enjoy a few days or a few weeks (completely) off social media. You will be amazed how good it feels and how much clarity and sanity you gain.

How did this experience feel? What did you do?

Things that made me feel good today:

Things I noticed about myself:

Things I am grateful for:

Thoughts on the daily exercise:

Would you like to add anything else?

Day 139

Today, I...

> *"I like to stretch myself and push the envelope, so anything that's new or different or not of my daily routine, I am so for."*
>
> ***- Merle Dandridge***

EXERCISE 139: Out of the Ordinary

Needless to say, everyone is more or less attached to a certain way of doing things – and while a routine can be helpful and comforting, stepping away from your habitual patterns can be instructive, fun, revealing, and exciting. If you always do the same things, or do things the same way, chances are you are going to grow weary, bored, stunted, and unhappy.

The status quo does not help you grow; on the contrary, it halts your personal development. It's not always easy to pull away from routines, but it also does not need to be complicated. Sometimes all that is needed to break out of a dull routine and bring excitement back into your days is to step out of your comfort zone by simply doing one stimulating, unfamiliar, or spontaneous thing after another.

Today, plan or organize something out of the ordinary. The key here is to completely step out of your habitual default patterns, and jump into an uncharted territory that appeals to you. To do that, begin by thinking about all the things you would usually do on a day like this one. Once you are done, improvise, change your routine, or do something that is exceptionally thrilling and different for you. Approach this activity with an adventurous and childlike spirit. With each new action or activity, consciously observe the thoughts and emotions that surface without criticism, and relish the new experiences. At the end of the day, share your experience on the following page.

Remember, it can be helpful to plan new experiences, until saying "yes" to new possibilities and spontaneity becomes more natural.

Examples

- Organize a food drive with family and friends.
- Invite your crush on a hike.
- Sign up for a marathon.
- Go on a road trip with your best friends.
- Organize a movie night with loved ones.
- Eat breakfast for dinner.
- Sign up for an art class.
- Invite your partner on a surprise date.
- Call a friend you haven't talked to in a long time.
- Introduce yourself to someone and make conversation.
- Stand in the street with a "Free Hugs" sign and give free hugs to strangers.
- Get your hair styled in a completely new way.
- Vlog in public.
- Go to a local event.
- Have a bonfire with loved ones.
- Volunteer at an animal shelter.

What did you do? How did it feel?

Things that made me feel good today:

Things I noticed about myself:

Things I am grateful for:

Thoughts on the daily exercise:

Would you like to add anything else?

Today, I...

> *"I hope I make people feel better. I hope I take people out of their situations a little bit and make them happier. That's really why I do what I do."*
> **- Ellen DeGeneres**

EXERCISE 140: A Reason to Smile

It's a beautiful thing to be given a reason to smile; it's a wonderful thing to be the reason someone smiles. Can you recall times when loved ones, acquaintances, or strangers have brightened your day, lifted your mood, and made you smile? As important as it is for you to smile, it's just as important that you walk through life uplifting other people and offering them reasons to feel enthusiastic.

Taking time to invest selflessly in the well-being and happiness of others can improve the quality of your day and completely transform the day of the receiver.

Today, spread love and give people a reason to smile. Begin by thinking of all the ways you can make people around you joyful, then brainstorm ways of making complete strangers happy. Once you have gathered your ideas, write them down on the following pages. Dedicate your day to this activity, and later record your results. Be conscious during the process, and notice how people react, behave, or connect with you once you have uplifted them. Along the way, appreciate and celebrate yourself for doing thoughtful acts of kindness, and enjoy yourself.

Remember, sometimes giving someone a reason to smile can completely change their day, their perspective, and their destiny. However, sometimes certain individuals can be dealing with personal issues and hurts that prevent them from opening up to any positivity, and insisting, being forceful or judgmental will only defeat the purpose of the exercise. Think about personal times of hardship; at times, we do not want to be uplifted. Do not let that distress or discourage you. Let it go and move on with a smile.

Examples

- Invite your coworker to lunch.
- Play a game with your child.
- Visit your elderly family member.
- Wear a t-shirt with a funny saying.
- Post a cute animal video.
- Share a funny joke.
- Make your dad his favorite dessert.
- Send someone a surprise gift.
- Hold the door open for someone.
- Let someone go ahead of you in line.
- Smile at people.
- Give a big hug to your best friend.
- Compliment the server.
- Send a sweet text to a loved one.
- Adopt an animal from a shelter or rescue group for your family.
- Give positive feedback to your employees.

Who?	Ideas	Results

Who?	Ideas	Results

Things that made me feel good today:

Things I noticed about myself:

Things I am grateful for:

Thoughts on the daily exercise:

Would you like to add anything else?

Today, I...

> ***"I love documentaries and I watch documentaries to no end."***
> ***- Michael Peña***

EXERCISE 141: Watch a Documentary

On average, people spend two to four hours a day watching traditional television or online television and videos. During this time, people usually watch fictitious films and shows that help them evade reality.

There is nothing wrong with occasionally wanting to escape the stresses of life by getting lost in some entertaining narratives. However, this could also be an opportunity to become educated and discover fascinating information through a compelling medium – documentaries.

Documentaries are nonfictional films that invite you to learn or expand your knowledge about a plethora of real topics, such as psychology, technology, social issues, health, arts, culture, spirituality, nature, sports, mystery, science, environmental issues, etc. Beyond the educational element, watching documentaries can also help you gain a greater understanding of the world, help you become aware of certain issues or solutions, spark your sense of adventure, inspire you to take action, or learn more about certain topics.

Finally, viewing documentaries with family and friends can be a great conversation starter or an opportunity to share different views and opinions.

Today, watch a documentary. You can choose to view a documentary you have been meaning to watch, begin an interesting docu-series, go to a screening at a theater near you, or look for a documentary based on a topic you are interested in exploring (e.g. Netflix, Amazon Prime Video, YouTube, or on a website such as http://watchdocumentaries.com). Do this activity on your own, or take the opportunity to invite family and friends to watch with you. Keep an open mind and enjoy learning something new and different.

Remember, documentaries are an entertaining way to broaden your worldly view and continue your schooling – whether you love the documentary you watch or not, there is always something to learn.

Helpful Tips: Here are some informative documentaries you might be interested in watching:

- Cosmos: A Spacetime Odyssey (https://www.nationalgeographic.com)
- A Brave Heart: The Lizzie Velasquez Story (http://imwithlizzie.com)
- Human (http://www.human-themovie.org)
- Embrace (https://bodyimagemovement.com)
- Happy (https://www.thehappymovie.com)
- Blackfish (http://www.blackfishmovie.com)
- He Named Me Malala (http://www.henamedmemalalamovie.com)
- Living on One Dollar (http://livingonone.org)
- Being Elmo (http://beingelmo.com)
- Minimalism (https://minimalismfilm.com)
- Samsara (https://www.barakasamsara.com)
- Man on Wire (www.manonwire.com)

Most of these documentaries are available on Netflix, Amazon, YouTube, Hulu, or Vudu.

What did you watch? Did you enjoy it? Explain

Things that made me feel good today:

Things I noticed about myself:

Things I am grateful for:

Thoughts on the daily exercise:

Would you like to add anything else?

Day 142

Today, I...

> *"I know of nothing else in medicine that can come close to what a plant-based diet can do. In theory, if everyone were to adopt this, I really believe we can cut health care costs by seventy to eighty percent. That's amazing. And it all comes from understanding nutrition, applying nutrition, and just watching the results."*
>
> **- T. Colin Campbell**

EXERCISE 142: Plant-Based

Nowadays, there is a growing body of evidence that supports that adopting a whole foods plant-based diet is healthier for people and for the environment.

Physicians and nutritionists agree that limiting or eliminating consumption of refined foods (sugar, oil, bleached flour, etc.) and processed foods (sugary drinks, fast food meals, breakfast cereals, potato chips, etc.) while eating a diet rich in vegetables, leafy greens, fruits, whole grains, legumes, nuts, and seeds is wonderful for anyone's health.

There is, however, a divergence of opinion among experts when it comes to meats, dairy products, and eggs – some suggest minimizing consumption of these products, while others suggest excluding them altogether.

There is a lot of controversy and emotional tension surrounding the anti-meat, dairy, and eggs movement, as it strikes a nerve, rattles core beliefs, and asks people to completely change their lifestyles.

Beyond the claims and the fears, these considerations and choices must be made individually through research, contemplation, and personal experience.

A balanced plant-based diet can offer remarkable health benefits, including fewer risks of developing heart disease, diabetes, and cancer. It can lower cholesterol levels, be anti-inflammatory, facilitate weight loss, improve skin health, and result in higher energy levels.

Today, eat whole foods (i.e. foods that are not processed) plant-based meals throughout the entire day. For the purpose of this activity, please abstain from consuming any animal products. Planning ahead of time will be helpful and ensure that you successfully accomplish this activity without stress or pressure. If you already eat a plant-based diet, try to eat foods you do not usually eat. Enjoy eating beautiful, vibrant, and colorful foods throughout the day. Take the time to appreciate each meal, and notice how you feel physically, emotionally, and mentally during and after.

Please remember, when it comes to your health and well-being, it is important that you take decisions based on your own research and experiences. Investigate different theories and opinions; consult professionals, and experiment until you find a way of life that is healthy for your body, mind, and spirit.

Helpful Tips: Here is some helpful information:

- Eat small portions of food throughout the day to prevent bloating.
- If you decide to transition to a plant-based diet, please do not shock your body and switch overnight. Make your research and consult with an understanding healthcare professional who can guide you through this process and recommend quality supplements such as vitamin B12.
- Do not worry about getting enough protein as plant-based protein options are abundant and rich in nutrients (ex: lentils, black beans, green peas, hemp seeds, chia seeds, quinoa, oatmeal, nutritional yeast, spirulina, broccoli, kale, collard greens, almonds, peanuts, etc.).
- Eating a whole foods plant-based diet can be more economical than other diets as long as you eat foods that are in season.
- Try to eat organic as much as possible.
- Do not blindly believe anyone's opinion about what and how you should eat. Educate yourself.

What did you eat? Did you enjoy it? Explain.

Breakfast	**Lunch**	**Dinner**	**Snacks**

Things that made me feel good today:

Things I noticed about myself:

Things I am grateful for:

Thoughts on the daily exercise:

Would you like to add anything else?

Today, I...

> *"Really big people are, above everything else, courteous, considerate and generous - not just to some people in some circumstances - but to everyone all the time."*
> *- Thomas J. Watson*

EXERCISE 143: Be Mindfully Courteous

Being absorbed by daily activities and thoughts, it's not unusual for people to behave robotically, indifferently, or impolitely.

Greeting individuals without listening to their answers, ignoring a person's request, staying on the phone when a person needs assistance, passing by people without acknowledgement, or bumping into people without an apology are all common behaviors. Regardless of whether this type of behavior is unintentional or not, the negative impact and consequences are the same.

We have all been on the receiving end of inconsiderate or rude people, and as a result we can empathize with how unpleasant, hurtful, or distressing it can be.

To live a balanced and happy life, it is essential to be kind, respectful, and polite toward others. Like you, most individuals appreciate being treated in a positive way.

Furthermore, treating people nicely is good for your three bodies (body, mind, and spirit) and has rippling benefits; it can make someone's day, bring you closer to people, expand your circle of friends, improve your reputation, open doors, result in opportunities and gifts, and boost your self-confidence.

Today, be mindfully courteous to people everywhere, including the people closest to you, especially children. Be aware of the world around you and be considerate in all your interactions. Even if you are well-mannered, this exercise may be a bit challenging; you must remain present and considerate, regardless of your mood, busyness, or circumstances. Do the best that you can with compassion and not self-criticism or judgment.

Remember, being courteous is partly for others but mostly for you, therefore, do not get upset if anyone chooses to ignore, stay indifferent, or be impolite when you attempt to be kind and gracious.

Examples

Greet people with "Hello," "Good morning," or "Good evening."	Be thoughtful and hold the door for others.
Express gratitude generously and say, "Thank You" (not thanks).	Offer your seat to the elderly, the ill, or pregnant women.
Be polite and say, "please."	Apologize when you are wrong.
Listen attentively while people are talking to you.	Offer sweet compliments to others.
Put down your phone when a customer needs your attention, or when someone is trying to have a conversation with you.	Smile any chance you get.
When someone offers you something, remember to say, "Yes, please," or "No, thank you."	Be mindful of respecting people's personal space – leave at least three to four feet between you and a person.
Do not interrupt.	Abstain from gossiping.
Be mindful to use your inside voice (whispers) when you are talking on the phone or speaking to people inside a structure, and also watch the volume of your voice when you are outside.	Be assertive if you need to be, but never yell at anyone, children included, unless it's an emergency.
Close doors without slamming them.	Do not eat people's food at work.
Abstain from any vulgarities.	Text back and reply to emails in a timely manner.
Abstain from biting your fingernails and picking your nose or your ears.	Wipe down equipment at the gym.
Politely call a waiter without whistling or snapping your fingers.	Never make derogatory or offensive comments.
Say "Excuse me?" when you need someone to repeat something and not "What?"	Praise, encourage, and congratulate people.
Say "Excuse me" when you need to walk past a person or when you bump into someone.	Call ahead of time if you are going to be late or apologize if you are.
Kindly say "Bless You" when someone sneezes.	Say "Goodbye" before you leave.

Things that made me feel good today:

Things I noticed about myself:

Things I am grateful for:

Thoughts on the daily exercise:

Would you like to add anything else?

Day 144

Today, I...

> ***"Procrastination is the bad habit of putting off until the day after tomorrow what should have been done the day before yesterday."***
>
> **- Napoleon Hill**

EXERCISE 144: Goodbye, Procrastination

Always doing things last minute? Often putting things off until tomorrow? No one likes to admit it, but quite frequently people choose to postpone things they ought to do for things that feel easy or comfortable.

Doing things that feel good is wonderful, however ignoring your to-do list or neglecting your responsibilities can result in stress, lack of productivity, broken trust, failed delivery, missed opportunities, self-sabotage, disappointment, pressure, etc.

There is a scientific explanation for this phenomenon: simply put, whenever you need to do an unpleasant endeavor or activity, two parts of your brain are at odds with each other, your prefrontal cortex and your limbic system. Your prefrontal cortex (the part of your brain responsible for thinking, decision-making, planning, etc.) needs your conscious attention to do any task; your limbic system (the part of the brain responsible for emotions, basic drives, memory, etc.) works automatically and spontaneously. Your limbic system is always seeking pleasure and will automatically resist anything that it perceives as being hurtful, undesirable, or a threat by triggering a multitude of suggestions that are more enjoyable or safe. Meanwhile, your prefrontal cortex takes longer to react and needs your conscious participation (unlike your limbic system) to bring any task to completion. As a result, more often than not your limbic system wins. For example, in your brain, it goes something like this: "I need to organize the garage. I don't feel like organizing the garage. Oh! What if I went on a hike? The garage can wait another week, it's not that bad! Yep, I'm going to enjoy the nice weather, go on a hike, and I'll get to the garage next weekend." Three hours later... "The garage is such a mess! I should have cleaned the garage! Why do I always do this? I'm so upset!"

Becoming aware of those patterns is a great way of stepping away from procrastination and becoming more of a doer. There are many techniques to help with overcoming procrastination, and I encourage you to do some research on the subject; however, for the purpose of this activity we will focus on a process which emphasizes eliminating a negative tendency by establishing a reward system.

Today, say goodbye to procrastination and do something you have been putting off. Make a short list of five significant things you have been postponing. Prioritize your list based on the level of importance instead of how you feel about it, and choose to accomplish the most pressing task – watch out for the resistance or the excuses that automatically surface. Before you begin, decide on a reward you will gift yourself after completing the task. Then, think of a few ways you can make the task at hand easier or more enjoyable (or simply focus on the task itself and not the feelings you have about the task). Finally, pull up your sleeves and get to work. Observe how your mind repeatedly complains and tries to convince you not to proceed with your endeavor; gently redirect your focus on thoughts that are encouraging or motivating, and keep your reward in mind. After you have reached your goal, reward yourself, feel proud, and rejoice without restraint. This is how you will retrain your brain to become more productive. At the end of the day, share your experience by answering the questions below.

Helpful Tips: Here are ideas to make tasks more enjoyable:

- Play some music and, if you can, dance.
- Think of how proud you will feel in the end or visualize the end result.
- Trick your brain and smile during the entire process.
- Have a healthy snack and a beverage next to you.
- Ask for help from family, friends, or colleagues.
- Work in a nicer environment like a terrace or a café.
- Work around motivated individuals.
- Practice positive self-talk and repeat affirmations.

What did you do? How did you reward yourself? How did it feel?

Things that made me feel good today:

Things I noticed about myself:

Things I am grateful for:

Thoughts on the daily exercise:

Would you like to add anything else?

Day 145

Today, I...

> *"To care for those who once cared for us is one of the highest honors."*
> *- Tia Walkers*

EXERCISE 145: Help an Elder

In various parts of the world, elders are seen and treated differently. While in some cultures the older generations are respected, regarded as wise, and cared for by the younger generations, in other cultures the aging population is neglected and disregarded. This negligence has become such an issue that in some countries, laws have been put into place to protect these older generations from abandonment.

Growing old is an amazing privilege, but unfortunately for many instead of being a happy and comfortable time, it can be a challenging one. Apart from (often) being the victims of ageism, becoming more fragile, and having to confront certain health issues, an alarmingly large percentage of the elderly community also suffers from isolation and loneliness.

It is important to remember that, life willing, one day we too will be seniors.

Older human beings are wells of wisdom; they have so much to teach and share, so much to offer and pass down to us – we just have to take the time to listen and care.

Today, be kindhearted and help an elder. There are many ways to step up and be kind toward the older generation, and you will be surprised to discover that you benefit just as much (if not more) from these interactions. You will learn new things, receive incredible advice, develop your patience and listening skills, make new friends, have a lot of fun, and finally, gain valuable wisdom, inspiration and perspective. You can plan an activity with someone you already know, volunteer, or be spontaneous and find other ways to be friendly to the older generation. Enjoy their companionship and have a good time! After your experience, journal your thoughts and feeling on the next page.

Examples

- Visit an older member of your family or an older friend.
- Teach a senior how to use a smartphone, computer, or tablet.
- Have a conversation with an older customer or neighbor.
- Join a volunteer program such as Meals on Wheels (https://www.mealsonwheelsamerica.org).
- Help a senior with their grocery bags.
- Make care packages and distribute them at a nursing home.
- Bring lunch to an elderly friend and enjoy the meal with them.
- Mow the lawn of an older neighbor.
- Teach an elder how to look out for scams.
- Go to bingo and converse with the older participants.
- Send a card to an elder you know or through a program such as Love for the Elderly (http://www.lovefortheelderly.org).
- Give a hug to an older adult.
- Play a fitness Wii game with a senior.
- Invite an elder to volunteer with you.
- Ask older individuals questions about "the good old days."

What did you do? What did you learn? How did it make you feel?

Things that made me feel good today:

Things I noticed about myself:

Things I am grateful for:

Thoughts on the daily exercise:

Would you like to add anything else?

Today, I...

> *"The world mirrors yourself back to you. If you love, nourish, and appreciate yourself internally it will show up in your external life. If you want more love, give more love to yourself. If you want acceptance, accept yourself."*
>
> **- Debbie Ford**

EXERCISE 146: Gratitude Letter

Everyone knows that gratitude is key to feeling good and attracting happy circumstances. Practicing gratitude regularly opens your heart and enables you to live a more serene and happy life. However, too often the focus of our gratitude is on beings, circumstances, and objects outside ourselves.

An important element of self-love involves recognizing your own worth and feeling appreciation for the whole of who you are: body, mind, and spirit.

Being thankful for who you are, regardless of imperfections, mistakes, and shortcomings, reminds you that you are a unique being, with amazing qualities, and limitless potential. It helps you acknowledge your accomplishments, your capacity to achieve greater things, and it helps you reconnect to your inner power.

Being able to appreciate yourself isn't always easy, but it's imperative if you are to love yourself completely.

Today, write a loving gratitude letter to yourself. Find a time during the day when you will not be disturbed, create a pleasant ambiance around you, and think of all the reasons you are grateful for YOU. Before you begin, close your eyes, take a few conscious breaths, and relax for a few minutes. Ask yourself "What do I appreciate about myself?" and see what comes through. If any negative thoughts surface, gently release them and refocus on feeling thankful for all that you are. When you are ready, write your letter in the space provided.

This exercise may feel uncomfortable for some of you. Many of us are taught that it's narcissistic and arrogant to feel good about ourselves. Nothing is further from the truth; without feeling grateful and loving toward yourself, you can never fully feel grateful or loving for anyone or anything else. Celebrate yourself!

Things that made me feel good today:

Things I noticed about myself:

Things I am grateful for:

Thoughts on the daily exercise:

Would you like to add anything else?

Today, I...

> *"As much as you can in your life, say yes."*
> *- Mary Carillo*

EXERCISE 147: Say Yes

It is quite normal for people to long for something more: a patch of greener grass, exciting experiences, exhilarating adventures, or simply a better story than the one they are living. However, often, it's not easy for people to get out of their comfort zone and open themselves to the opportunities that lay ahead of them. For one, routines are comfortable and secure; secondly, people allow their fears to hold them back from breaking through their so-called boxes. They dread the unknown, imagine all the possible dangers and worst-case scenarios, panic at the idea of failure or ridicule, and are imbued with insecurities. Too afraid to live life on their own terms, they substitute by living vicariously through others, such as movie characters, successful figures, role models, peers, mentors, or celebrities.

Life is constantly offering you opportunities, and you often deny yourself amazing experiences by simply saying "no." To live an incredible life filled with synchronicities and magic, you do not need to do something drastic like quitting your job and travelling the world – the adventure can start with you just saying "yes" to possibilities, people, opportunities, and the voice of your intuition.

Is there a chance that things won't work out or go as planned when you say yes? Of course. Every so often, you will not get the results you want or hope for; on the other hand, the more you step out of your comfort zone and the more you agree to dance with life, the more you will be amazed and the more you will experience miracles and magic. You will have more fun, meet more people, make greater connections, discover more places, learn new things, have unique and extraordinary experiences, create brilliant memories, become braver, develop self-confidence, but most of all, you will stop sitting on the sideline of your life and you will become an active participant.

Today, step away from your comfort zone and say "YES!" Be brave and have fun saying "yes" as much as you can. Be conscious of how you feel during this activity and realize how often your mind tries to stop you from enjoying new experiences. In the space provided, write a list of things you agreed to do during the day that you would have normally turned down. From this point forward, consider saying "yes" more often.

Remember, saying "yes" does not mean agreeing to do things that could be dangerous, illegal, harmful (to yourself or others), or terrifying (for you or others). This is also not about being someone's doormat. This activity is about agreeing to stretch yourself and experience life more fully. Always check in with your inner compass (your intuition), as it will always guide you toward your best life.

My 'Yes' List

Things that made me feel good today:

Things I noticed about myself:

Things I am grateful for:

Thoughts on the daily exercise:

Would you like to add anything else?

Day 148

Today, I...

> ***"The beauty of poetry is that the creation transcends the poet."***
> ***- Mahatma Gandhi***

EXERCISE 148: Blackout Poetry

Making time to connect with your inner artist and tapping into your creativity can offer an abundance of positive advantages. Whether you are a novice or an expert, regardless of your preferred art form (music, photography, calligraphy, painting, writing, sculpting, quilting, etc.), finding ways to express your creativity can facilitate a meditative state, relieve stress, uplift your mood, improve your self-esteem and confidence, alleviate pain, and even heal certain diseases.

Today, you will explore a charming art form called "Blackout Poetry." To complete this activity, you will need an existing text from an old book, a newspaper, or a printed document, a pencil, and a permanent marker (e.g. Sharpie). Before beginning, create an enjoyable atmosphere and make yourself comfortable. When you are ready, take your text, and create a poem by lightly circling or drawing boxes with a pencil around words or sentences that either stand out to you, inspire you, or resonate with you. Be present, allow your intuitive process to guide you, and have fun. Your poem can be long or short – just make sure it makes sense to you. Once you are happy with your creation, carefully trace over your pencil lines with the marker, and blackout the rest of the text taking care not to go over words you want to keep. In the end, you may end up with a poem that is completely different from the topic of the original text, you may be surprised by the underlying tone (humorous, optimistic, serious, sad, loving, etc.), or you may gain some personal insight. Take a moment to contemplate your final piece. Blackout poems can be incredibly revealing and thought-provoking. When you are done, either attach your original blackout poem in the space provided, paste a photo of your work, or write down your poem.

Helpful Tips: Here are different avenues of inspiration:

- Instead of only using a black marker you can choose to use colored markers and crayons or paint.
- Instead of blacking out the text, make a drawing around your circled words. Or draw a simple design or shape, and circle words within that drawing.
- Use a text aligned with the kind of poem you want to write. It may seem less spontaneous, but it can be easier to begin.
- Instead of using a single page, purchase a second-hand book or use an old book to create your own blackout poetry book.
- For some practice or fun, go to The New York Times (https://www.nytimes.com/interactive/2014/multimedia/blackout-poetry.html) to create an interactive blackout poem.
- Look up images for Blackout Poetry on Google, Pinterest, Tumblr, or Instagram.
- Look up the creations of Austin Kleon at Newspaper Blackout (http://newspaperblackout.com), or visit Tom Phillips' page (http://www.tomphillips.co.uk/humument/slideshow/1-50).

My Blackout Poem

Things that made me feel good today:

Things I noticed about myself:

Things I am grateful for:

Thoughts on the daily exercise:

Would you like to add anything else?

Day 149

Today, I...

> ***"A good, sympathetic review is always a wonderful surprise."***
> ***- Joyce Carol Oates***

EXERCISE 149: A Positive Review

There is no question that online reviews are as important for consumers as they are for professionals and businesses. Before hiring a professional, buying a product, or visiting a business, shoppers will often do their research, look at ratings, read reviews, and make a decision based on those reviews. On the other hand, professionals and businesses gain a lot of insight from consumers' feedback – it helps them assess how shoppers feel about their services or products and gives them the opportunity to make any necessary rectifications or improvements.

Unfortunately, reviews are not always dependable and do not always reflect actual quality or value – excluding the honest reviewer, a few factors come in to play. For one, unhappy buyers are (usually) more inclined to leave reviews than happy consumers; next, there are "professional" reviewers who are predisposed to leave biased feedback in exchange for payment or incentives, and finally, there are the false reviews put out by unethical professionals or businesses.

Nevertheless, people continue to count on online reviews and allow this feedback to influence their purchasing decisions. Considering these facts, it is clear that leaving genuine positive and negative reviews is important for you and others.

Today, focus on professionals, products, and businesses that you have enjoyed, and leave a positive review extolling their virtues. You can choose to leave one or more reviews as long as you take the time to write up a compelling account. Think of information or details that are important to you or appeal to you when you read online reviews. Sharing your experience is valuable to others – it is a nice way to assist your fellow consumers as well as your favorite professionals and businesses.

Examples

- Leave a positive review for a book or a game on Amazon.
- Leave a helpful review for your favorite physician or restaurant on Yelp.
- Leave a kind review for a business or contractor on Angie's List.
- Leave a useful review for a hotel or resort on TripAdvisor.

Things that made me feel good today:

Things I noticed about myself:

Things I am grateful for:

Thoughts on the daily exercise:

Would you like to add anything else?

Today, I...

> *"I am my own muse. I am the subject I know best. The subject I want to better."*
> ***- Frida Kahlo***

EXERCISE 150: *Bi-Weekly Report*

It is time to pause and reflect on the past two weeks. Complete this exercise when you can have at least one hour of undisturbed time. Make yourself comfortable by creating a soothing ambiance: get a warm drink, put on some music, or light a candle. Take a few deep breaths, relax, and when you are ready, answer the following questions honestly and thoroughly.

1. Summarize the past two weeks in a sentence.

2. Looking back, what are you most proud of?

3. What are some inner blocks and fears you noticed?

4. What important lessons did you learn?

5. What brought you the most joy?

6. What surprised you the most?

7. How are you doing in terms of loving yourself?

8. How has your relationship with yourself evolved?

9. How has your relationship with others evolved?

10. How has your attitude toward life evolved?

11. What tools, practices, or teachers have helped you the most?

13. What were your favorite and least favorite exercises? Explain.

14. What are you most grateful for at the moment?

15. What are things you would like to improve on in the upcoming two weeks?

Would you like to add anything else?

Today, as the daily exercise, either repeat your favorite exercise of the past two weeks or do an activity that feels good to your soul.

What did you do?

Today, I...

> ***"Saying no can be the ultimate self-care."***
> ***- Claudia Black***

EXERCISE 151: Say No

In exercise 147, you were encouraged to step out of your comfort zone and say "yes" more often. Now, we will explore the importance of saying "no."

It's undeniable that saying "yes" will open doors and invite amazing experiences into your life; however, honoring and preserving yourself by placing healthy boundaries and saying "no" is also essential to your well-being.

Too often, we feel compelled to agree to things we would prefer not to do, and we allow our decisions to be influenced by feelings of obligation, other people's agendas, potential repercussions, fear of missing out, guilt, and other worries. Having been raised to comply with authority figures and our ever-present desire to be accepted makes standing up for ourselves or confronting others – by denying, disagreeing, or rejecting them – uncomfortable. Nevertheless, feeling manipulated into saying "yes," or sticking your head in the sand (i.e. ignoring requests by avoiding to answer or commit) causes major stress and inner tension that result in negative feelings and emotions (e.g. embarrassment, anger, resentment, shame, sadness, hopelessness, guilt, unhappiness, etc.), unhealthy relationships, and physical conditions and illnesses.

Saying "no" can certainly be a bit difficult and awkward, but continually ignoring your own inner voice and desires will keep you from enjoying inner harmony and peace of mind. Becoming your authentic self and being true to you is the most loving and caring thing you can do for yourself.

Today, practice saying "no." Be conscious of any situation where you want to genuinely say "no," and do your best to honor that inner desire. This process will not be easy for many of you, and for that reason it's important to be gentle and compassionate toward yourself whenever you are unable to respond authentically. It is also vital that you celebrate and compliment yourself each time you say a real "yes" and a real "no." At the end of the day, write a list of things you refused to do that you would have ordinarily agreed to on the next page.

Remember, saying "no" does not mean neglecting or ignoring your responsibilities. It's about spending less time doing things that drain you, declining to hang out with people who are toxic, delegating tasks, refusing additional duties or activities you cannot handle, and asking for help – it's about being loving to yourself. Furthermore, it's not about being passive aggressive or rude. Choose a compassionate and kind approach, but never hesitate to contact authorities if you need assistance and always pay attention to your intuition and gut feeling.

Helpful Tips: Here are tips to help you become proficient at saying "no":

- Evaluate your standards and values. Decide what you will tolerate and accept, versus what you will not.
- Mentally rehearse different (possible) scenarios where you are saying no.
- Ask for time or give yourself time before giving permanent answers.
- Instead of "no," use an alternative (e.g. "This is not a great time," "I have other plans," "Maybe some other time," "Thank you, but unfortunately," etc.).
- Think about pleasing yourself instead of pleasing everyone else.
- Keep your "no" answers short and sweet. Do not ramble or give excuses.
- Be kind but be assertive.
- Scared of missing out? Remind yourself of the potential consequences.

My 'No' List

Things that made me feel good today:

Things I noticed about myself:

Things I am grateful for:

Thoughts on the daily exercise:

Would you like to add anything else?

Day 152

Today, I...

> ***"Everyone is influencing the people around them one way or another."***
> ***- Robin Sharma***

EXERCISE 152: The Quality of Your Presence

Every day we come face to face with individuals who affect us with their words, behaviors, moods, and energies. It's easy to focus on how a person impacts you – how they uplift you, inspire you, drain you, or break you.

Indeed, it is important to evaluate how people influence you, what effect they have on your life, and to take appropriate measures. But, what about you? What influence do you have on others? How do you behave? How do you talk to people? How do you dismiss or approach others? What does your energy say about you? Everything you feel and notice about people, they feel and notice about you.

While you cannot control how others behave and the kind of energy they emanate, you can be mindful of your personal impact on others. Paying attention to the quality of your presence around others, and working on yourself to achieve a personality and energy print you are proud of, is the only responsibility you have.

Today, be mindful of the quality of your presence. Do not attempt to be any different than your usual self, just make sure to observe yourself (as objectively as possible) within the context of your relationships and in situations where you come in contact with strangers. Notice your thoughts, feelings, emotions, behaviors, and actions. Finally, carefully watch how people respond to you – closely look at their body language and listen to the tone of their voice. Becoming aware of the effect you have on others will not be an easy process, and it may trigger certain defense mechanisms such as denial, or negative emotions such as guilt and shame. If you experience any unpleasantness, be forgiving and kind toward yourself. Remind yourself that the more aware you become and the more you learn about yourself, the more you can make empowering and transformative changes in your life. At the end of the day, journal about what you discovered on the following page.

Remember, it's better to be aware and willing than to be oblivious and incapable of making changes. As you become conscious of your influence and realize the vastness and value of your impact, you can choose to make improvements that benefit you and others.

What did you discover? How did you feel? What do you plan to do about it?

Things that made me feel good today:

Things I noticed about myself:

Things I am grateful for:

Thoughts on the daily exercise:

Would you like to add anything else?

Day 153

Today, I...

> ***"I love anything quiz related."***
> ***- Natasha Hamilton***

EXERCISE 153: Quiz it Out

Most days, hectic schedules and commitments do not leave much time for play. Yet, in order to live a more harmonious and balanced life, it is essential to make time for unstructured or even (unproductive) leisurely activities. Creating a space for fun gives you the opportunity to momentarily disengage and unwind from your daily hustle and bustle – this can be incredibly therapeutic as it helps you de-stress, slow down, and replenish your energy.

Among many options, a quick entertaining and amusing activity is taking online quizzes. Quizzes are a fun pastime that require no planning or brain matter and, although it is scientifically unfounded, they have a way of provoking some level of personal insights.

Today, take a break and quiz it out. Have fun finding out what kind of superhero, sandwich, or emoji you are. Go explore which career path is best suited for you, look into some "Who am I?" quizzes, and find out your personality type or IQ. Do not take it seriously; just enjoy yourself, have some giggles, and maybe even share your results with family and friends. This exercise, while being a little goofy, is a reminder that even when your schedule seems chockfull of to-dos, you can always find time for self-care and a bit of fun.

Helpful Tips: Here are some quiz providers you may enjoy:

- Buzzfeed (https://www.buzzfeed.com/quizzes)
- My Personality Test (https://my-personality-test.com)
- Human Metrics (http://www.humanmetrics.com)
- My Next Move (https://www.mynextmove.org)
- Zimbio (http://www.zimbio.com/quiz)
- Mensa (https://www.mensa.org/workout)
- Visual DNA (https://www.visualdna.com/quizzes)
- Playbuzz (http://www.playbuzz.com/Quizzes)
- Brainfall (http://brainfall.com)
- Spirit Animal (http://www.spiritanimal.info/spirit-animal-quiz)
- Truity (https://www.truity.com)
- A Real Me (https://www.arealme.com)

Things that made me feel good today:

Things I noticed about myself:

Things I am grateful for:

Thoughts on the daily exercise:

Would you like to add anything else?

Day 154

Today, I...

> ***"Start where you are. Use what you have. Do what you can."***
> ***- Arthur Ashe***

EXERCISE 154: Clean Up, Shape Up

Every day people prioritize their to-do lists and push aside activities that would significantly improve their lives. Among those neglected activities we often count exercise and cleaning. Two essential elements that directly impact our health and well-being but that are often ignored because of crammed schedules, lethargy, and fatigue.

It is imperative to remember that your home is your haven and that your body is the temple of your spirit – to be healthy physically, mentally, emotionally, and spiritually – both must be clean and cared for.

Keeping your body active and your home clean will raise your spirit, boost your sense of accomplishment, increase your level of fitness, relieve stress and anxiety, preserve peace of mind, and improve your overall health.

Today, clean up and shape up. Carry out two important tasks with one effort. Take on chores or a house project you have been neglecting, and enjoy a great workout in the process. Put on some music, ask family members and friends to join you, or simply practice being present and mindful. Push yourself if you want to turn this activity into a real workout – the higher the intensity, the greater the results! Remember, the more you enjoy this activity, the more likely you are to repeat it. So, have fun moving your body and take pleasure in beautifying your space.

Examples

- Do some yard work.
- Perform a complete house cleaning.
- Wash, wax, or clean your car.
- Move and rearrange your furniture.
- Build a deck, a tree house, or a garden tool shed.
- Clean out your closets, cupboards, and cabinets.
- Sweep, vacuum, or wax your floors.
- Paint your walls.
- Reorganize your garage, your attic, or your basement.
- Power wash your deck or the siding of your house.
- Clean all your appliances.
- Install a fountain, a swing table, or solar panels.
- Scrub all the showers, sinks, and bathtubs.
- Wash, iron, and fold your clothes.

What did you do? How did it feel?

Things that made me feel good today:

Things I noticed about myself:

Things I am grateful for:

Thoughts on the daily exercise:

Would you like to add anything else?

Day 155

Today, I...

> ***"You gotta have fun."***
> ***- Derek Jeter***

EXERCISE 155: Spontaneous Celebration

Celebrations hold a special place in people's lives. They are an opportunity to praise life, rejoice, have fun, share, laugh, and enjoy family and friends. Considered "special occasions," they are usually observed on specific holidays, birthdays, anniversaries, achievements, and other noteworthy dates.

Why is it that we need a calendar or a planner to decide if and when we can celebrate? Every new day deserves to be appreciated and commemorated.

Regardless of your circumstances or what you may think, you are lucky to be alive today, and that is reason enough to celebrate. Finding ways to honor each day will remind you to appreciate your blessings, value the important people in your life, acknowledge your experience, enjoy the present moment, and most importantly feel reverence for your life.

Today, enjoy a spontaneous celebration. You can either mark this day by being festive in your own unique way, or you can choose to get inspired by looking up today's holidays (links in examples below) and commemorating a theme of your choosing. Get in a celebratory mood and have fun marking this day in a way that is special to you. Invite loved ones over, dress up, have a party, play music, dance, eat cake, get a piñata, or wear beads and party hats – just have a blast! At the end of the day, make sure to journal your experience on the following page.

Remember, it's important to find simple ways to celebrate your life every day.

Helpful Tips: Here are different ideas to inspire you:

- Find "daily holidays" by going to websites such as Days of the Year (https://www.daysoftheyear.com/), Checkiday.com (https://www.checkiday.com/), or National Day Calendar (https://nationaldaycalendar.com/).
- Make some fun party snacks and bring them to work to celebrate your team.
- Let the kids choose dinner and dessert.
- Go dancing at your favorite club.
- Get a piñata, fill it up with goodies for children and/or adults, and have fun with your favorite people.
- Buy some plain shirts and decorate them.
- Have a picnic breakfast or dinner.
- Put together little treat bags and hand them to your friends.

How did you celebrate? Did you enjoy yourself? Explain.

Things that made me feel good today:

Things I noticed about myself:

Things I am grateful for:

Thoughts on the daily exercise:

Would you like to add anything else?

Day 156

Today, I...

> ***"Perhaps the most important thing we ever give each other is our attention."***
> ***- Rachel Naomi Remen***

EXERCISE 156: Put Your Phone Down

Nowadays it's not surprising to see couples holding up their phones at restaurants instead of enjoying a conversation, teenagers texting the people sitting next to them instead of chatting, parents too entranced by their phones to pay attention to their children, or pedestrians bumping into one another mesmerized by their smartphones. Although most people openly admit this kind of behavior is inappropriate, disrespectful, offensive, or hurtful, this has become our new "normal."

Human beings need to make meaningful connections in order to be happy, to be healthy, and to thrive. Continually putting up a wall between you and people keeps you from forming and establishing new connections, prevents you from bonding with loved ones, and can cause conflict or trouble in your relationships. We all seek to be seen and heard, and just as you enjoy having someone's undivided attention, you must realize that others enjoy receiving the same kindness. Giving your time to others without distractions can translate to them feeling acknowledged, appreciated, respected, or loved.

Today, put your phone down whenever you are in the presence of other people – exceptionally, if you must, take the important call or read the urgent email. Do your best to connect with others around you and have some pleasant conversations. Give people your full attention, carefully listen to them, and enjoy your different exchanges. Be present and conscious, observe the people you are talking with, appreciate them, and delight in creating or deepening relationships throughout the day.

Helpful Tips: Here are some conversation ideas that can help you:

- Don't know what to talk about? Head to Conversation Starters World (https://conversationstartersworld.com/) for some ideas.
- Give nice compliments to people everywhere.
- Ask people questions about themselves or their opinions about upcoming events.
- Exchange pleasantries with people wherever you go.
- Ask people about their profession and get curious.
- Ask your children about their day.
- Comment about the weather.
- Watch a documentary or film with friends and discuss it afterward.

Things that made me feel good today:

Things I noticed about myself:

Things I am grateful for:

Thoughts on the daily exercise:

Would you like to add anything else?

Today, I...

> *"You have to take care of yourself, your body, your mind, take care of your soul-be your own keeper."*
> *- Jennifer Lopez*

EXERCISE 157: Self-Care List

There are different perspectives and opinions about what self-care is and what it is not. I believe self-care encompasses all the habits, rituals, or activities that participate in your holistic well-being. Self-care begins with attending to your most basic health needs, such as eating properly, bathing daily and getting good rest, and extends to more abstract necessities, such as the need for laughter, having supportive relationships, and knowing how to self-soothe.

Caring for yourself allows you to recharge your personal battery – it helps you recover and replenish your energy. Neglecting yourself, on the other hand, is reckless because it jeopardizes your health, your happiness, and your peace of mind.

In order to care for yourself properly, it's wise to adopt healthy methods that will empower your three bodies (body, mind, and spirit), however I do recommend that you also include a few indulgences here and there.

The key to positive self-care is to become aware of the needs of your three bodies – to pay careful attention to your energy levels, what drains them, and what restores them. However, sometimes when restlessness, fatigue, and exhaustion set in, it's not easy to connect with yourself, understand core needs, and remember what options could assist.

Today, put together a helpful self-care list itemizing your favorite ways to care for yourself. Make sure to cover activities that answer to your physical, mental, emotional, and spiritual needs. If you have a challenging time coming up with ideas, close your eyes, take and few deep breaths, relax, and ask yourself "What makes me feel good?" – see what comes up. If you are still unable to complete the list, do not worry about it, just add to it as you discover new ways of caring for your being. Use your self-care list anytime you need some inspiration.

Examples

- Spend time with my favorite people.
- Drink plenty of water.
- Take a nap.
- Watch Christmas movies.
- Cuddle with my puppy.
- Have a good cry.
- Meditate or pray.
- Do some stretching exercises.

Self-Care List

Things that made me feel good today:

Things I noticed about myself:

Things I am grateful for:

Thoughts on the daily exercise:

Would you like to add anything else?

Day 158

Today, I...

> *"I keep all of my letters, postcards, and thank you notes. I'll keep them forever!"*
> *- Jane Levy*

EXERCISE 158: Send a Card or a Letter

In this digital age, where a phone, a laptop, and the internet are the most common means of communication, letter writing is becoming obsolete. Nowadays it's really easy to keep up with family and friends around the world and stay connected through social media. So, why bother writing?

Despite our ability to receive updates or send well-meaning wishes in an instant, everyone still enjoys receiving a handwritten card or letter. In a world where most exchanges happen instantaneously and effortlessly, sending mail to someone shows care and appreciation.

Today, think of someone you know who would really appreciate a card or a letter from you and send them one. Keep in mind that while everyone enjoys receiving mail, children and seniors truly relish finding a surprise in their mailboxes. Take your time to choose a lovely greeting card, a beautiful postcard, or some nice paper. If you feel inspired, decorate your gift with some drawings or a few stickers, write in different colored inks, or include a few pressed flowers or photographs. The objective of this activity is to brighten someone's day, warm their hearts, and let them know how much you care. When you are done, mail it, but do not tell the receiver anything. Have a bit of fun and keep it a surprise.

Helpful Tips: Here are some ideas that can inspire you:

- Send a funny singing card to a friend that needs a boost.
- Send a love letter to your partner.
- Send postcards to an older family member.
- Send a "Thank You" note to a teacher or mentor.
- Send a letter to your favorite author.
- Send pop-up cards to your nieces and nephews.
- Send a letter to a pen pal through a group such as Interpals (https://www.interpals.net/) or the PenPal World (www.penpalworld.com).
- Send an apology letter to someone you have hurt.
- Send a nice letter to your sponsored child.
- Send holiday greeting cards to family and friends.

Who did you write to?

Things that made me feel good today:

Things I noticed about myself:

Things I am grateful for:

Thoughts on the daily exercise:

Would you like to add anything else?

Day 159

Today, I...

> *"The beautiful thing about learning is nobody can take it away from you."*
> **- B. B. King**

EXERCISE 159: Life Hacks

Once upon a time, people depended on their parents, elders, teachers, and books for recommendations and knowledge that could make life easier. Nowadays, all this information (and more) is available online. Among all this data you can find brilliant tips, tricks, and advice, commonly called life hacks, which have been shared by people all over the world. Looking for a smart place to hide your money? Want to score higher on exams? Want to be more organized? Interested in learning how to waterproof your shoes? All these answers can be found at the tip of your fingers.

Today, think of areas of your life or specific issues you could use help with, and look for ten life hacks that can simplify your life. Have fun finding answers and enjoy exploring different ideas. When you are done jotting down your favorite solutions, consider sharing your findings with family and friends, or on your different social media accounts.

Helpful Tips: Here are some websites where you can find some ideas:

- 1000LifeHacks (1000lifehacks.com)
- HowStuffWorks (https://www.howstuffworks.com/)
- Lifehack (https://www.lifehack.org/)
- DumbLittleMan (https://www.dumblittleman.com/)
- Pinterest (https://www.pinterest.com/)
- YouTube (https://www.youtube.com/)

Life Hacks

Things that made me feel good today:

Things I noticed about myself:

Things I am grateful for:

Thoughts on the daily exercise:

Would you like to add anything else?

Day 160

Today, I...

> ***"Even as we get older, we get in these routines -and routines are nice and comfortable -but I think that it's important to live life to its fullest and try different things. Because you never know what you're going to learn. You might not like it, you might like it."***
>
> ***- Masi Oka***

EXERCISE 160: Let Someone Pick Your Meal

Aside from dietary restrictions, most people are very selective and particular about the foods they eat. They find comfort rotating between their preferred meal options and feel uneasy stepping away from their usual food choices. Even those who are more adventurous and open to trying new things prefer having some level of control over their food selections – they typically opt for dishes that still feel "safe."

Living life to the fullest means stepping out of your conventional ways, boldly exploring, and experiencing new things. There are so many great dishes to choose from, so many flavors to discover, and so many cultural foods to enjoy. Worst-case scenario you don't like something, and you turn it down, but best-case scenario you get to appreciate a fantastic meal.

Today, be brave and let someone pick all your meals for you, or, if that's too scary, give it a go for at least one of your meals. Make sure to inform the chooser of your dietary preferences or restrictions if they are not already accustomed to your diet. Finally, let the person know about the foods you personally dislike and any other information that can help them, such as price limits or time constraints. Have fun with this activity and be proud of yourself for being so bold and daring. If the meal is tasty, be mindful, enjoy the experience, and savor each bite. If it isn't, pat yourself on the back for being adventurous and trying something different. Either way, moving forward, choose to expand your culinary palate, and try new foods whenever the opportunity presents itself. At the end of the day, share your experience on the following page.

Examples

- Ask a waiter to suggest a meal from the menu.
- Have a nutritionist create a meal plan for you.
- Let a friend choose the restaurant and the meal.
- Take your kids to the store and have them pick all the daily meals.
- Ask someone at work to recommend a good restaurant and menu item.
- Ask connections on social media to share their favorite recipes and try one.
- Ask a food truck vendor to sell you their most popular dish.
- Ask your partner to prepare their favorite childhood meal for you.

Meals	Who Helped?	Opinions

Did you enjoy this experience? Explain.

Things that made me feel good today:

Things I noticed about myself:

Things I am grateful for:

Thoughts on the daily exercise:

Would you like to add anything else?

Today, I...

> ***"That's the way I do things when I want to celebrate, I always plant a tree."***
> ***- Wangari Maathai***

EXERCISE 161: *Remember the Trees and the Plants*

You breathe in oxygen; you breathe out carbon dioxide. The plants and trees breathe in carbon dioxide; they breathe out oxygen. Such a symbiotic relationship.

That said, we depend on trees and plants for much more than the air that we breathe – we rely on them for food, shelter, health, protection, preservation, and for purifying our air. Unfortunately, with the growing deforestation worldwide, we are now confronting a global environmental crisis. Loss of animal habitat, loss of biodiversity, species endangerment and extinction, climate change, surge in greenhouse gases, increased flood and fire hazards, and geological changes are some of the alarming and growing issues that the world is now confronting because of the massive removal of trees and plants.

There are many ways that you can get involved to help counteract this disaster, but one of the best ways to give back to Gaia is to plant or grow trees and plants.

Today, remember the value of trees and plants, and decide to lend a hand by either planting a seed, buying and caring for a plant, or donating to an organization that is involved in reforestation or conservation. Stretch yourself to do something meaningful for the plant world. Take time to notice and appreciate the vegetation around you, hug a tree or two if you feel compelled to, and feel gratitude for Mother Nature and our beautiful planet. At the end of the day, share your experience on the following page.

Helpful Tips:Here are a few ideas to inspire you:

- Instead of throwing away the seeds and pits of the fruit and veggies you eat today, plant them in your yard, urban gardens, forests, or in containers that you can then offer for free on a space like Craigslist (https://www.craigslist.org/).
- Buy a mini greenhouse and plant different varieties of plants.
- Buy a seedling or young tree, and plant it in your yard.
- Purchase a house plant, a cactus, or a succulent, and care for it.
- Donate to an organization such as Arbor Day Foundation (https://www.arborday.org/), Haiti Reforestation Partnership (haitireforest.org), or One Tree Planted (https://onetreeplanted.org/).
- Join a community garden and grow some fruits and veggies.
- Grow an herb garden for family, friends, and neighbors.
- Purchase (Non-GMO, heirloom, and organic) seed kits and donate them to individuals who have edible gardens or organizations who help their community through urban agriculture.
- Help save lives and plant gardens around the world by donating to organizations such as Seed Programs International (https://seedprograms.org/), Hope Seeds (hopeseeds.org), or Charity Seeds (https://charityseeds.org/).

What did you do? How did it make you feel?

Things that made me feel good today:

Things I noticed about myself:

Things I am grateful for:

Thoughts on the daily exercise:

Would you like to add anything else?

Day 162

Today, I...

> ***"It's a helluva start, being able to recognize what makes you happy."***
> ***- Lucille Ball***

EXERCISE 162: A Few Favorite Things

People often choose to focus on things they dislike or things that bring them down. Yet, taking the time to refocus on more positive aspects (i.e. all the beings and things that you love and enjoy) can help cultivate an attitude of gratitude and develop a more optimistic outlook.

Today, take a moment to list a few of your favorite things by filling in the blanks on the following pages. This is just a beginning; I encourage you to add as many favorites as you want to this list and to add to it anytime you discover a new favorite. With time, this list will change and evolve as you do, but it will always be a great source of joy and inspiration. Choose to answer these prompts on your own or invite family and friends to help you – they could even join in the fun and create their own list. If at any time you draw a blank and cannot think of an answer, skip to the next prompt and come back to it when you have one.

Helpful Tip: Create a scrapbook (hardcopy or virtual) dedicated to all your favorite things. Decorate it with photos, illustrations, images, stickers, and mementos. Place labels with titles and dates. Write up short summaries or reviews. This will become a special keepsake capable of making you smile in good times and more trying times.

My Favorite Things

Favorite person as a child:

Favorite game/toy as a child:

Favorite childhood memory:

Favorite movie of all time:

Favorite subject in school:

Favorite TV show of all time:

Favorite memory ever:

Favorite documentary of all time:

Favorite affirmation or quote:

Favorite book of all time:

Favorite song of all time:

Favorite cartoon character:

Favorite artist of all time:

Favorite superhero:

Favorite villain:

Favorite boss you have ever had:

Favorite role model/inspirational figure:

Favorite pet you have ever had:

Favorite quality about yourself:

Favorite animal:

Favorite quirky habit:

Favorite breakfast:

Favorite part of your body:

Favorite nickname:

Favorite pet name (ex: sweetheart, pookie, etc.):

Favorite compliment ever:

Favorite self-care ritual:

Favorite accomplishment:

Favorite pastime:

Favorite form of exercise:

Favorite sport:

Favorite job you have ever had:

Favorite season:

Favorite lunch:

Favorite dinner:

Favorite beverage:

Favorite number:

Favorite color:

Favorite scent:

Favorite sound:

Favorite place/location:

Favorite mode of transportation:

Favorite type of weather:

Favorite social media website:

Favorite holiday:

Favorite gift you have ever received:

Favorite store:

Favorite website:

Favorite app:

Favorite charity:

Favorite activist:

Favorite quality in others:

Things that made me feel good today:

Things I noticed about myself:

Things I am grateful for:

Thoughts on the daily exercise:

Would you like to add anything else?

Today, I...

> *"Every morning, my dad would have me looking in the mirror and repeat, 'Today is going to be a great day; I can, and I will."*
>
> *- Gina Rodriguez*

EXERCISE 163: Mirror Pep Talk

"You are amazing! You've got this! You are capable, intelligent, talented, and powerful! You can do anything! You are great, and every day you get better and better! Focus! Commit! Stay strong and keep moving forward! I love you! I believe in you! I am here for you! I've got your back! Now, get out there and seize the day!"

From time to time, it's lovely to be on the receiving end of an uplifting pep talk. Feeling that someone supports you and believes in you can be encouraging and life-changing. However, you do not need to depend on family members, friends, or mentors to provide motivation or inspiration. What if I told you that you can easily get similar results by holding positive self-talk sessions with yourself?

Standing in front of a mirror and talking to your reflection with the same passion and enthusiasm that you would put in a talk aimed at helping someone you love or care about will help you think more positively, improve your behavior patterns, build self-confidence, and gain determination. With regular practice, you will improve your posture, refine your speech and syntax, and organize your thoughts more easily. More importantly, this practice will help you cultivate a kinder relationship with yourself, while also teaching you how to become self-reliant and self-trusting.

Today, take some time to have a mirror pep talk with yourself. Do this exercise in the morning before you begin your day. Think about what you most need encouragement with at this very moment and what you would really love to hear. When you are ready, allow yourself to freely dive into this personal conversation – speak passionately, use your body powerfully, and look into the eyes of your reflection. If you are worried people will hear you, put on some music and talk more quietly. When you are done, take a moment to smile at yourself, and appreciate yourself. Doing this exercise once will raise positive feelings, but practicing this method daily will result in amazing inner and outer changes.

Remember, this activity may feel awkward at first, but with time it will become enjoyable.

Things that made me feel good today:

Things I noticed about myself:

Things I am grateful for:

Thoughts on the daily exercise:

Would you like to add anything else?

Today, I...

> ***"Drink warm water with lemon first thing in the morning. It's a good way to detox and alkalize your body."***
>
> ***- Valentina Zelyaeva***

EXERCISE 164: Lemon Water

Lemon water is often recommended by alternative healthcare professionals, health enthusiasts, and beauty experts. Drinking freshly squeezed lemon juice in some lukewarm water first thing in the morning is wonderful for your body.

By themselves, these two ingredients offer their fair share of benefits – together they rehydrate your body, boost your immune system, promote diuresis, rejuvenate your skin, and help with digestion and detoxification.

Today, drink a glass of lemon water during the day (preferably first thing in the morning). Squeeze the juice of a lemon wedge in a glass and dilute it with 10 to 12 ounces of lukewarm water. Be mindful to drink your lemon water slowly; with each sip enjoy the freshness, the smell, and the flavor of your drink. Pay attention to how your taste buds react and how your body feels during the process. To witness real changes, you must continue the daily practice for a couple of weeks.

Remember, lemons are acidic; drinking too much lemon water can cause tooth erosion. Limit your consumption to one or two glasses per day, drink with a straw to bypass your teeth, and rinse your mouth thoroughly with clean water after drinking your lemon water.

If you do not like or have lemons, feel free to use limes instead. They may look slightly different – lemons are yellow and bigger in size, while limes are green and smaller – however, they have similar nutritional benefits.

Helpful Tips: Here are a few tips to help you make a good lemon water:

- Use organic lemons, if possible.
- Do not use bottled lemon juice.
- To make juicing easier, roll lemon on a counter under the palm of your hand with a little pressure.
- Use filtered water.
- Do not use sweeteners.
- Use a wedge or half a lemon per serving depending on your taste preference.
- Get creative and add other fruits, veggies, roots, and herbs to your lemon water (e.g. ginger, cucumber, mint, strawberries, basil, turmeric, etc.).
- Drink at least half an hour before eating your meals.

Things that made me feel good today:

Things I noticed about myself:

Things I am grateful for:

Thoughts on the daily exercise:

Would you like to add anything else?

Today, I...

> *"Without reflection, we go blindly on our way, creating more unintended consequences, and failing to achieve anything useful."*
> *- Margaret J. Wheatley*

EXERCISE 165: Bi-Weekly Report

It is time to pause and reflect on the past two weeks. Complete this exercise when you can have at least one hour of undisturbed time. Make yourself comfortable by creating a soothing ambiance: get a warm drink, put on some music, or light a candle. Take a few deep breaths, relax, and when you are ready, answer the following questions honestly and thoroughly.

1. Summarize the past two weeks in a sentence.

2. Looking back, what are you most proud of?

3. What are some inner blocks and fears you noticed?

4. What important lessons did you learn?

5. What brought you the most joy?

6. What surprised you the most?

7. How are you doing in terms of loving yourself?

8. How has your relationship with yourself evolved?

9. How has your relationship with others evolved?

10. How has your attitude toward life evolved?

11. What tools, practices, or teachers have helped you the most?

13. What were your favorite and least favorite exercises? Explain.

14. What are you most grateful for at the moment?

15. What are things you would like to improve on in the upcoming two weeks?

Would you like to add anything else?

Today, as the daily exercise, either repeat your favorite exercise of the past two weeks or do an activity that feels good to your soul.

What did you do?

Day 166

Today, I...

> ***"Excuse me while I kiss the sky."***
> ***- Jimi Hendrix***

EXERCISE 166: Look Up

Whether it's delighting in a sunrise or a sunset, cloud watching, or stargazing, looking up at the sky has fascinated and inspired human beings for thousands of years. Sadly, nowadays, people are often looking down, forgetting to appreciate the sky in all its splendor and mysteries.

By simply raising your head skyward and getting lost in the vastness, you are likely to witness mesmerizing spectacles. Rain or shine, day or night, the sheer beauty of the heavens can offer new insights and generate incredible emotions and feelings (e.g. peace and gratitude, a sense of awe, hope, etc.).

Today, slow down and look up. Take the time to enjoy and appreciate the immensity of the sky. Open your mind to bigger questions and marvel at the exquisiteness. Let emotions and feelings blossom within you, and delight in them. Be present, relax, and allow sentiments of peace and expansiveness to fill your heart and spirit. Share your experience on the space provided.

Remember, for your safety and the welfare of others, be mindful to look up at appropriate moments and in suitable locations. During daylight hours make sure to protect your eyes with a good pair of sunglasses.

Examples

- Enjoy watching the moon.
- Sit quietly and enjoy a blue or gray sky.
- Delight in observing a beautiful rainbow.
- Wake up before the first light and go watch a glorious sunrise.
- Try to recognize the cloud types (e.g.: cumulus, stratus, cirrus, nimbus, etc.).
- Have fun and spot shapes in the clouds.
- Revel in the movement of the clouds.
- On a clear night, try to recognize the constellations.
- Take your telescope out and enjoy watching the stars.
- Try to catch as many shooting stars as possible.
- Visit an observatory with family and friends.
- Gather your closest friends and go enjoy a sunset.

What did you do? Did you enjoy it? Explain.

Things that made me feel good today:

Things I noticed about myself:

Things I am grateful for:

Thoughts on the daily exercise:

Would you like to add anything else?

Today, I...

> ***"Not only do I think being nice and kind is easy but being kind, in my opinion, is important."***
> ***- Dwayne Johnson***

EXERCISE 167: Nice Comments

It's unfortunate that in today's world, trolling and cyberbullying have become common place. People who spew negativity and behave in horrifying ways are all over the internet. Ranging from passive aggressive to dangerously violent, most people will admit being on the receiving end of negative or inflammatory comments at one time or another. In the best cases, the damage amounts to hurt feelings, but in the worst cases it's resulted in suicide. Although there is increased public awareness, regrettably, aside from the blocking and reporting options, not much is being done to improve this growing problem – for this reason, positive feedback and positive interactions are more important than ever.

Being nice and kind to people makes a real difference for you and for them. Saying sweet things, being encouraging or supportive, and having pleasant exchanges or conversations are significant to developing positive relationships in both the physical and the cyber worlds. If we want a more loving and peaceful world, it is up to you and me. We must take steps to make a positive difference whenever possible, and we must turn the negatives into positives whenever an opportunity presents itself.

Today, be benevolent, and leave nice comments on blogs and social media platforms. Think of ways you can make the recipients smile but also of how you can positively influence other people reading your comments. Do not avoid the comment section and do not be shy; just show some kindness and share some cyber love. Don't know what to say? Try not to give generic answers; think of the comments you appreciate receiving and let that inspire you. Be mindful during this activity; purposefully create high energy messages and enjoy commenting in a meaningful way. At the end of the day, share your experience on the following page.

Remember, this activity is not about confronting naysayers, trolls, or bullies; it's about shining your own individual light by writing uplifting comments.

Examples

- Post a welcome comment.
- Explain why you enjoyed a particular video.
- Comment on the lovely details of a photo.
- Show support toward someone.
- Tag your friends inviting them to follow the account.
- Express gratitude for a blog post, podcast, or video.

What did you do? How did it make you feel? Explain.

Things that made me feel good today:

Things I noticed about myself:

Things I am grateful for:

Thoughts on the daily exercise:

Would you like to add anything else?

Today, I...

> *"Today is life-the only life you are sure of. Make the most of today. Get interested in something. Shake yourself awake. Develop a hobby. Let the winds of enthusiasm sweep through you. Live today with gusto."*
>
> **- Dale Carnegie**

EXERCISE 168: A New Hobby

Do you regularly take time to enjoy a special hobby? Do you even have a hobby? If you are like most people, the answer to both questions is no. People often avoid partaking in fun activities because they don't feel that they have the time to indulge in such "extravagances," or they feel that pursuing leisure is irresponsible, childish, and unproductive.

Making space in your life for activities that you enjoy is one of the essential pillars of having a balanced lifestyle. The quality of your life is only as good as you allow it to be, and by neglecting your inner needs for relaxation and leisurely pleasures you cannot blossom. This can negatively affect your inner well-being and create stress, anger, anxiety, moodiness, and fatigue. Listening to your inner child's need to play can be immensely fulfilling, exciting, and soothing.

Taking time off to explore and pursue your passions is always a good idea, and will often result in unexpected, positive outcomes. Here are some of the advantages you can expect to gain from enjoying a hobby: improved physical, mental, emotional, and spiritual health, new relationships, deeper bonds, career opportunities, and improved talents and skills.

Today, regardless of whether you already have a hobby or not, take up a new hobby. Think about something you would really like to do that can fit in your life and your present schedule. You may come up with something related to health, home life, career, goals, or just a whimsical desire. Have a fun time exploring different possibilities, weigh the pros and cons, and dive into a new experience. On the next page, write about the hobby you have decided to adopt.

Helpful Tips: Here are a few ideas to successfully keep up with your new hobby:

- Plan ahead each week for this activity (i.e. mark it in your calendar or planner).
- Create time by canceling activities such as watching television, surfing the internet, or wandering on social media.
- Join a group or create a group in the field of your interest.
- Learn from the pros or people who have more experience.
- Try several hobbies until you find the perfect fit for you.
- Have patience; learning something new takes time.

Examples

- Genealogy
- Golfing
- Making YouTube videos
- Urban exploration
- Rock Painting
- Archery
- Filming
- Origami
- Building dioramas
- Upcycling
- Travelling
- Meditation
- Photography
- Snorkeling
- Crocheting
- Drawing Zentangles
- Creating Fairy gardens
- Rock climbing
- Going to garage sales
- Creating terrariums

What hobby did you choose? Why did you choose this particular hobby?

Things that made me feel good today:

Things I noticed about myself:

Things I am grateful for:

Thoughts on the daily exercise:

Would you like to add anything else?

Day 169

Today, I...

> ***"If you're happy, if you're feeling good, then nothing else matters."***
> ***- Robin Wright***

EXERCISE 169: Comfy Day

Day in and day out, many of us deal with increasing amounts of pressure due to some recurring stressors such as overscheduling, expectations from others, worries or concerns, responsibilities, and exhaustion. This can take a toll on someone's mental, emotional, and physical well-being.

To counteract the effects of stress, it's important to take time to do things that rejuvenate the mind, body, and spirit. Slowing down the pace, doing things that feel good, and taking time to focus on the wants, the needs, and the yearnings of your authentic self are all important steps to replenish and balance your whole being.

Today, disconnect from the hustle and bustle, prioritize your well-being, and have a comfy day. Take time to do all the things that make you feel warm and cozy inside. Every individual has a different concept of comfort; therefore, you will have to think of the things that generate feelings of relaxation, pleasantness, and contentment within you. To help, fill in the list in the space provided, recording all the things that warm your heart, soothe your soul, and relax your body. Allow yourself the space and freedom to be, without stress, guilt, or negative judgments. Let feeling good be your guide throughout the day, and take the opportunity to check some things off your "comfy list."

Examples

- Wear jammies all day.
- Eat comfort foods.
- Snuggle with my children.
- Pet my fur babies.
- Watch heartwarming movies or documentaries.
- Take a long nap.
- Wear comfortable clothes.
- Wrap myself in a warm blanket.
- Do some yoga.
- Read a good book.
- Drink a cup of something warm and delightful.
- Take walks with my sweetheart.
- Eat scrumptious pastries or desserts.
- Listen to soothing music.
- Light candles in the whole house.
- Have a small get together with close friends.
- Work on a large jigsaw puzzle.
- Wear fuzzy socks.
- Spend time in a hot tub.
- Cuddle by the fire pit or fire place.

Helpful Tips: Here are a few ideas to assist you:

- Try to stay off your phone or social media.
- Stay away from toxic people.
- Tell your family your plans for the day.
- If possible, do not look at your clock.
- If you would like to incorporate more coziness in your daily life, look up the Danish practice called hygge or the Norwegian koselig.

Comfy List

Things that made me feel good today:

Things I noticed about myself:

Things I am grateful for:

Thoughts on the daily exercise:

Would you like to add anything else?

Day 170

Today, I...

> ***"Anything I can not transform into something marvelous, I let go."***
> ***- Anais Nin***

EXERCISE 170: Wash Away the Stress

Taking a shower in the morning and in the evening both have their benefits. On a physical level, your morning shower helps you wake up and invigorates you for the day ahead; your evening shower relaxes your muscles and cleanses your body of the day's impurities, toxins, and smells. Beyond that, during your showers, you often come up with your most creative and brilliant ideas.

However, for many, time in the shower can also spark negative thoughts and unpleasant memories. To counteract this negativity, doing a quick clearing and releasing exercise in the shower can be effective.

Today, during your shower(s), wash away the stress. Close your eyes, take a few conscious breaths, relax, and feel the water running down your body. Imagine that the water is washing away all your suffering; visualize soaping away all your sorrow, angst, and fears, and envision them spiraling down the drain – if you find it helpful, you can strengthen the process by making declarations such as "This water is now purifying me!" "I now release all negativity from my being!" or "I am grateful for the inner and outer cleansing that is now taking place." When you feel that you have released all the negativity, end the process by visualizing that you are now showering in health, joy, happiness, peace, and love. Remain present during the entire process and allow feelings of relief, gratitude, peace, and empowerment to uplift you. Once you are done, turn off the shower, and step out with a clearer and happier state of mind.

Remember, be mindful about water conservation. This activity can easily be done in a few minutes.

Helpful Tips: Here are a few ideas to include if you have a bit more time:

- Light some candles and turn off the lights.
- Burn some all-natural incense.
- Play some nature sounds or some instrumental music.
- Before your shower, hang your towel on a towel warmer, to enjoy wrapping yourself in a warm towel – it will feel like a warm hug.

Things that made me feel good today:

Things I noticed about myself:

Things I am grateful for:

Thoughts on the daily exercise:

Would you like to add anything else?

Today, I...

> *"I'm big on hydrating internally and externally, so there's a lot of oils and hydration that I use. I love moisturizing. I'm the girl on the plane who will go wash my hands, spritz, and add a layer."*
>
> **- Tracee Ellis Ross**

EXERCISE 171: Massage and Moisturize

With tight schedules and the busyness of life, people often forgo applying a moisturizer on their skin. However, not taking the time to hydrate your skin could result in an unhealthy, uncomfortable, and irritated epidermis.

Your skin is a sensitive organ, and it's often impacted by damaging factors. Beyond health issues, dehydration, and a poor diet, there are other components responsible for skin conditions – the soap you use, the elements, the weather, air conditioning or heating, and the pollution around you all cause dry, cracked, itchy, and flaky skin. Taking the time to hydrate your skin daily will not only result in soft, glowing, and healthy skin, but will also have the added benefit of relaxing your muscles and easing your mind. Massaging your own body with a moisturizer is a beautiful act of self-love. It's a wonderful way to calm your nervous system, deepen your appreciation for your body, improve blood circulation, rehydrate your skin, and practice being present.

Today, make time to massage and moisturize your body. Take a nice warm shower or bath, gently pat your skin dry, and apply your favorite oil or moisturizer. Beginning with your feet, slowly and gently work your way up. Relax your body, breathe consciously, be mindful of the sensations you feel, and let your intuition guide you through the process. Enjoy connecting with your body, and when you are done, wait a few minutes before putting your clothes on.

Helpful Tips: Here are a few things to keep in mind when choosing a moisturizer:

- Your body absorbs whatever you put on it, therefore the more natural a moisturizer, the better.
- Avoid moisturizers that have ingredients such as alcohol or benzoyl peroxide as they have a drying effect on the skin.
- When purchasing a moisturizer, keep in mind that many products are unregulated and may contain carcinogens and toxic chemicals. For more info, visit EWG's Skin Deep (https://www.ewg.org/skindeep/).
- Many companies test their products on innocent animals. For an extensive list of animal-friendly and cruelty-free companies and products, visit PETA (features.peta.org/cruelty-free-company-search) or CRUELTY-FREE KITTY (https://www.crueltyfreekitty.com/).

Things that made me feel good today:

Things I noticed about myself:

Things I am grateful for:

Thoughts on the daily exercise:

Would you like to add anything else?

Day 172

Today, I...

> *"Often we treat certain aspects of ourselves as junk, having no value. We try to throw parts of ourselves in the garbage. But a human being is an ecosystem, and everything in that system is of value to the whole."*
>
> ***- Stephen Schwartz***

EXERCISE 172: Health and Well-Being

For many people, the words "healthy lifestyle" resonates with living fully and enjoying a healthy mind and body. For others, it implicates nightmarish visions of doctor's orders, regimented fitness plans, painful diets, and the elimination of all things fun and delicious. Being healthy should always be a priority because without health, life can become restrictive. Taking care of your health should be seen as an act of self-love toward your whole being and never as a tedious task. Dropping the negative associations and changing them to more mindful and empowering correlations can be helpful in awakening to what it truly means to live a healthy lifestyle – to live with such a reverence for your life that you lovingly, consciously, and willingly care for your three bodies (body, mind, and spirit) to the best of your ability.

Adopting healthy habits does not have to be painful; it can be a matter of noticing things that would enrich your life and taking action. It can begin with small daily changes and improvements that support a healthier way of life.

By having an intention to be kinder and more loving to your body, mind, and spirit, and repeatedly making small choices that are aligned with a more vibrant version of yourself – without stress – you will create a positive momentum that will naturally result in a healthier you.

Today, take your health and well-being into your own hands, and do one or more acts of love in favor of your entire being. Take a moment to consider the different decisions you could make throughout the day that would be beneficial to your health. Create a small to-do list (or TLC list) and check off as many of these activities as you can. Each time you carry out a healthy activity, be attentive, thank yourself, and feel gratitude for your achievement. At the end of the day, record your accomplishments on the following page.

Examples

- Purchase a water filter.
- Do not take the elevator, climb up the stairs.
- Eat lots of fruits and veggies.
- Purchase a standing desk.
- Sing and dance to some fun music.
- Complete a brain teaser puzzle.
- Meditate or pray.
- Purchase a new air conditioner filter.
- Clean your phone, tablet, and/or computer.
- Drink more water.
- Have a good laugh.
- Diffuse essential oils.
- Purchase a glass water bottle.
- Go for a swim.
- Get rid of your toxic cleaning products and purchase more environmentally friendly ones.
- Listen to a podcast.
- Purchase a new toothbrush.
- Take a healthy supplement.
- Chat with your best friend.
- Get a good night sleep (7 to 9 hours).

How did you care for your health and well-being today?

Things that made me feel good today:

Things I noticed about myself:

Things I am grateful for:

Thoughts on the daily exercise:

Would you like to add anything else?

Today, I...

> *"Make it a habit to tell people thank you. To express your appreciation, sincerely and without the expectation of anything in return. Truly appreciate those around you, and you'll soon find many others around you. Truly appreciate life, and you'll find that you have more of it."*
>
> **- Ralph Marston**

EXERCISE 173: Express Gratitude

We are often told that it is the little things that matter most. Nothing could be truer when it comes to showing gratitude to another. A little investigating will reveal that, despite how much people wish to be acknowledged and appreciated, in reality, they seldom receive any form of appreciation. Sadly, examples of parents not thanking children, bosses not thanking employees, spouses not thanking one another, customers not thanking staff members, and people everywhere forgetting to show gratitude are plentiful. Some, lost in thought, forget; others were not taught proper etiquette, and still others feel that it may diminish them in some way.

When you speak words of gratitude, in essence you are saying, "you are valuable and what you do matters to me." To acknowledge a person and remind them of their significance is one of the best gifts you can give any human being.

Today, be mindful and express gratitude wherever you go. Pay attention to people everywhere and take the time to offer genuine words of appreciation whenever someone shows you a kindness. Be conscious of how you feel each time you thank someone, and be observant of how people react to your thoughtfulness. At the end of the day, journal your thoughts on the following page.

Remember, saying "thanks" is not a positive shortcut – it's cold and impersonal. Take the time to direct your appreciation by saying "thank you," and include the name of the person you are speaking to if possible. You can also choose to expound your heartfelt gratitude by saying something like "I appreciate you for...," "I am grateful to you because...," or simply "Thank you so much!"

What did you learn today?

Things that made me feel good today:

Things I noticed about myself:

Things I am grateful for:

Thoughts on the daily exercise:

Would you like to add anything else?

Day 174

Today, I...

> ***"My story is definitely going to be a happily ever after, no matter what."***
> ***- Rihanna***

EXERCISE 174: Your Personal Timeline

When was the last time you contemplated the entirety of your lifespan? Your fondest and worst memories? Your greatest accomplishments and your hardest setbacks? Crucial events that deeply affected you? All the moments that have come together to create your story.

Taking time to look closely at your history can help you make peace with your past, appreciate yourself more authentically, and have an overall sense of gratitude for your life. It can also be valuable in helping you gain perspective, realize certain patterns, and inspire your direction for the future.

Today, step back in time, move forward to the present, and envision your future by creating your personal timeline. Use the blank timeline on the following page to write down all the important dates you feel have shaped your life up to the present moment. You can be crafty and include some photos, some illustrations, or some stickers. Once you get done with the current year, think of all your dreams and intentions for the future, all the things you would like to accomplish, and the timeframe in which you would like to experience those things. With a different colored pen, fill in your "dream timeline," and decorate it if you feel inspired to do so. This activity will take at least one hour to complete, so make yourself comfortable and create an enjoyable ambiance to work in. As emotions surface, welcome them without judgment, and allow them to rise and dissipate freely. Celebrate the positive feelings, but if negative feelings arise, remember to be kind and compassionate toward yourself. When working on the second part of the activity, make sure to have some fun envisioning your wildest dreams. Do not allow doubts or your limited understanding of what is possible to dictate what you "should want" versus what you "would love to experience." When you are finished with your timeline, look at your past with gratitude, embrace where you stand today, and feel excitement for the future – most of all, have faith in your own "happily ever after."

My Timeline

10

20

30

40

50

60

70

80

90

100

Things that made me feel good today:

Things I noticed about myself:

Things I am grateful for:

Thoughts on the daily exercise:

Would you like to add anything else?

Day 175

Today, I...

> ***"Have nothing in your home that you don't know to be useful or believe to be beautiful."***
> ***- William Morris***

EXERCISE 175: Beautify Your Space

Take a moment to look around you. Does your space uplift you, or does it demoralize you? Are you happy with the placement of your furniture? Do you like the color of the paint on the walls? Is it clean? Is it cluttered?

Whether you are conscious of it or not, the spaces you spend the most time in influence your mood, your thoughts, your feelings, and your well-being. Key rooms such as your bedroom, your living room, your kitchen, or your office should all be pleasant and inspiring. They should be decorated in a way that makes you feel good and in a way that is aligned with your dreams, your goals, and your desires.

Today, evaluate your surroundings and beautify your space. Begin by spending time in the areas where you hang out the most and assess how you feel. Pay attention to the things that uplift you and to the things that irritate or upset you. Be conscious of the things that give off a good vibe and things that drain your energy. Finally, think of your goals and intentions for each space. Do you need the space to uplift you, relax you, or energize you? Allow your inner voice and your feelings to guide you. Start doing a few things to enhance and embellish your favorite areas. Have fun during the process and enjoy modifying your space to your unique style and taste. In the end, just make sure these changes produce the best feelings within you and an atmosphere that suits your needs and desires.

Remember, interior design can sometimes feel overwhelming, so remind yourself that there is no rush, and take your time to intuitively and slowly make adjustments – rearrange a few pieces of furniture here and there, add some color, change the lighting, reorganize an area, or buy some beautiful decorations until you feel happy in your space. Decorating your space should always be an ongoing process. Like you, your space has life and should evolve as you do.

Helpful Tips: Here are a few ideas that could assist you with this activity:

- Research the principles of Feng Shui, an ancient Chinese art of placement.
- Clean and declutter your space.
- Get some indoor plants.
- Look into the principles of Minimalism.
- Purchase some accent cushions.
- Explore Color Psychology to understand how colors affect you.
- Think about adding natural scents with diffusers, incense, or potpourri.
- Add some quality lighting, a few salt lamps, or some beautiful candles.
- Choose artwork and decorations that uplift your spirit.
- Consider repurposing or upcycling some of your belongings.

Things that made me feel good today:

Things I noticed about myself:

Things I am grateful for:

Thoughts on the daily exercise:

Would you like to add anything else?

Day 176

Today, I...

> ***"All human beings have an innate desire to overcome suffering, to find happiness. Training the mind to think differently, through meditation, is one important way to avoid suffering and be happy."***
>
> ***- His Holiness the 14th Dalai Lama***

EXERCISE 176: Loving-Kindness Meditation

Loving-kindness meditation, also known as "Metta" or "compassion" meditation, is a practice that encourages expanding deep love and compassion to all sentient beings, including ourselves. It is based on the premise that like us, most beings long to be free of suffering and desire to experience well-being and happiness. It teaches that cultivating compassion toward all life eventually leads to being kinder, more understanding, loving, equanimous, and altruistic. This meditation shows you the way to compassion through a progressive technique that guides you to, first, cultivate feelings of love and benevolence toward yourself, next extending those feelings to those you care most about, then continuing with strangers, then to those who have hurt you or for whom you feel a certain aversion, and finally ending by encompassing all beings worldwide.

This practice is a wonderful exercise to develop a deeper love toward yourself and all beings, and if done regularly, it has the potential to offer outstanding advantages. It can calm your mind, reduce angst, lower stress, help with forgiving yourself and others, ignite pleasant feelings, as well as heal certain illnesses, conditions, and disorders.

Today, open your heart to compassion by practicing loving-kindness meditation. Read the instructions on the following page and record them on your phone if you wish to. Choose a time during the day when you will be undisturbed and make yourself comfortable. If this is your first time practicing this type of meditation, do not be surprised if you feel some resistance. Depending on your current state of mind, you may find it challenging to feel love and/or compassion for people you know, strangers, people you loathe, or yourself. Do not worry, it is perfectly fine. It can take time to develop such feelings, but as with anything, the more you practice, the easier it will get, and the better the results will be. Remember to be loving, kind, and compassionate toward yourself and make peace with where you are on your journey. Like with any meditation you can make it last for as long as you want, and stop anytime you begin to feel uncomfortable.

Commonly, loving-kindness meditation begins with the self; in my experience, when beginning the practice this often causes resistance because people generally have a hard time feeling love and compassion for themselves right off the bat. I have found the following progression to give the greatest results for beginners, but feel free to begin in any way you prefer and see what works best for you. Additionally, in some schools of thought, the use of mantras is also recommended. If you would like, try repeating mantras during the process and see if you enjoy it. To help, I have included potential mantras, but you can create your own.

Helpful Tips: Here are a few potential mantras:

- Mantra for you and others: "Love, kindness, forgiveness, compassion."
- Mantra for yourself:
  "May I be... (safe, protected, etc.)."
  "May I be... (peaceful, happy, free, etc.)."
  "May I be... (healed, healthy in body and mind, etc.)."
  "May I be filled with (love, kindness, joy, etc.)."
- Mantra for others:
  "May you/she/he/they (all beings) be... (safe, protected, etc.)."
  "May you/she/he/they (all beings) be... (peaceful, happy, free, etc.)."
  "May you/she/he/they (all beings) be... (healed, healthy in body and mind, etc.)."
  "May you/she/he/they (all beings) be filled with... (love, kindness, joy, etc.)."
- Mantra for the world:
  "May all living beings/the world/Gaia and its creatures be... (healed, at peace, etc.)."

Steps:

1. Sit in a comfortable position. It is up to you whether you want to sit in a lotus position, on a chair, or in any way that feels good to you.
2. Close your eyes. Take a few conscious breaths and relax your body completely.
3. When you are ready, begin contemplating the fact that hostility and suffering are hurtful energies for you to hold on to, while love and kindness are nourishing energies. Think of how the world could evolve if we all embraced cultivating compassion toward others and ourselves. Gently begin to open your heart area to the energies of love and kindness.
4. Visualize a being you love dearly and who loves you as much, who is alive or who has passed. See that being looking at you joyful and smiling. Let love, caring, kindness, and compassion flow from yourself to that being freely and happily. If you choose, complement this loving energy by silently repeating your chosen mantra. Continue doing that as long as it feels good. When you are done, take a few conscious breaths and relax.
5. Visualize someone you barely know, or a stranger you have crossed paths with. See them warmly smiling at you. Realize that, like you, they desire to experience happiness and well-being in their lives. Feel friendliness and kind-heartedness toward them, and let loving feelings freely flow in their direction. If you choose, complement this benevolent energy by silently repeating your chosen mantra. Continue doing that as long as it feels good. When you are done, take a few conscious breaths and relax.

6. Visualize someone for whom you feel hostility (at first, you will want to begin with someone that simply bothers you, and with time, as you practice more regularly, you will be able to take on more challenging personalities). See that individual in a way that is not threatening or confrontational, but in a way that helps you be more accepting, altruistic, and forgiving. In no way does this mean that you condone their behavior. This simply is a way to free yourself of the negative feelings that bind you to them and recapture your heart's power. Try to think of one or several things that help soften your heart toward them. Remind yourself of their humanity; remind yourself of their sufferings, remind yourself of a quality they have, or reminisce of a particularly good memory of them. Even if you are not able to feel love, feel as much compassion as you possibly can toward them (it can be helpful to release your opinions about the personality they presently embody, forget what you know about them, and instead visualize their essence, their soul, or their spirit). If you choose, complement this compassionate energy by silently repeating your chosen mantra. Continue doing that as long as it feels good. When you are done, take a few conscious breaths and relax.
7. Visualize the entire planet and all living beings. Human beings from all over the world, animals from all the kingdoms, the plants and the trees, and the earth itself. Realize that like you, they all deserve to be happy, peaceful, and free from suffering. Allow heartfelt loving-kindness feelings to naturally flow to them all. If you choose, complement this all-encompassing loving energy by silently repeating your chosen mantra. Continue doing that as long as it feels good. When you are done, take a few conscious breaths and relax.
8. Visualize yourself. See yourself, radiant, healthy, and smiling back at you in the most loving way. If you have a difficult time imagining this, imagine a much younger version of yourself. Feel the energy of unconditional love, kindness, acceptance, and gratitude emanate from that vision of yourself back toward you. There is no judgment, only love. When you are ready, let feelings of love, care, kindness, and gratitude flow toward that representation of yourself. If you choose, complement this loving energy by silently repeating your chosen mantra. Continue doing that as long as it feels good. When you are done, take a few conscious breaths and relax.
9. Finish this meditation by extending those beautiful feelings of loving-kindness as long as it feels comfortable and good to you. Once you are done, take a few conscious breaths, relax, put your hands over your heart in gratitude, and when you are ready slowly open your eyes.

Things that made me feel good today:

Things I noticed about myself:

Things I am grateful for:

Thoughts on the daily exercise:

Would you like to add anything else?

Day 177

Today, I...

> *"With every act of self-care your authentic self gets stronger, and the fearful, critical mind gets weaker. Every act of self-care is a powerful declaration: I am on my side. I am on my side, each day I am more and more on my own side."*
>
> **- Susan Weiss Berry**

EXERCISE 177: Favorite Activities

For the past 176 days, you have been encouraged to perform daily activities and answer questions relating to self-love and self-care. Now that the program is ending, it is time to go back and review all the exercises. Which ones were your favorite?

Today, make a list of the 30 activities you loved the most throughout this journey. Take a moment during the day where you can relax and enjoy perusing through your workbook. Get yourself a drink and a snack, create a pleasant atmosphere, and start browsing. Have fun looking through your notes, recall your most enjoyable memories, and appreciate how far you have come. Take as much time as you need for this activity. The list you are putting together is meant to be a quick reference sheet that you can easily pull out in the future. It will complement other lists you have completed along the way, such as WEEK 23's "Exercise 157: Self-Care List" and WEEK 25's "Exercise 169: Comfy Day list." Together, these lists will all be helpful anytime you need a reminder or a little inspiration.

Favorite Activities

Things that made me feel good today:

Things I noticed about myself:

Things I am grateful for:

Thoughts on the daily exercise:

Would you like to add anything else?

Day 178

Today, I...

> ***"Reflecting on where I came from helps me to appreciate and balance what I have now."***
> ***- Meghan Markle***

EXERCISE 178: Time to Reflect

Do you remember who you were and how you felt about yourself when you began this journey? Who have you become, and how do you feel about yourself today? What has happened in the last 177 days?

Contemplating such questions will help you gain perspective concerning the last few months. It will give you a deep appreciation for you and your progress, and it will help you better understand what you still need to work on.

Today, take some time to reflect on your self-love journey. Do this activity during a time of day when you will be undisturbed, and be mindful to create a relaxing atmosphere. When you are ready, take a few deep breaths, relax your body, and begin your introspection. Look back at who you were on DAY 1 and at how things were going in all areas of your life. Think of all the experiences, the achievements, and the setbacks you have gone through since beginning this program. Now, look at who you have become today and what has improved or changed in your life. Think of all your milestones, your present intentions, and all the objectives you still want to achieve for yourself. But, most of all, muse on how your relationship with yourself has evolved, how you used to feel about taking care of your body, mind, and spirit in contrast to how you feel presently, and where you stand at this precise moment in terms of loving yourself compared to that very first day. Take all the time you need to reflect and when you are finished, journal your reflections on the following page.

Helpful Tips: Here are some self-directed questions that can help your inquiry:

- What did I learn?
- What did I learn about myself?
- Did I truly invest myself in this program?
- What would I do differently?
- What were my greatest accomplishments?
- What challenges did I face?
- What setbacks did I have to face?
- What am I most proud of?
- Am I grateful for doing this program?
- What are my biggest takeaways?
- How have I changed?
- How has every area of my life changed?
- Can I say that I love, honor, and respect myself more today?
- Will I continue embracing self-love and self-care?

Reflections

Things that made me feel good today:

Things I noticed about myself:

Things I am grateful for:

Thoughts on the daily exercise:

Would you like to add anything else?

Day 179

Today, I...

> ***"When I was around 18, I looked in the mirror and said, 'You're either going to love yourself or hate yourself.' And I decided to love myself. That changed a lot of things."***
>
> ***- Queen Latifah***

EXERCISE 179: Love Letter

During this journey, you have learned to cultivate authentic self-love and explored many ways in which you can tend to the needs of your three bodies (body, mind, and spirit).

Today, you will discover a sacred and intimate way to connect to your heart space by writing yourself a love letter. This is one of the most powerful ways to commune with your whole being, as it will help you contemplate all the ways in which you are delightful and deserving of love.

To get the most out of this activity, choose to write yourself the letter during a time of day when you feel your best – early morning hours, before the agitation of the day, are usually best. Close your eyes, take a few conscious breaths, and relax your body and mind. When you are ready, allow your heart space to open and think about all the things you truly love about yourself. As you do this, let feelings of self-appreciation and self-love blossom within you. Gently surrender to the sweetness of this moment and these beautiful feelings.

Begin writing the moment you feel inspired and let your words flow unto the page. If you feel some resistance, do not be harsh or impatient with yourself; simply ask yourself a few questions such as "What do I love about myself?" or "Why am I lovable?" Once you are done writing your letter, take a moment to sit with yourself and enjoy your own company. Finally, when you feel ready, slowly get back to your daily activities.

The more regularly you write yourself love letters, the more you will witness wonders in all areas of your life – you will experience positive emotions, greater self-love, improved self-esteem, increasing confidence, self-trust, transformations and healings of the three bodies (body, mind, and spirit), deeper connections with loved ones, more synchronicities, heightened intuition, etc.

Dear Self,

Things that made me feel good today:

Things I noticed about myself:

Things I am grateful for:

Thoughts on the daily exercise:

Would you like to add anything else?

Day 180

Today, I...

> ***"I'd like to congratulate myself, and thank myself, and give myself a big pat on the back."***
> ***- Dee Dee Ramone***

EXERCISE 180: Final Assessment

It is time to assess where you are today. Choose to complete this exercise when you can have at least an hour of undisturbed time. Make sure to make yourself as comfortable as possible by creating a soothing ambiance: get a warm drink, put on some relaxing music, or light a candle. Take a few deep breaths, relax your body and mind, and when you are ready, answer the following questions as honestly and thoroughly as possible.

Do not peak at your first assessment.

1. As you end this journey, what are your thoughts? Did you accomplish everything you had hoped for? Be as specific as possible.

2. On a scale of 1 to 10, with 10 being the most satisfied, how would you rate each area of your life? Circle the answer that best characterizes the way you feel at the moment.

Spiritual (connection with the Divine, mindfulness, meditation, etc.)	1	2	3	4	5	6	7	8	9	10
Relationship with yourself (self-love, self-care, self-awareness, etc.)	1	2	3	4	5	6	7	8	9	10
Family relationships	1	2	3	4	5	6	7	8	9	10
Romantic relationships	1	2	3	4	5	6	7	8	9	10
Friends and social relationships	1	2	3	4	5	6	7	8	9	10
Health	1	2	3	4	5	6	7	8	9	10
Fitness	1	2	3	4	5	6	7	8	9	10
Growth and learning (personal development, education, therapy, reading, etc.)	1	2	3	4	5	6	7	8	9	10
Career, business, occupation (student, stay at home parent, etc.)	1	2	3	4	5	6	7	8	9	10
Finances (income, savings, investments, etc.)	1	2	3	4	5	6	7	8	9	10
Philanthropy and community (volunteering, charity work, acts of random kindness, etc.)	1	2	3	4	5	6	7	8	9	10
Fun and recreation (hobbies, travel, entertainment, game nights, etc.)	1	2	3	4	5	6	7	8	9	10

3. On a scale of 1 to 10, with 10 being the happiest, how happy would you say you are? Circle the answer that best characterizes the way you feel at the moment.

Very Unhappy				Neutral					Very Happy
1	2	3	4	5	6	7	8	9	10

4. On a scale of 1 to 10 with 10 being the most positive, how would you rate the amount of love you feel for yourself presently?

I loathe myself				Neutral					I love myself completely
1	2	3	4	5	6	7	8	9	10

5. Please write down words you would use to describe yourself (mentally, emotionally, physically, and spiritually).

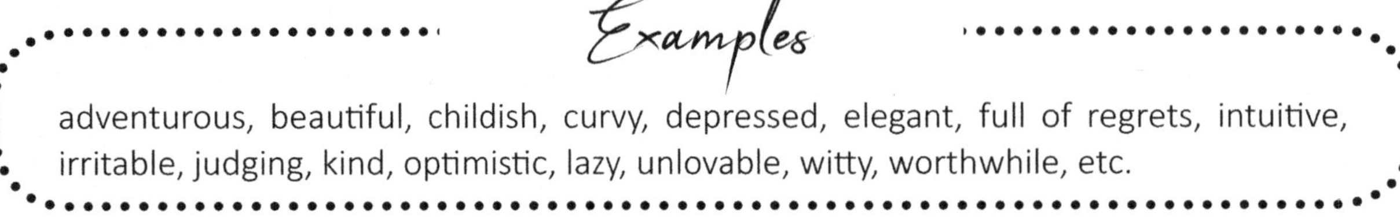

adventurous, beautiful, childish, curvy, depressed, elegant, full of regrets, intuitive, irritable, judging, kind, optimistic, lazy, unlovable, witty, worthwhile, etc.

6. Are you able to spend time alone and enjoy your own company? Explain.

7. Do you think you are lovable and worthy of love? Explain.

8. Do you make time daily to do the things you love and enjoy? Explain.

9. When you look in the mirror, what do you see?

10. How do you feel about your body? Do you like or dislike it? Explain.

11. Do you allow circumstances and people to dictate whether you feel good or bad, or are you in control of your own well-being?

12. Do you rely on others to make you feel good about yourself, or do you have a good amount of self-esteem? Explain.

13. Do you feel you can be yourself around other people? Explain.

14. How are you unfair, hard, and abusive toward yourself?

15. How are you loving, kind, and gentle toward yourself?

16. Name your top five favorite things about yourself.

17. What are the most recurring thoughts and feelings you have about yourself?

18. If you continue treating yourself the way you do, what do you expect will happen in the long term? Explain.

19. Do you think things will be different in your life once you love yourself completely? Explain.

20. Do you connect to a higher intelligence and listen to your intuition daily? Explain.

Once you are finished with your assessment, feel free to compare it with the first one you completed.

Things that made me feel good today:

Things I noticed about myself:

Things I am grateful for:

Thoughts on the daily exercise:

Would you like to add anything else?

Congratulations! You Did It!

Pause. Breathe. Take a moment to appreciate the journey from where you were at the beginning of this program to where you are today. Be proud of yourself!

So, what now?

Chances are, after reflecting on the past 180 days and looking ahead to what you want for yourself, you are celebrating a lot of wonderful accomplishments, but also realize that you still have a way to go.

I want to remind you that falling in love with yourself genuinely and holistically will take time. Changing your inner self-talk, your thinking patterns, your emotions, your behaviors, and your habits is quite a process; one you must deliberately and consciously take part in. It requires continual mindfulness and action. It demands perseverance, courage, practice, and determination. It entails immersing yourself into new ways of thinking, talking, feeling, and being until it all becomes a natural part of you.

I recommend that you consider starting this program over and that you do it as many times as needed, until loving yourself and caring for yourself become instinctive.

If you decide not to, please continue to take good care of your mind, body, and soul. Continue nurturing the relationship you have with yourself – it's the surest way to an exceptional life and a happy you.

Wherever you find yourself at the end of this program, always know that you deserve the very best! You are precious and deserving of unconditional self-love. May you care for yourself, treat yourself, and grow into the happiest version of yourself.

I always welcome any questions or suggestions, and I would love to hear about your personal experience with our program, so please contact us, or share your story and photos with us at https://www.melodyrohr.com/, on our Facebook Group page (Loving Me 180), or on social media (@rohrmelody) using the hashtag #LOVINGME180. I am looking forward to hearing from you!

Now, go and celebrate yourself!

Today, to celebrate accomplishing this program I

Helpful Resources

BOOKS

As a Man Thinketh – James Allen

The Alchemist – Paulo Coelho

Breaking the Habit of Being Yourself Book – Dr. Joe Dispenza

You Are the Placebo: Making Your Mind Matter – Dr. Joe Dispenza

Excuses Begone!: How to Change Lifelong, Self-Defeating Thinking Habits – Dr. Wayne W. Dyer

Peace Is Every Step: The Path of Mindfulness in Everyday Life – Thich Nhat Hanh

You Can Heal Your Life – Louise L. Hay

What to Say When You Talk to Your Self – Shad Helmstetter Ph.D.

Ask and It Is Given: Learning to Manifest Your Desires Paperback – Esther Hicks, Jerry Hicks

Who Moved My Cheese?: An Amazing Way to Deal with Change in Your Work and in Your Life – Spencer Johnson

Loving What Is: Four Questions That Can Change Your Life – Byron Katie

The Four Agreements: A Practical Guide to Personal Freedom (A Toltec Wisdom Book) – Don Miguel Ruiz

The Fifth Agreement: A Practical Guide to Self-Mastery (Toltec Wisdom) – Don Miguel Ruiz, Don Jose Ruiz, Janet Mills

Dying to Be Me: My Journey from Cancer, to Near Death, to True Healing – Anita Moorjani

The Power of Your Subconscious Mind – Joseph Murphy

Love Yourself Like Your Life Depends on It – Kamal Ravikant

Year of Yes: How to Dance It Out, Stand in the Sun and Be Your Own Person – Shonda Rhimes

The 5 Second Rule: Transform your Life, Work, and Confidence with Everyday Courage – Mel Robbins

You Are a Badass: How to Stop Doubting Your Greatness and Start Living an Awesome Life – Jen Sincero

The Untethered Soul: The Journey Beyond Yourself – Michael A. Singer

The Power of Now: A Guide to Spiritual Enlightenment – Eckhart Tolle

A New Earth: Awakening to Your Life's Purpose – Eckhart Tolle

The Top Five Regrets of the Dying: A Life Transformed by the Dearly Departing – Bronnie Ware

The Wisdom of Sundays: Life-Changing Insights from Super Soul Conversations – Oprah Winfrey

The Seat of the Soul – Gary Zukav

DOCUMENTARIES AND THOUGHT-PROVOKING FILMS

What the #$*! Do We Know!? – William Arntz, Betsy Chasse, Mark Vicente

The Secret – Rhonda Byrne

The Shift – Wayne Dyer

Mindfulness: Be Happy Now – Larry Kasanoff

You Can Heal Your Life, the movie – Louise L. Hay

Discover the Gift: The Movie – Demian Lichtenstein

10 Questions for the Dalai Lama – Rick Ray

I am – Tom Shadyac

Notes

Made in the USA
Coppell, TX
11 March 2020

16753507R00306